The Historic Gardens of England
Warwickshire

For Christopher Francis & Jinny Krish

The publication of this volume has been made possible by a grant from
THE LEVERHULME TRUST
to cover all the necessary research work

First published in 2011 by Redcliffe Press Ltd.,
81g Pembroke Road, Bristol BS8 3EA
T: 0117 9737207
E: info@redcliffepress.co.uk
www.redcliffepress.co.uk

ISBN 978-1-908326-01-0

British Library Cataloguing-in-Publication Data
A catalogue record for this book is available from the British Library

Designed by Stephen Morris, smc@freeuk.com www.stephen-morris.co.uk
Printed by HSW Print, Tonypandy, Rhondda

The Historic Gardens of England
Warwickshire

Timothy Mowl

Diane James

Stoneleigh Abbey from Humphry Repton's 1809 Red Book
Stoneleigh Abbey Ltd

Contents

Acknowledgements

As with the last seven books in this series, my first thanks go to Professor Sir Richard Brook and his Trustees at the Leverhulme Trust, whose generous funding of the research has made the Warwickshire travelling and garden visiting a pleasure rather than a financial worry. Their generosity has made it possible for Diane James, a former MA student and resident of Warwick, to be appointed as consultant for *Warwickshire*. She has undertaken all the research and co-ordinated the site visits, with thoughtful support from her husband Philip, in a calmly professional manner. I should also like to thank Dr Clare Hickman, Research Fellow of the project, who has not only overseen the progress of the writing and research with her usual efficiency, but has also written Chapter 8.

Jamie Carstairs has photographed most effectively the archival images from my own university's Special Collections and I must thank Michael Richardson for bringing many important texts to my notice. Jo Elsworth, Director of the University's Theatre Collection, has been most helpful over Julia Trevelyan Oman's archive, and in particular the designs for the Bear and Ragged Staff Spectacle at Warwick Castle. John Sansom has been an encouraging and enthusiastic editor, and Stephen Morris has achieved another elegantly designed volume.

Alexandra Denman has proofed the typescript most conscientiously, and Douglas Matthews has produced yet another definitive index.

Thanks are due to the staff at the Bodleian Library in Oxford, Warwickshire County Record Office, Birmingham Library and Archives, Shakespeare Centre Library and Archive, Kendal Record Office, Coventry History Centre, Bristol Reference Library, the RIBA Archives, the Royal Horticultural Society's Lindley Library, Sandwell Community History and Archives Service, Catherine Wood and Kasia Howard at the Landmark Trust, Mary Daniels at the Francis Loeb Library, Harvard University, Giles Carey and Ben Wallace of Warwick Museum Field Services, Stephen Falk at Warwickshire Museum, Huw Jones of the Herbert Art Gallery & Museum, Maria Singer at the Yale Center for British Art, and Pamela Bromley of Warwick Castle Archives.

Owners, archivists, friends, and colleagues who have been particularly helpful include Sir Roy Strong, the Viscount and Lady Daventry, the Earl and Countess of Denbigh and Desmond, the Earl of Aylesford, Brenda Newell, David Ridgeon, Sir William and Lady Dugdale, Benjamin Wiggin, Geri Reaves, Cathy Hurst, Maja Foster, Ludovic and Camilla de Walden, Deborah Williams, Gwyn Perry, John Carson, Hamish and

Gillian Cathie, Joanne Hammick, Karen Threadgold, Peter Kirk, Dr Sarah Richardson, Peter Freeman, Tony and Marion Dowding, Raphael Gonzalez, Julie Griffith, David Adams, Sir Peter Rigby, Marian Carter, Chris Holdsworth, John Dobbs, Jane Kinnaird, Richard Keble, Igor Kolodotschko, Les Baker, David Whitehead, Felix Dennis, Caroline Rush, Ron Terry, Nick Williams, Jonathan Squire, Bill and Jane Colman, Martin Holton, Mike Hill, Michael Heber-Percy, Mike and Diana Poole, Terry Roberts, Sarah Ridgeway, James Hill, Pattie Hall, Mike Sheldon, Jenny Dodge, George Mills, Kari Dill, Marcus Dill, Miranda and Martin Taylor, Tim Morgan, Sarah Baker, Charlotte Bayliss, Jane Carwithen, Rosemary Fetherston-Dilke, Matthew Dugdale, David Kirkland, Malcolm Bumford, Judy Bruce, Carol and Billy Smith, Roy Cockel, Simon Marcus, Tania Cowan, Stephen Browning, Louise Stow, Kay Gleeson, Dr and Mrs Mark Cecil, Will Hewitt, David and Karen Richards, Sam Harvey, Dr Dianne Barre, Jeri Bapasola, Marion Mako, Dr Jane Bradney, Dr Laura Mayer, Lesley Smith, Jane Whitaker, Dr Christine Hodgetts, Claire Burns, Robin Smith-Ryland, Sarah Smith-Ryland, Kim Nutton, Lynne Lacey, Shahab Seyfollahi, Cynthia Woodward, Paula Cornwell, Ron Adams, Mick Hogan, Sarah Jones, Joanna Coward, Katie Kelland, Gerald Lesinski, Suzanne Pery, David and Julia Russell, John Fenwick, Robert Waley-Cohen and the Hon. Felicity Waley-Cohen, Nicolette Diment, John Goom, Geraint and Jackie Lewis, Greg Fehler, Clive Gunter, David Orchard, Alison Darby, Pam Vanderstam, Julie Folkes, Ashton Hall, Anthony George and Ron Trenchard.

Warwickshire has been researched along-side my teaching of Bristol University's MA in Garden History, so I must thank my fellow university colleagues for their lively support. The research and visiting for this latest volume has coincided with the curating, by a Bristol garden history team, of a major exhibition on Capability Brown in the Midlands to be held at Compton Verney between June and October 2011. The gallery's director, Dr Steven Parissien, has monitored the progress of both book and exhibition with thoughtful and informed encourage-ment. My agent, Sara Menguc, has continued to support the project with her affectionate enthusiasm. My wife, Sarah, and daughter, Olivia, went with me to check out the visitor attractions at Warwick Castle after a family hog roast. The staff at the Warwick Arms Hotel gave me a warm welcome and provided a perfect base for garden visits in the county. My son Adam, who was teaching in Rome for most of 2010, and who is now researching for a PhD in intellectual history at King's College, London, was quietly encouraging via text and email. Finally, I should like to thank Christo-pher Francis and Jinny Krish, to whom this book is dedicated, for their warm and caring friendship at a particularly difficult time. I now leave the Midlands in search of the plummy brick villages and lush valleys of Marcher Herefordshire.

Timothy Mowl, Bristol, July 2011

A county of legends, heroes and historical revivals

WARWICKSHIRE STRETCHES FROM STAFFORDSHIRE AND LEICESTERSHIRE
IN the north to Gloucestershire and Oxfordshire in the south, while
Northamptonshire flanks it on the east and Worcestershire on the west.
Much of its north-western corner is now subsumed within Birmingham
and the West Midlands. Consequently, its specific character is hard to
define, and in topographical terms it has no recognisable features like the
moors and miniature hills of Somerset or the vast Plain of Cheshire.
Birmingham and Coventry, two sprawling conurbations, and Nuneaton, a
nondescript town, dominate the low-lying northern sector, which was
once covered by the Forest of Arden. This flourished on the underlying
coal measures and sandstones, but has now mostly disappeared. The
historic region of Arden is separated from the un-wooded, more fertile
Feldon area by the River Avon, which meanders diagonally through the
county from near Rugby in the north-east to Salford in the south-west.[1]

In contrast, south Warwickshire is a much gentler, rolling country,
reaching down to the honey limestone cottages of the north Cotswolds.
Here there are delightful villages of timber-framing, Georgian brick and
vernacular stone. In the centre of the county, both threaded by the Avon,
are tourist-haunted Stratford and Warwick, the shire's most beautiful
town, which was almost entirely rebuilt in warm red brick after a disas-
trous fire in 1694.

Even though the county lacks a distinctive visual character, it has a
strong sense of its own historic past. Throughout the ages it has recycled
its particular history, with the recreation by English Heritage of Robert
Dudley's garden, originally laid out at Kenilworth Castle in 1575 for a visit

by Queen Elizabeth I, being the most recent evocation of a historic event. Not surprisingly, the Edgehill ridge in the south-east has encouraged annual re-enactments of the first pitched battle of the Civil War, fought there in October 1642, but its importance in garden history terms is as the site of the first substantial eighteenth-century Gothick garden structure in the country: the Edgehill Tower. This was consciously modelled on the late-fourteenth-century Guy's Tower at Warwick Castle and raised by Sanderson Miller, the squire of Radway Grange in the field below, to which it was connected by a dramatic carriage drive. Miller, known to his close friends as the 'Great Master of Gothick', was a pioneer of the medieval revival. He dominated Warwickshire landscape and garden design in the middle decades of the eighteenth century, either designing or advising on the grounds at Arbury; the eclectic landscape at Honington with its Cascade, Grotto and Chinese Seat; the Temple Pool below Upton House; and Farnborough's sweeping viewing terrace, aligned on Edgehill, its classical temples sited for landscape appreciation and alfresco dining.

Warwickshire is characterised by such revivalism, which was often conceived to celebrate its legendary heroes. Celia Fiennes, that indomitable traveller, spotted this phenomenon when she reached Warwick in 1697, soon after the fire had destroyed most of the town's medieval core. Although some of the old stone houses survived, most were newly built in 'brick and coyn'd with stone', but the parish church was still in ruins and had yet to be reconstructed.[2] Fortunately, the chancel was still standing, and there she saw the extraordinary 1439 gilded brass monument to Richard Beauchamp, Earl of Warwick, the sinews and veins of his face so delicately cast that they conveyed 'the very aire of his countenance much to the Life or like a lieving man'.[3] The Earl's feet rest on a bear, one of the heraldic supporters of the earls of Warwick. Richard Beauchamp's son-in-law, Richard Neville, Earl of Warwick – Warwick the Kingmaker – was the first to use the bear together with the ragged staff in the 1450s. Of the other monuments that had been saved from the fire Fiennes noted particularly that of 'the great Earle of Leisters and his Ladyes in stone curiously wrought with their garments, and painted and gilded'.[4] Robert Dudley, who died in 1588, is commemorated by a wildly polychromatic alabaster tomb chest, backed by a canopy supported on

1 Julia Trevelyan Oman's 1981 design for a fountain at Warwick Castle to accompany the Bear and Ragged Staff Spectacle in the Conservatory. Designer: Julia Trevelyan Oman. *Courtesy: Sir Roy Strong and University of Bristol Theatre Collection*

coupled Corinthian columns, all lavishly decorated with riotous strap-work. The Dudleys became earls of Warwick in 1547, which accounts for the insistent use in the decorative patterning of the bear and ragged staff, a free-standing sculpture of which tops the central heraldic achievement.

Typically, given Warwickshire's fascination with its aristocratic fore-bears, this heraldic badge was incorporated into its coat of arms in 1931. In 1981 the emblem was the centrepiece of an exhibition held at Warwick Castle entitled: 'A Spectacle in the Conservatory – The Bear's Quest for the Ragged Staff'.[5] This was conceived by the theatre designer Julia Trevelyan Oman, and featured a statue and fountain raised on a plinth of volcanic rock from Mount Vesuvius in the pool which fronts the Conservatory (*1*). Astrid Zydower sculpted the Bear, and the Spectacle, which was created in the style of the eighteenth century and illustrated the legend of the Bear and Ragged Staff, was set up in the Conservatory. It included a narration by Trevelyan Oman and was accompanied by music by Carl Davies.[6] There is another Warwick garden nearby which survives, and that features a modern sculpture of the Bear and Ragged Staff, at Lord Leycester's Hospital. The Knot Garden, sited in a paved courtyard behind the main building, was created in 2000 by Geoffrey Smith to mark the Millennium. His simple, but historically appropriate, Tudor-style layout is dramatised by a metal sculpture of the Bear by Rachel Higgins. It was commissioned to celebrate the life of David Eliot Mycroft, who died in 1998 at the very young age of 28 (*colour plate 1*).

After her tour of the monuments in St Mary's, Fiennes went on to Warwick Castle, was taken around the apartments and then went outside to see the gardens, which she pronounced were 'fine with good gravell and grass walks, squares of dwarfe trees of all sorts and steps to descend from one walke to another'.[7] She viewed all this from the 'top of the Mount, together with the whole town and a vast prospect all about, the Mount being very high and the ascent is round to an agen [a spiral walk] secured by cut hedges'.[8] The porter then diverted her with the history of the legendary Guy, Earl of Warwick, and she was shown 'his walking staff 9 foote long and ye staff of a Gyant wch he kill'd thats 12 foote long; his sword, helmet and shield and breast and back all of a prodigious size'.[9] These Brobdingnagian survivals included 'the pottage-pott for his supper, it was a yard over the top', and 'the bones of severall Beasts he kill'd, the Rib of ye Dun-Cow as bigg as halfe a great cart wheele'.[10]

The legend of Guy appears to have begun as oral history and was then written down in the thirteenth century; the earliest existing record is *Gui de Warewic*, an Anglo-Norman poem, which later appeared in Middle English in fourteenth- and fifteenth-century versions.[11] Geoffrey Chaucer mentions Sir Guy in his *Rime of Sir Thopas* in the *Canterbury Tales*. There seems to be no real evidence that Guy and his wife Felice (Phyllis) ever existed. The names of Guy and Felice are probably of Norman derivation, and the storyline more compatible with the period of chivalry around the time of the Crusades than of Anglo-Saxon derivation.[12] The tale's main purpose was probably to enhance the status of the Warwicks, as like many other Anglo-Norman families established after the Conquest they lacked a long English family history.

Fiennes' eighteenth-century equivalent, Dr Richard Pococke, also visited Warwick in his tours of the country and reached the town on 30 May 1757. Like Fiennes before him, he made straight for St Mary's church to view the Beauchamp and Dudley memorials. Then he went to the Castle that, two generations later, had been recently restored by Earl Brooke, 'who has greatly beautifyed the park and the whole place by plantations'.[13] The Earl's 'very handsom apartments' displayed the usual mix of Flemish tapestries, paintings by van Dyck and Lely, and 'some beautiful marble tables...brought from Italy by the present Earl'.[14] Further evidence of the Earl's Grand Tour collecting was evident in his study, which was 'adorn'd with drawings of the capital statues in Rome and Florence, and also of several views of buildings'.[15]

However, what intrigued Pococke most, and seemed typical of the town's obsession with its legendary historic past, was an 'out-office', in which there were 'some things preserv'd, which they say belong'd to Guy Earl of Warwick, as his armor, all of immense size, and his sword'.[16] Local folklore had it that Guy was 'nine feet high', no doubt as a result of the walking stick that Fiennes had seen back in 1697. Certainly the size of his iron shield, his helmet and part of his coat of mail suggested to Pococke that the legend had some veracity.[17] Furthermore, Guy had been 'drawn on the walls as encountering another giant' and another tapestry, 'left as an heirloom', depicted his actions.[18] As well as the rib of the Dun Cow there was a vertebra of the wild boar that Guy was also reputed to have killed, 'which seem'd to be of the size of the largest ox'.[19] Pococke was told that in Henry VIII's reign a William Hoggeson was paid 2 pence a week for 'showing these acoutrements',[20] so they must have been one of the earliest visitor attractions in the country. The exhibit has long since disappeared, but Guy's sword, fork and porridge pot are still preserved in the Great Hall of the Castle.

After spending a day in Warwick, where he saw Sanderson Miller's Shire Hall with the stones of its frieze still to be carved, Pococke headed for Coventry, missing another site associated with the legendary Guy. He was told about it some time afterwards: 'I have been inform'd since I left that place that a mile from the castle on the Avon is Guy or Gib Cliff, where there is a cave with trees and water rising about it; to which place they say Guy retir'd after all his conquests'.[21] Fiennes had been ahead of him in 1697. She reported:

> 2 miles from the town is his Cave dugg out by his own hands just ye
> dimention of his body as the common people say, there is also his
> will cut out on stone, but the letters are much defaced; these are the
> storyes and meer fiction, for the true history of Guy was that he was
> but a little man in stature, tho' great in mind and valour, which
> tradition describes to posterity by being a Gyant.[22]

About two miles from Warwick, where the spectacular ruins of Guy's
Cliffe lower over the Avon, there is still a towering image of Earl Guy,
carved from the living rock (2), in a chapel that serves now as a Freema-
sonic Lodge. There are also several caves hewn out of the rock below the
ruined house, into which he might once have retreated, hermit-like,
taking his leave of the world. A much later owner of Guy's Cliffe, Bertie
Greatheed, was to make it his life's work to reconstruct the house in
medieval style as a celebration of the daring deeds of the legendary Earl.
A brass memorial in the chapel, set up by Greatheed after 1818, records
that 'Richard Beauchamp, Earl of Warwick, caused this image to be
carved out of the rock in the reign of Henry VI'. That would date the
carving and the chapel which encloses it to the early fifteenth century,
between 1422, when Henry acceded to the throne as a minor, and 1439,
when the 13th Earl died.

    If Guy is the most enduring of all Warwick's legendary medieval
heroes, William Shakespeare must rate as the county's most famous son,
one around whom an entire industry has grown since John Dryden first
praised his work in the 1668 *Essay of Dramatick Poesie*; this followed the
publication of the second edition of Shakespeare's First Folio in 1663.
Dryden was the first critic to evaluate the work of the Elizabethan drama-
tists, and particularly that of Shakespeare, whom he regarded as 'the man
who, of all modern and perhaps ancient poets, had the largest and most
comprehensive soul. All the images of nature were still present to him,
and he drew them not laboriously, but luckily; when he describes
anything, you more than see it, you feel it too'.[23] Seven more editions of
the First Folio were published between 1685 and 1768, one of which was

2

This medieval
carving of the
legendary Guy of
Warwick in the
Chapel at Guy's
Cliffe is almost
nine feet in height

brought out by Alexander Pope (1723-25), by which time Shakespeare had become a national figure. This celebrity was also due in part to a statue of the Bard that had been set up in Westminster Abbey in 1741. The idea for this was first promoted in 1738 by a group of women who called themselves 'Shakespeare's Ladies', and who persuaded the manager of Drury Lane theatre to put on a benefit performance of *Julius Caesar* to raise funds. Both Pope and Lord Burlington were on the organising committee, so it was not surprising that Burlington's protégé William Kent was commissioned to design the statue and Peter Scheemakers to execute his design. The monument was placed in what is now known as Poets' Corner

3 The Great Booth or Amphitheatre set up on Bancroft Gardens in 1769 to celebrate the Shakespeare Jubilee. *University of Bristol, Special Collections*

and was the catalyst for further memorials there to the literati.

When the actor and theatre manager David Garrick took over at Drury Lane in 1747, incidentally the year when a further edition of the First Folio was published by William Warburton, he determined to make his theatre the home of the Bard. He produced twenty-seven of Shakespeare's plays there between 1747 and 1776, but his greatest Shakespearian achievement, one that would bring the Bard to international recognition, was the Stratford Jubilee of 6-8 September 1769. Shakespeare's birth town had no theatre, and until the 1760s his only memorial was the 1616 alabaster monument in Holy Trinity church. Pococke was moved when he saw this in September 1756, reporting that 'the comedians who were here some years ago repair'd and adorn'd it, and added a canopy over it'.[24] This was a reference to its restoration in 1746 with monies raised by a performance of *Othello* by James Ward's company.[25] This brought an influx of pilgrims to the places in Stratford associated with Shakespeare. It resulted, in 1756, in the cutting down by the Revd Francis Gastrell of the ancient mulberry tree in the garden of New Place, the house in which Shakespeare had died, because too many people wanted to see it. Not content with this desecration, three years later, after a dispute with the borough authority, Gastrell demolished the house itself. Thomas Sharp, a local watch and clock maker who was an accomplished carver, bought some of the mulberry wood and did a brisk trade in memorabilia. Garrick bought some of the wood and got William Hogarth to design a serpentine chair to be carved from it for the Shakespeare Temple at his Thameside house in Hampton.[26]

It would seem, therefore, that it was high time for Stratford to acknowledge its famous poet. Consequently, in 1764, there was vague talk of an event for the bi-centenary of Shakespeare's birth, but unfortunately Garrick, who would be needed as the driving force for such a celebration, was abroad and nothing happened. However, in 1767 the Corporation decided to rebuild the Town Hall and resolved to raise a statue to Shakespeare, which they hoped would be provided by Garrick. To flatter the great Shakespearean actor, a portrait of the Bard in his study by Benjamin Wilson was to be hung facing another picture of the thespian by Gainsborough at the other end of the chamber.[27] The statue was to be copied from a replica of Scheemakers' Westminster Abbey statue, which had been made in 1743 for Lord Pembroke of Wilton House in Wiltshire. In the event the statue, cast in lead by John Cheere, was erected in a niche on the new Town Hall where it survives today with the inscription: 'The Statue of Shakespeare and his Picture within were given by David Garrick Esq'.

If all this Shakespearean hagiography seems a little removed from garden history, Garrick's Jubilee had as its centrepiece the 'Amphitheatre', also known as the 'Great Booth', which was sited by the Avon on what is now Bancroft Gardens. This circular building (3) was loosely modelled on the great Rotunda at Ranelagh Gardens in London, which had been designed by James Lacy, Garrick's co-manager at Drury Lane.[28] The *Gentleman's Magazine* for September 1769 carried an illustration and description of the structure, which was built of wood with a dome supported by 'a colonnade of the Corinthian order, distant about ten feet from the sides'. It accommodated over a thousand people, with the Drury Lane orchestra, the singers and the Shakespeare statue sited at one end. It was constructed by the Drury Lane technical staff, who came up from London once the large tract of land on the riverbank had been cleared.[29] Garrick's letters of the summer of 1769 are full of references to the

Jubilee. Two are particularly interesting, which he wrote on 16 and 27 August to William Hunt, Stratford's town clerk. He expressed surprise that 'the Country People did not seem to relish our *Jubilee*, that they look'd upon it to be *popish* & that we shd raise ye Devil', but he was more hopeful of the impact of the Amphitheatre: 'I hope ye Building is forward enough. If that great & striking Object turns out as it ought to do, it will make other matters very Easy'.[30]

Although there were no plans for a garden of riverside walks on the Bancroft, the banks of the Avon were decorated with transparencies, some based on designs by Joshua Reynolds, together with firework set-pieces and other lighting effects contrived by Domenico Angelo.[31] In addition, thirty cannon were sited along the river to open the Jubilee and to be fired at intervals throughout the celebrations. There were further transparencies at the Birthplace – Shakespeare struggling through clouds to enlighten the world – and at the Town Hall, where the Bard was flanked by Falstaff and Pistol on one side and Lear and Caliban on the other. In spite of the masquerade ball, pageant, fireworks, music and horse race, the last two days of the Jubilee were washed out by torrential rain, but Garrick's performance of his *Ode upon Dedicating a Building, and Erecting a Statue, to Shakespeare*, delivered in the Amphitheatre with music and choruses composed by Thomas Arne, was electrifying. James Boswell, who witnessed the scene, wrote: 'While he repeated the Ode, and saw the various Passions and Feelings, which it contains, fully transfused into all around him, he seemed in Extacy, and gave us the Idea of a Mortal trans-formed into a Demi-god'.[32]

Scheemakers' statue of Shakespeare was modern for its time, in that it was one of the first memorials to depict its subject in contemporary costume rather than the classical style usually favoured for important statuary in this period. It shares a link, therefore, with a whole host of other heroes – literary, scientific, sporting, engineering, computing, popular – that form the nucleus of an extraordinary sculpture garden of bronzes. These were laid out for Felix Dennis at Dorsington, in the far south-western corner of the county where it connects with both Worces-tershire and Oxfordshire. Scrambling RAF fighter pilots dash for a sortie, while King Kong, the creation of Merian Caldwell Cooper, roars from a

4

Shakespeare as
poacher in the
Garden of Heroes
at Felix Dennis'
Dorsington Manor

gunnera-leaved pool. In the distance Carl Payne's breathless Roger
Bannister is in mid-stride as he completes the mile in just under four
minutes, and then the visual axis funnels out down a long tree-lined
avenue, studded with the heroes that have shaped Dennis' imagination
and, in many respects, his career as publisher, entrepreneur, poet and
philanthropist. They stand proudly, many by different sculptors, but all
united by a sparkling light bronze patina: Galileo next to Dorothy Parker,
Stephen Hawking by Sherlock Holmes and Watson, Einstein alongside
Rudyard Kipling, Robert Crumb, creator of Zap Comics, and the rock

guitarist, Chuck Berry. At the end of the avenue, next to a group of sinisterly helmeted warriors from the Battle of Thermopylae, stands William Shakespeare. Anthony Stones' bronze is not the bald Bard of the theatre, but the youthful poacher with his dog, bow in hand, a deer shot with an arrow lying at his feet (4). This is Shakespeare caught in the act in Sir Thomas Lucy's deer park at Charlecote: the stuff of Warwickshire legend.

endnotes on pages 263-264

1

Maximum consumption for a visiting monarch – Elizabethan gardens

▼

Kenilworth Pleasance, Warwick Castle, Kenilworth Castle
Combe Abbey

THE EARLIEST RECORDED DESIGNED LANDSCAPE IN WARWICKSHIRE, APART from the many deer parks dotted around the county, appears to have been the rectangular 'Pleasance in the Marsh' at **Kenilworth**, which Henry V had built as a hunting retreat in the 1420s. Payments for it have been lost, but an April 1427 commission for a 'new work at Kenilworth' may relate to its construction. John Leland calls it a 'praty banketynge house of tymbre', so it must always have been intended as a place for leisure and entertainment.[1] The timber ranges, set inside two rectangular moats, once enclosed a garden, which was commanded by tall corner towers. The moats were linked to the Mere surrounding Kenilworth Castle by a harbour where Henry's boat would dock. Henry VIII abandoned the Pleasance, but one of its banqueting houses was re-erected in the base court of the Castle. The moated site survives to the west of the Castle and is clearly visible in aerial photographs.

If Kenilworth was an important royal seat for hunting and entertainment in the fifteenth century, it came into its own as a place of regal pageant when the thirty-year-old Robert Dudley, Earl of Leicester, was granted the Castle in 1563. He was intent upon a glittering career at Queen Elizabeth's court and managed to lure her to Kenilworth four times: in 1566, 1568, 1572, when she made a surprise visit, and finally in 1575. On her last stay he put on one of the most magnificent and memorable of all the entertainments staged for her annual progresses through the realm.[2] During these she visited the major towns of her kingdom, which held civic pageants in her honour, and then lodged at nearby courtiers' houses. Her 1572 visit to Warwick town began in high ceremony and then descended into farce and fire. It is recorded in a manuscript 'Black Book' that John Nichols, an antiquary who collected original documents relating to the Queen's journeys, published in 1788.[3]

As with so many of the events created for the Queen's amusement, there were high points and lows. She had to endure a long speech by the town recorder before she made a ceremonial entry into the town, accompanied by the Bailiff and burgesses as far as **Warwick Castle**. It is not known whether the Earl of Warwick or his Countess had made any new private gardens for the Queen's use, but it seems unlikely, as after two nights she made her impromptu visit to Kenilworth where she enjoyed 'princely sports'.[4] She also surprised Thomas Fisher, who had made an immense fortune by the acquisition of 'dissolved' land, buying Warwick Priory and its park in 1546.[5] When his queen arrived Fisher was stricken with gout and had to be brought out into the gallery for an audience. With royalty and nobility as guests the Priory gardens were presumably as spectacular as the house, although little evidence survives today. Neither is there a record of the sixteenth-century gardens around Charlecote, where Sir Thomas Lucy entertained Elizabeth in the Great Hall.

When she returned to Warwick she was treated to country dancing in the Castle courtyard, followed by a firework display in Temple park across the Avon.[6] The centrepiece was a mock fort made of 'slender timber covered with canvas' and 'against that fort was another castlewise prepared of like strength'.[7] The townspeople, dressed as soldiers, holding one of the forts, laid siege to the other, which was commanded by the dashing Edward de Vere, Earl of Oxford. The battle raged:

> they in the fort shooting again, and casting out divers fires, terrible
> to those that have not been in like experiences, valiant to such as
> delighted therein, and indeed strange to them that understood it
> not; for the wildfire falling into the river Avon, would for a time lye
> still, and than again rise and fly abroad, casting forth many flashes
> and flames, whereat the Queen's Majefty took great pleasure.[8]

When it was decided that the townspeople's fort should be taken, 'a dragon flying, casting out huge flames and squibs, lighted upon the fort, and so set fire thereon to the subversion thereof'.[9] That was not all. A fireball then struck a house at the end of the medieval bridge across the Avon and set it alight. The Earl of Oxford and Sir Fulke Greville had to rescue the couple that had been sleeping through it all, and the following morning Elizabeth organised a collection among her courtiers to compensate them.

This blend of romantic revivalism, theatricals, mock battles and pyrotechnics characterises the progresses, the Queen either carried aloft by her retinue into towns and cities, riding on horseback in the hunt, or walking through the landscape parks of the great Elizabethan houses of her subjects. In order to understand how the more sylvan entertainments were staged, one need only read Sir Philip Sidney's epic poem of 1590-3, *The New Arcadia*, much of which, as its title suggests, has a woodland setting.[10] The action in Book Three opens in a forest to which Basilius, King of Arcadia, has retired and where he has built himself two fine lodges. Basilius and his wife, Queen Gynecia, live in one lodge with their daughter Philoclea, while their other daughter, Pamela, lives in the second lodge with attendant servants. Like a scene from one of the pastoral masques put on for Elizabeth's pleasure, six maids come to the door of Pamela's lodge dressed

> all in one livery of scarlet petticoats which were tucked up almost to their knees, the petticoats themselves being in many places garnished with leaves; their legs naked, saving that above the ankles they had little black silk laces upon which did hang a few silver bells – like which they had a little above their elbows upon their bare arms; upon their hair were garlands of roses and gillyflowers.[11]

Each maid has a musical instrument, 'which, consorting their well-pleasing tunes, did charge each ear with unsensibleness that did not lend itself unto them'.[12] The maids then walk in the forest, to the sound of their music, and come to a clearing, 'a little square place, not burdened with trees' where a board is laid before them 'covered and beautified with the pleasantest fruits that sunburned autumn could deliver unto them'.[13]

5

The Elizabethans alfresco – an illustration from George Gascoigne's 1575 *Noble Arte of Venerie* of a picnic during a hunt.
University of Bristol, Special Collections

Relaxing after this 'collation'[14] they are suddenly surprised by twenty armed men who put hoods over their heads and carry them off on horseback to a 'castle stood in the midst of a great lake, upon a high rock, where partly by art, but principally by nature, it was by all men esteemed impregnable'.[15] The whole episode, with its pastoral setting, picnic, music, abduction and flight to a castle, reads like the Kenilworth Entertainment, staged by Dudley in the landscape around his stronghold, which, like that in the *Arcadia,* floated above a peerless lake.[16]

Elizabeth was entertained by these alfresco picnics and had already enjoyed one at Dudley's seat at Kew. Dudley used Kew as his country base when he was not attending Court. His household accounts for 1558-9 have an item for 'the banketing stuff prepaird at the Quenes highness being at your lordship's tents within the Parke'.[17] By 1565 Kew had been sold off and Dudley was resident in Durham House in the city. He was not granted Kenilworth until 1563, and before 1568 had only visited it for the Queen's 1566 Progress. In 1570 he bought Paget Place, near St Clement Danes, renaming it Leicester House, and this became his principal London residence. This was convenient for the London palaces but, owing to Elizabeth's constant moving between these and her outlying houses, Dudley needed a suburban seat. In 1576-7 he leased Wanstead House, which was close to Greenwich, and then bought it in 1578. He visited **Kenilworth** annually, but most of the garden activity took place at Wanstead, as the household accounts record. The Queen's Privy Garden at his Warwickshire castle was run up quickly and then, no doubt, as quickly forgotten.

In addition to these pastoral interludes and mock sieges, every Royal Progress was punctuated with hunting expeditions, Elizabeth being a keen huntswoman. Dudley employed the author and soldier George Gascoigne to devise the masques, pageants and speeches for Elizabeth's 1575 visit to Kenilworth, the very year that Gascoigne published anonymously his *Noble Arte of Venerie or Hunting*.[18] This was a translation from the French of treatises by Jacques du Fouilloux and Gaston de Foix.[19] The addition of 'noble' in the title suggests that Gascoigne was trying to curry favour with the Queen and solicit patronage. He did this in person at the Kenilworth Entertainment, when she was returning from a late afternoon's hunt on the Monday of her stay, surprising her, dressed like a Savage Man, a precursor of the eighteenth-century hermit, 'with an oaken plant plucked up by the roots in his hand, himself forgrone all in moss and ivy'.[20] As each Progress was a quest in which the Queen would take part, her journeying to the parent house through the landscape park 'became fraught with adventure. Satyrs and Wild Men lurked behind every tree, ready to address her'.[21]

The *Noble Arte* has several interesting woodcuts, two of which feature, not surprisingly, the Queen. The first (5), which recalls Sidney's Arcadian picnic, is entitled: 'Of the place where and howe an assembly should be made, in the presence of a Prince, or some honourable person'.[22] Two pages of rhyming couplets describe the perfect place for such an assembly:

The place should first be pight, on pleasant gladsome greene,

Yet under shade of stately trees, where little sunne is seene:

And neare some fountaine spring, whose chrystall running streames,

May help to coole the parching heate, yeaught by Phoebus beames.[23]

Significantly, given that most sixteenth-century garden design constrained flowers and herbs within rigid geometric patterns – either knots or parterres – this forest clearing was not to be full of 'forced flowers', but 'must of it selfe, afforde such sweete delight'.[24] The settings for these alfresco repasts are the flip side of the Elizabethan garden: a conscious evocation of wild, rather than tamed, nature where a nobleman or a monarch could relax during a hunting expedition. A similar scene is enacted in Edmund Spenser's 1579 *Shepherd's Calendar*:

See, where she sits upon the grassie greene,

  (O seemly sight)

Yclad in Scarlot like a mayden Queene,

  And Ermines white.

Upon her head a Cremosin coronet,

With Damaske roses and Daffodillies set:

  Bayleaves betweene,

  And Primroses greene

Embellish the sweet Violet.[25]

The other hunting illustration concerns fewmets (6), or deer droppings, which one of the huntsmen would present to the Queen for close inspection so that she could chose which of the harts might give her the best sport. The Queen is shown on a purpose-built, but temporary, hunting stand set in a forest clearing; the woodcut is accompanied by another piece of verse:

Before the Queene, I come report to make

The husht and peace, for noble Trystrams sake,

6

A huntsman presenting deer droppings or 'fewmets' for the Queen's inspection from Gascoigne's Noble Arte. *University of Bristol, Special Collections*

From out my horne, my fewmets first I drawe,
And them present, on leaves, by hunters lawe.[26]

But what must concern us principally at Kenilworth is Dudley's sumptuous Privy Garden, created expressly for the royal visit. Robert Laneham's general description of the layout is so precise and detailed that it is worth quoting at length:

Unto this, his Honour's exquisite appointment of a beautiful Garden, an acre or more of quantity, that lyeth on the North there: wherein hard all along the Castle wall is reared a pleasant terrace, of a ten foot high, and a twelve broad, even under foot, and fresh of

fine grass; as is also the side thereof toward the garden: in which, by
sundry equal distance, with obelisks, spheres, and white bears, all of
stone upon their curious bases, by goodly show were set: to these,
two fine arbours redolent by sweet trees and flowers, at each end
one, the garden plot under that, with fair alleys green by grass, even
voided from the borders at both sides and some (for change) with
sand, not light or too soft or soily by dust, but smooth and firm,
pleasant to walk on, as a seashore when the water is availed: then,
much gracified by due proportion of four even quarters: in the
midst of each, upon a base a two foot square, and high, seemly
bordered of itself, a square pilaster rising pyramidally of a fifteen
foot high: symmetrically pierced through from a foot beneath, until
a two foot of the top: whereupon for a capital, an orb of a ten inches
thick: Every of these (with its base), from the ground to the top, of
one whole piece; hewn out of hard porphyry, and with great art and
heed (thinks me) thither conveyed and there erected. Where,
further also, by great cast and cost, the sweetness of savour on all
sides, made so respirant from the redolent plants and fragrant herbs
and flowers, in form, colour, and quantity so deliciously variant; and
fruit trees bedecked with apples, pears, and ripe cherries.[27]

In addition to Laneham's text, there are two important visual sources for
the Queen's Privy Garden. These are an eighteenth-century copy of a lost
seventeenth-century wall painting, formerly at Newnham Paddox House,
of the Castle as it appeared in 1620, and a simple plan of the inner
precinct illustrated in Dugdale's 1656 *Warwickshire*. The evocative
painting (*colour plate 2*) shows the walled Castle surrounded to the north
and south by calm blue waters, the Mere or 'Poole' as Dugdale calls it. The
Castle is depicted from the south with Lunn's Tower and the Water
Tower in the foreground, the 'Great Gatehouse' to the right with the
Privy Garden beyond. Its east wall has a towered projection, oddly shown
as a concave tower on the Dugdale plan, and the Swan Tower defends the
north-east corner. The area is laid to grass with the Atlas Fountain
surviving in splendid isolation at the centre. A ziz-zag wall extends from
the Swan Tower to enclose a triangular area which has a three-gabled

building complex attached to the rear curtain wall. This is marked on the Dugdale plan as the 'Pleasance'. By 1656 the garden had been altered and an eight-part parterre created in the grassy enclosure centred by a circular *rond point*, the Atlas Fountain having been dismantled.

The gardener, Adrian, let Laneham sneak in and see the Fountain and the Aviary while Elizabeth and Dudley were out hunting. Laneham encountered 'a very fair fountain, cast into an eight square, reared a four foot high; from the midst whereof a colum up set in shape of two Athlants joined together a back half'.[28] The water cascaded from the globe into the basin 'wherein pleasantly playing too and fro, and round about, carp, tench, bream, and, for variety, perch and eel'.[29] Dudley's heraldic bear was emblazoned throughout the garden, and the ragged staff topped the globe.

There were, of course many precedents for fountains in England inspired by both Italian and French precedent.[30] There was a Diana Fountain and a Table Fountain at Nonsuch, similar to one set up for the Queen's visit to Kelston Manor in Somerset, under which she dined in the summer of 1591.[31] The most beautiful fountain of the period, certainly the most strikingly Italianate, is at Wilton House, Wiltshire. This fountain of the modest Venus was set up in 1577 to celebrate the marriage of Henry Herbert, 2nd Earl of Pembroke, to Mary Sidney, sister of the poet Sir Philip.[32] But perhaps of more direct influence on the fountain at Kenilworth was that at Cardinal Georges d'Amboise's chateau of Gaillon, near Rouen in France, which Dudley is thought to have seen. Carved by Genoese sculptors, it was sited in the central courtyard, was twenty-two feet high, topped by a sculpture of John the Baptist, and had an octagonal marble basin decorated with classical reliefs and family heraldry.[33] The detached formal garden at Gaillon had at its centre a tall domed building, housing another fountain, with cage-like projections suggesting that it also served as an aviary: these were the two main garden features constructed at Kenilworth. Another possible influence was the great garden at Amboise, which had no fewer than ten parterres – all quartered – the enclosure centred by a domed aviary.[34]

Laneham described the great Aviary at Kenilworth as 'a square cage, sumptuous and beautiful, joined hard to the North wall...of a rare form and excellency'.[35] Every part of it was 'beautified with great diamonds,

7

The 'Queens seat of freestone', now acting as an entrance porch to the Gatehouse at Kenilworth Castle, was originally set up by Robert Dudley for Elizabeth's pleasure on her 1575 visit

emeralds, rubies, and sapphires; pointed, tabled, rock and round; garnished with their gold, by skilful head and hand, and by toil and pencil so lively expressed'.[36] The Elizabethans delighted in highly overwrought decoration in both architecture and furnishings: Laneham's description of the Aviary makes it seem like an arched and meshed jewel casket patterned with cabochon ornament. Both Fountain and Aviary were of the highest quality in design and, given that Dudley employed a Frenchman as his head gardener, first at Kew and then later at Wanstead – the Adrian that had let Laneham into the Garden – and had travelled widely in France, it is safe to assume that the Queen's Privy Garden was intended to display the very latest in French garden technology and planting. But it was more than just a piece of cutting-edge design. It offered all the delights that Elizabethans had come to expect from their gardens. Laneham summed it up perfectly:

> A garden then so appointed, as wherein aloft upon sweet shadowed
> walk of terrace, in heat of summer, to feel the pleasant whisking
> wind above, or delectable coolness of the fountain spring beneath:

to taste of delicious strawberries, cherries, and other fruits, even from their stalks: to smell such fragrancy of sweet odours, breathing from the plants, herbs, and flowers: to hear such natural melodious music and tunes of birds...whereby, at one moment, in one place, at hand, without travel, to have so full fruition of so many God's blessings, by entire delight unto all senses (if all can take) at once: for etymon of the word worthy to be called Paradise.[37]

As well as this walled garden of earthly delights, there were views out towards the Mere and the Chase beyond with its deer, which could also be seen from 'the East arbour in the base court'.[38] This may well have been the little banquet house brought from the Pleasance. There was another viewing seat – the 'Queens seat of freestone' – mentioned as such in a later valuation, which is shown on the plan of the Castle in Dugdale's *Warwickshire*.[39] Dudley wrote to Lord Burghley on 17 May, just weeks before the Queen's arrival in Warwickshire, that he was pleased his lordship saw fit to 'help me that I may have some stone toward the making a little banquet-house in my garden'.[40] The façade of this seat survives (7), now set against Leicester's Gatehouse, where it serves as an entrance. Its form is of a Doric triumphal arch decorated with Dudley's heraldic cinquefoils and his initials.

Dudley's Paradise Garden, fit for a Faerie Queene, was probably left to decay gently after his death in 1588. His household disbursements for 1584–6 list payments to 'Awdryan [Adrian] the gardneir at his goyng to Kenelworth',[41] but more specific garden activity was taking place at Leicester House in February 1585 when 'John Varnham of Westminster gardneir' supplied 'turffes from Tuthill'.[42] Earlier, in April 1584, Dudley had paid 'fower gardneirs which made and sett a knott in the garden at Wanstead',[43] while Robert Adams was rewarded in October of the same year 'for making the [sun] dyall in the garden at Leicester House'.[44] At some point, after the early seventeenth-century painting was commissioned and the Dugdale plan drawn, the garden enclosure was simplified, the Aviary was taken down and a parterre laid out. Might the parterre garden have been planted as a theatrical enclosure for Ben Jonson's 1626 *The Masque of Owls*, which was performed at Kenilworth by the ghost of Captain Cox, mounted on his hobby-horse, for Prince Charles, the future Charles I?

What then does a modern visitor make of the recent reconstruction of the Queen's Privy Garden, carried out at vast expense by English Heritage? It reeks of conspicuous consumption and its overall effect is flashy and brash, just as it must have looked in 1575. What must be stated at the outset is that its reconstruction was achieved after a thorough archaeological excavation, carried out in 2004 by Brian Dix, who had previously worked on the Hampton Court Privy Garden in London and at Kirby Hall in Northamptonshire.[45] Similar scholarly attention to detail was employed by garden historian David Jacques, when he was choosing plants for the four knot gardens of African marigolds, sweet bays, straw-berries and carnations. Certainly the first glimpse of the Atlas Fountain and the Aviary beyond (8), as the visitor walks through the Castle keep, is breathtaking. So too is the scale of the enterprise. As English Heritage's Chief Executive, Simon Thurley, has stated: 'Never before has something like this been attempted and never before has anything on this scale been achieved'.[46] What then palls? The impact is overwhelmingly artificial, new, shiny and garish. It is to be hoped that the plants will take over, the paint will weather down and the gravel paths take some stain of wear-and-tear. What might have evoked more romantically that 1575 royal visit would have been the flooding of the marshy fields surrounding the Castle, thereby rein-stating the Mere, from whence the Lady of the Lake, in true Arthurian fashion, rose to yield to the Queen her sovereignty over the waters.

Dudley's horticultural extravagance must have had resonances within the county, and it may well have inspired a garden laid out at **Combe Abbey** by one of his neighbours, Sir John Harington. That they were close friends is borne out by Dudley's informative household accounts, where a disbursement for February 1585 records a payment to 'Sir John Harington's man for presenting a pyde [piebald] horsse to your lord-ship'.[47] It is not known precisely what kind of garden Harington created at Combe, but there are clues in a later memoir, and also in an intriguing portrait of Princess Elizabeth (*colour plate 3*), daughter of James I and his queen, Anne of Denmark. This was painted by Robert Peake, just months after the death of Queen Elizabeth I in March 1603. The seven-year-old – her age is inscribed on the fan she holds in her left hand – stands some-

8 Two marble Atlas figures support a globe in the restored Queen's Privy Garden at Kenilworth. In the background, the Aviary is fronted by four knot gardens, which are filled with flowers of the correct period

what rigidly, close to the picture plane, against the backdrop of a land-scape. This appears to be an imagined scene, with huntsmen in a paled deer park on one side, and on the other a spiral mount with an ornamental tree arbour under which sit two women in conversation. The Princess poses primly on an open lawn separated from the parkland by a stream, over which there is a wooden bridge leading to the arbour and a three-arched stone bridge leading to a gate in the wooden pale. This portrait is linked to another, also by Peake, of Elizabeth's brother, the young Prince Henry; he is standing proudly beside a dead stag. Sir John, whose son John attends the Prince, commissioned both paintings as gestures of welcome to the new royal family, which had just arrived in England.

Harington's main country seat was Exton Hall in Rutland, but through his marriage to Anne, daughter of Robert Keilwey, he had acquired Combe Abbey on her father's death in 1581. Harington divided his time between Exton, Burley-on-the-Hill and Combe. He had no need to undertake extensive works at Exton and Burley, for his father had renovated both. Any new improvements would, therefore, have been carried out at Combe.

This raises the intriguing possibility that the landscape depicted in Peake's portrait of Princess Elizabeth might not be artificial, but a close representation of what Harington had achieved in the grounds before his royal guest arrived at Combe in June 1603 on her journey south, and before Harington was appointed her guardian in October of the same year.

It is clear from a later account by one of Elizabeth's ladies-in-waiting, Frances, Lady Erskine, that Sir John took his guardian's duties very seriously and instructed Elizabeth in botany, astronomy, philosophy and cosmology, so that before she and her ladies left Combe, '*Copernicus*'s System of our World's diurnal and annual Motion round the Sun, was quite familiar' to them.[48] Harington had 'one of the best Telescopes' through which he allowed Elizabeth to look at the 'Moon and other Planets' for pleasure rather than for studious erudition; it was 'granted as a Favour, as well as looking at Things in the Microscopes'.[49] Harington seems to have been the perfect guardian who 'never debarred her [Elizabeth] of her Liberty, in the Choice of her Amusements, though he endeavoured to turn them to her Improvements'.[50] What is also apparent is that Combe Abbey had an important ornamental landscape that Harington encouraged Elizabeth to enjoy and to improve while she was in his care.

Moreover, Lady Erskine's account of the time spent at Combe is so revealing of the designed landscape that Harington laid out there after 1581 that it deserves to be quoted at some length:

> The first Days after our arrival at Comb-abbey, were spent in admiring the Beauties of the Place, which made so great an Impression upon me, that I still remember it well enough to give you some Account of it ...The House stood rather low, as most old ones do, but had a pleasing, though not an extensive Prospect; and under the Windows of the Princess's Apartment, was a Parterre filled with the greatest Variety of Flowers, that ever I saw; beyond which, a Lawn of a beautiful Verdure, peculiar to that Country, relieved the Eye, which otherways, would have been fatigued with the dazzling Colours of the Flowers.[51]

This sounds like a typical late Elizabethan layout with formal flowerbeds beneath the windows of the house and an enamelled lawn further out. But the description then extends to the wider landscape where there were elements that accord in part with the Peake portrait:

> The Prospect was terminated by a Cascade, falling into a Canal, that looked like a River, and seemed to lose itself in a fine Wood on the right Hand which Wood came right round from the other Side of the House, and one could go through it in the Shade, all the Way to the Park, which was a very fine one; through it there were many Gravel Paths, that made Walking agreeable in Winter, when the Greasiness of the Soil, would not admit of it on Grass.[52]

Admittedly, there is no mention of the mount or its arbour, but the Peake painting has a river-like canal and there are gravel paths leading up to the arbour.

However, what delighted the Princess particularly was a wilderness garden way out in the park:

> Nothing took the Princess's Fancy so much, as a little Wilderness at the End of the Park, on the Banks of a large Brook which ran winding along, and formed in one Place; a large irregular Bason, or rather a small Lake, in which there was an Island covered with Underwood, and flowering Trees and Plants, so mixed and disposed, that for nine Months in the Year, they formed a continual Spring. This Place, and the adjoining Thicket, my young Mistress begged to have the Disposal of, during her Stay, which was granted with great Pleasure, by Lord and Lady Harrington, who made it their Study to render their Habitation agreeable to her.[53]

The Princess 'was extremely fond of the feathered Tribe', and collected all kinds of different birds and fowl.[54] She had an aviary 'made like that she had heard Queen *Elizabeth* had admired so much, at the late Earl of *Leicester's*, in Imitation of which, the Top of this was round, with coloured Glass, that looked at a little Distance, like rough Emeralds and Rubies,

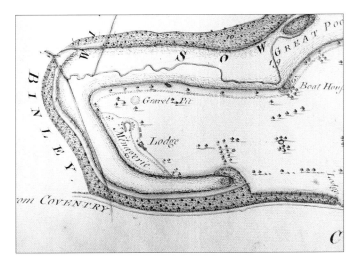

9

Matthias Baker's
1778 plan of the
Combe Abbey estate
marks the present
Menagerie, probably
close to the site of
Princess Elizabeth's
early seventeenth-
century Wilderness
Garden.
*Warwickshire County
Record Office,
CR8/184*

seemingly the Produce of a Rock, overgrown with Moss, which formed the Back and Roof of the Aviary'.[55] The walls were 'enclosed with a Net of gilt Wire' and inside there were bushes for perches, while water fell 'continually from the artificial Rock, into a shallow Marble Bason, in which the pretty little feathered Inhabitants drank and bathed at Pleasure, and Recesses were made in the Rock for them to build their Nests in'.[56] As well as living specimens, the Aviary was decorated with the skins and feathers of exotic birds that could not cope with the English climate and had been stuffed for display.

The Aviary appears to have been sited on an island on which there was a thatched cottage that the Princess had had repaired for a poor widow and her children who were to take care of the birds. In improving the building she gave it 'the Appearance of an Hermitage, and near it a Grotto, the Adorning of which with Shells and Moss, was the Amusement of many of her leisure Hours, in which, as in every Thing else, she shewed a Genius above her Years'.[57] This cottage and Aviary were surrounded by 'representations of other Creatures', which 'were placed in different Parts of the Wood, and the Pictures of such, whose Skins could not easily be had, adorned the little wooden Buildings'.[58] In an extraordinary foretaste of the eighteenth-century eclectic garden, these huts were constructed in 'all the different Orders of Architecture, which was a Science Lord *Harrington* thought a Princess ought to understand....Some of the Edifices were after the Draughts, given in Books of Travels, of those of *India*, and in them Figures drest according to the Manners of those Countries, so that this was a kind of World in Miniature'.[59] Harington was obviously taking seriously the King's view that women were 'all naturally addicted to Vanity', and his urging that her guardian should not 'attempt to make the Princess a Latin or Greek Scholar...but to endeavour to make her truly wise, by instructing her thoroughly in Religion, and by giving her a general Idea of History'.[60] Tantalisingly, Lady Erskine describes the Princess' 'Garden and Greenhouse', which were 'as well stored with Curiosities, and exotic Plants, as her Minagerie, with Creatures', but fails to elaborate on them.[61]

If all this encyclopaedic amusement were not enough, in the adjacent meadows the Princess had a 'Fairy-farm' stocked with diminutive cattle, which were looked after by the children of a neighbouring farmer.[62] He managed the farm, while the children tended the animals, dressed as shepherdesses. It is as if a scene from Sidney's *Arcadia* or Spenser's *Faerie Queene* had miraculously come alive; clear evidence that, in this north-western pocket of Warwickshire, an informal Elizabethan Arcadian wilderness had been created by a royal princess. But where in the land-scape did Elizabeth achieve her garden of earthly delights? It must have been some way off from the main house, as Lady Erskine recalls that it was at the 'End of the Park, on the Banks of a large Brook which ran winding along'. The only places that correspond to the description are on a bend in the river opposite the island or, not surprisingly, where the present Menagerie is sited. It seems extremely likely that this secret corner of the estate is where the Princess created her exotic garden and where Henry Holland built his Menagerie in 1771 for Lord Craven. The building is shown on Matthias Baker's estate survey of 1778, at the south-western corner of the park (9) where the Great Pool doubles back in a U-shaped curve.[63] At the end of the lake is another small, tree-cloaked island where the Princess may have delighted in the birdsong of the 'feathered Inhabitants' of her Aviary.

endnotes on pages 264-265

2

Pools and earthworks – lost gardens of the early seventeenth century

Wormleighton Manor, Astley Castle, Warwick Priory, Arlescote Manor
Chesterton House, Packwood House, Weston House, Blyth Hall

THE OFTEN SCANTY REMAINS OF LOST GARDENS AND LANDSCAPES ARE notoriously difficult to date, but one site in the county at **Wormleighton**, near Fenny Compton on the border with Northamptonshire, has a strange water feature that seems to have been associated with the manor house built by John Spencer in 1516-19. This modest brick building was sited close to the parish church on the ridge above the medieval village, which by 1634 had been deserted. The village site was recorded on an estate survey (*10*) of that year made by Richard Norwood.[1] This, together with a later plan of 1734 by John Reynolds, gives a fascinating insight into the steady demise through the seventeenth century of a small landed estate.[2]

Today, almost all the courtyard buildings of the Manor have disappeared, but a green drive leads from the T-junction of suburban roads in the village to an imposing Gatehouse built in iron-rich Hornton stone. This was erected by John Spencer's descendant, Robert, who was elevated to the peerage in 1603. It is dated 1613 and, together with the adjacent Manor, served as Prince Rupert's headquarters before the battle of Edgehill, which is about seven miles to the south-west. The 1634 survey shows small enclosures to the east of the Manor, but these are likely to have been service yards rather than gardens. To the west, along the ridge, the area is wooded, and it funnels down to one of the four 'charges', or pastures, named 'The Old Town'. At its centre is a strange kite-shaped water feature, which aerial photographs show has survived, though it is now silted up.[3] It was, no doubt, a series of fishponds and a great breeding tank constructed for the Tudor manor house. By 1634 it formed the central ornamental element of an enclosed wooded park.

Throughout the first half of the seventeenth century the Spencers rose steadily in status, with William, Lord Spencer, being made a Knight of the Bath in 1634, and Henry Spencer, the 3rd Baron Spencer, elevated to the earldom of Sutherland in 1643. William had begun to sub-divide his lands in Wormleighton into compact blocks to lease to tenants, suggesting that his interests lay elsewhere. Dugdale records that in 1646, during the Civil War, the house was 'burnt by his Majesties forces of

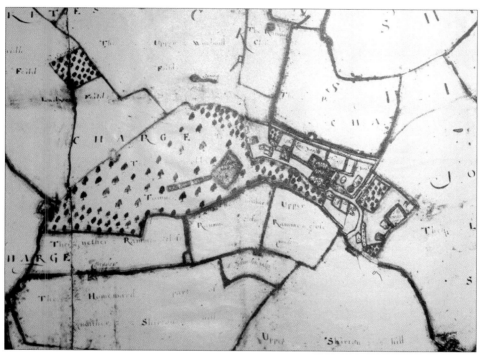

10 The deserted village at Wormleighton, shown on a 1634 survey by Richard Norwood. The kite-shaped feature in the field marked 'The Old Town' is the medieval fishpond and breeding tank associated with the Tudor manor house. *From the Collection at Althorp*

Banbury, to prevent the Rebells making it a garrison'.[4] Thereafter, the Spencers abandoned Wormleighton for the major family seat at Althorp in Northamptonshire. So by 1734, when Reynolds surveyed the estate, the wooded park had reverted back to pasture, as it remains today, and the only indications that the village once had an important house and land-

11 The surviving earthworks and watery channels of the early-seventeenth-century New
Garden at Astley Castle

scape are Robert Spencer's evocative Gatehouse and the ghostly outlines
of the great rectangular fishpond in the fields below the church.

Further intriguing garden earthworks survive at **Astley Castle**, due
west of Arbury Hall near Nuneaton, once part of the Arbury estate. This
ownership is signified by the Gothick trim of the stable block on the
approach to the moated Castle, while several Gothick features on the
main building itself are further proof of a mid- to late eighteenth-century
Gothicisation. This is likely to have been carried out by Sir Roger Newdigate when his sister-in-law, Mary Conyers, was living at the Castle. Astley
is now ruinous, having been abandoned after a fire in 1978, but is in the
process of being restored by the Landmark Trust, which has commissioned a conservation management plan that charts the major
chronological developments on the site.[5] What is clear from the research
carried out is that the medieval Castle was substantially remodelled
before 1627 and again in the early nineteenth century.[6] Below the
entrance front there are remnants of a circular flower parterre of indeterminate date, its beds defined by box, surrounded by building materials.

However, more significant in terms of garden history is the possibility that there was an important seventeenth-century garden at Astley on an open field on the other side of the moat.

Robert Hewitt's 1696 map of the 'Lordshipp of Astley' (*colour plate 4*) shows the Castle on its moated island with a garden laid out in eight rectangular enclosures divided by paths.[7] This may have been a productive kitchen garden, though there appears to be a small building, perhaps a banqueting house, at the north-east corner, overlooking the moat. Further out to the west across the moat is a field called 'The Plash', which separates the moated site from the 'Great Pool', still in evidence today. To the east of the Castle and north of the parish church is an irregularly-shaped enclosure marked 'New Garden', rendered plainly except for three mature trees. The only access to this, given that it is separated from the Castle by the western arm of the moat, is via the lane to Ansley east of the church. The main stone causeway bridge is to the south and its approach is cut off from the field by the churchyard. There was, apparently, a timber bridge across the north arm of the moat in the late nineteenth century, which gave access to a shrubbery, but that has since disappeared.[8] All surviving illustrations of the Castle and its grounds date from the late eighteenth and nineteenth centuries, while two further estate maps were made in 1807 and 1825. There is, therefore, no other visual evidence for this 'New Garden' and no indication in the archival record as to what it comprised.

A possible date of construction is during the ownership of Richard Chamberlain. His father, Sir Edmund, had bought the estate in 1601, and Richard restored the chancel of the parish church in 1607, fitting up part of the Castle for residential use and inscribing the date 1627 on the parapet of the east front. The Chamberlains seem not to have spent much time at Astley, and in 1674 it was bought by Sir Richard Newdigate of Arbury. It is likely, therefore, that Richard Chamberlain laid out the New Garden before 1627, when he was remodelling the Castle. There are several wide ditches, which were full of standing water on our visit after rain (*11*), at the northern corner of the field. This suggests that there was originally a series of trapezoid-shaped ponds with banked causeways. At the north-western corner is an earth mound, now topped with a mature tree, that might well have been a viewing mount overlooking the formal water garden one way, the moat on the other, while offering views out to the 'Little Parke' beyond the Garden.[9] There can be no definitive proof as to what precisely existed at Astley, but the surviving earthworks, like those at Wormleighton, are indicative of an early seventeenth-century formal water garden.

Water also featured in perhaps the most important gentry grounds in the county, at **Warwick Priory**. As we have seen, in the Elizabethan period it was the seat of Thomas Hawkins, alias Fisher, who had not only created a park, but also developed a series of pools from existing monastic fishponds to the north-west of his house.[10] After his death in 1577 the estate passed briefly to his wastrel son and was then sold in 1581 to John Puckering, later knighted and Keeper of the Great Seal of England. His son Sir Thomas Puckering inherited in 1596 and before his death in 1637 he created an important formal garden at the Priory.[11] Almost all trace of this has gone in a late seventeenth-century remodelling, possibly by the landscape gardener, Henry Wise, and during later nineteenth-century improvements. Furthermore, the great Priory house itself, apart from a small range and a section of walling, has been demolished, its site now occupied by a banal 1970s building which houses the Warwickshire County Record Office. Any retrieval of Thomas Puckering's early seventeenth-century garden must, therefore, rely entirely upon archival and cartographic evidence.[12] What is certain is that Puckering's formal garden was at the cutting edge of style and fashion, for he was well connected at Court, being part of a group of noblemen who were companions to Prince Henry, himself a great garden maker. This friendship with the Prince is commemorated on Puckering's memorial in St Mary's church, which was designed in austere Corinthian classicism by Nicholas Stone, to whom we will return at Chesterton. Puckering was also well travelled, visiting France and Italy between 1610 and 1611. He was knighted in 1612, married in 1616 and began work on his new garden in 1620.

In March of that year '32 ballisters' and twelve posts for three staircases in the 'Great Garden' were turned and cut, while the gardener and two labourers were working for three days gravelling the walks.[13] In June workmen were paid 'for making splints and railes (the splints cut in the

12 Thomas Puckering's formal garden, with its plain parterres and gravel walks, is shown on this 1711 bird's-eye view of Warwick Priory. *Warwickshire County Record Office, CR26/2/2*

forme of flower de luce, and the posts of achornes)'.[14] It is interesting that Puckering did not use his family crest of a stag, but a *fleur de lys*, which may well have been an allusion to the Prince of Wales. These 'posts' were, no doubt, heraldic poles set within a balustrade, like similar contemporary examples at the royal palaces of Nonsuch and Richmond, and particularly those in the Great Garden at Whitehall.[15] Masons were also at work on stone walls and a 'causey' on the side of his 'Turnabout'.[16] A causey was a raised terrace (causeway) similar to those in other early seventeenth-century gardens. There was one at Somerset House in London, and earlier examples abroad such as that at Saint-Germain-en-Laye in Paris, which in turn was modelled on the Villa Lante at Bagnaia in Italy.[17] Evidence of Puckering's terrace walk was found in excavations made in 1937: 'On the first day that we commenced to excavate we found the foundations of a wall which has since proved to be the wall of a formal garden ....In the centre there were steps leading up from the garden to the top of the wall.'[18] The raised terrace to the south of the Priory enclosed and overlooked three sides of Puckering's formal garden, which is shown on a much later 1711 bird's-eye view (12). By that time it was laid out as a rectangular grass-covered *parterre à l'Anglaise*, defined by rows of evenly spaced, clipped evergreen shrubs. It was more likely to have been planted with knots when Puckering created it in the 1620s.

The 'Turnabout', parallel to the west side of the viewing terrace, was essentially a place in the garden in which to take a turn, or a walk, and was enlivened by a pedimented gateway in an overwrought Jacobean style; it carried the date 1620.[19] A drawing of the archway is inscribed: 'This was the Side Entrance and stood in the Front of the Priory with the Pilars & Iron Gates now standing at the end of the Long Walk'. While the viewing terrace was being constructed Puckering was also building a banqueting house in the grounds, the exact location of which is not known. However, a later description suggests that it was on an island in one of the Priory pools: 'a banqueting house now gone to ruin, where Bacchus had used to be adored in flowing bumpers of stout October, brought from the hospitable cellars of the old Priory'.[20] The 1620-1 accounts give details of the completion of building, including stone steps, ironwork for the windows and wainscoting for the interior.[21] A blacksmith called Henbury was paid 2s 8d for 'making of 4 pick-leads for the posts of the staircases of my Banqueting house', and Roger Edgin, a plasterer from Bromsgrove, was in charge of 'plaistering my Banqueting house both without and within'; he worked on the site from 21 May until 21 December.[22] The entries in the accounts include lime, hair to bind the plaster and 630 tiles sent from London, 'half of them greene, and half of them yellowe'.[23] These may have been for the roof, or for external cladding like tile-hanging; wherever they were used the building must have had a richly polychromatic impact. During the construction members of Puckering's family went to see the contemporary garden at Sir Baptist Hicks' Campden House in Gloucestershire, which had two banqueting houses facing each other along a terrace.[24] Puckering paid the gardener there for showing his 'nephew Pakington my brother Grantham and Sir Will Brown...that house and garden'.[25] This suggests that, like the buildings at Campden, the Priory banqueting house was a structure of some architectural pretension.

While the banqueting house seems to have been built amongst the pools, at a distance from the Priory, the main features of the 1620 formal garden were set below the south front of the main house. The parterre gave onto a grand terrace at a higher level, offering views out towards the town, with Caesar's Tower of Warwick Castle the main visual focus, though Guy's Tower and St Mary's church, before its reconstruction after the great fire of 1694, must also have been visible. Given Puckering's considerable knowledge and experience of continental gardens, it is likely that, as well as the ornamental gateway, the terrace and 'Turnabout' were punctuated with statuary, though this can only be speculation. What is certain is that the raised walk, thought to have been created by Henry Wise in conjunction with Charles Bridgeman almost a century later, is of Thomas Puckering's campaign. It reveals a surprisingly early interest in the picturesque qualities of the historic Warwick skyline, the same view of which would be drawn in the 1750s by Canaletto.[26]

A far more modest house than Warwick Priory, nestling under the lee of Edgehill, has further relics of a water garden, but of an indeterminate seventeenth-century date. At first sight **Arlescote Manor** seems an archetypal post-Restoration house, with its high, hipped roof, dormer windows and sedate seven-bay entrance front. However, seen through a break in the front garden wall, its three-bay centrepiece framed by two tall gate piers, all is not what it appears. The cross-mullioned windows betray an earlier date, suggesting that a sixteenth-century building was remodelled in the late seventeenth century. This is more evident on the former entrance front to the north, which is E-shaped and lit entirely by cross-mullions. This was the house that either Richard Cooper or his son Manasses constructed after Richard had bought the property in 1572 from Sir Gerald Crocker, although a house may have existed on the site as early as 1553.[27] Manasses inherited in 1594, after which little appears to have been done at Arlescote, the family fortunes having dwindled.

During the Battle of Edgehill in October 1642 the house was the refuge of princes Charles and James, and in 1648 it was bought by William Goodwin. His son, another William, was probably responsible for remodelling the gabled Elizabethan roofline, introducing sash windows to the advancing wings on the south front and laying out the forecourt garden

13 One of two Gazebos at the end of a raised walk in the forecourt garden of Arlescote
Manor under the lee of Edgehill

with its twin Gazebos (*13*). These match the house in their rich golden
Hornton stone and are topped by ogee-domed clay tile roofs. There is a
further pavilion to the rear, the survivor of another original pair. Most
intriguing, however, is the substantial body of water to the north and also
a more formal canal behind the south-western Gazebo, suggesting that
this was once a moated site. In 1784 Arlescote passed through marriage to
John Loveday of Caversham, who kept an informative diary that gives a
good impression of the gardens in his ownership.[28] On the north side, the
garden was divided into quadrants planted with fruit trees, centred by a
mount with yews. The walks were edged with roses set in grass paths,
while others were bordered by hazelnut hedges. Close by the canal there
was a skittle alley and another mount. All these features must pre-date
Loveday's tenure and are likely to be elements associated with the Good-
wins' late-seventeenth-century campaign.

Perhaps the most eerily evocative seventeenth-century site in the
county survives at Chesterton, south-east of Warwick and close to the
Fosse Way. This is a series of earth banks surrounding a rectangular

14 Sir Edward Peyto's great 1632 Windmill at Chesterton once acted as a classical eye-catcher to be seen from the house, which itself overlooked a formal garden by the parish church

depression, a water-filled ditch now choked with bushes and the remnants of a moated site, all presided over by a solitary brick archway of insistent rustication. This last provided access between the ornamental gardens, which were set far below Chesterton House, and the churchyard of St Giles. On the hilltop platform to the north of the church Sir Edward Peyto, known as the Royalist, commissioned the greatest classical house in the county, which was sadly demolished as long ago as 1804.[29] The Archway is not the only survivor of the Peytos' architectural campaign in the most advanced classicism of the period. Further out beyond the site of **Chesterton House**, to the north-west on the aptly-named Windmill Hill, his father Sir Edward, known as the Parliamentarian, perhaps acting as his own architect, built in 1632 the great Windmill (*14*), a circular structure set on a round-arched arcade of stone piers. Finally, having begun the new house in 1655, Sir Edward commissioned in 1657 a sturdily classical Mill House. The site is, therefore, unmatched in any county for the strength of architectural vision of two patrons and their architects. For the new house Sir Edward commissioned John Stone, a statuary mason of real distinction and considerable flair, whose father Nicholas had served as master mason on Jones' Whitehall Banqueting House, with which Chesterton House has stylistic affinities.[30] Nicholas Stone had already carved the busts of Sir Edward's grandfather, William and his wife in St Giles' church. Busts of Sir Edward the Parliamentarian, who died in 1643, and his wife were carved by John Stone. The two Peyto memorials by the Stones, father and son, which contain these portrait busts, chart the subtle development of classical forms in the early century. Significantly, given the possible attribution of the Windmill to Sir Edward the Parliamentarian, the Latin inscription on his monument states him to have been a 'Most noble and experienced man of letters and mathematics'.[31] He would, therefore, have been well equipped to work out the stereotomy of the circular windmill.[32]

An undated, mid-eighteenth-century map of Chesterton (*colour plate 5*) gives a good indication of what existed on the estate and offers clues that help to interpret the surviving earthworks.[33] The Windmill can be seen in the wider landscape west of the Mill and the vast 'Mill Pool'. To the north of the water is a square plantation marked 'Lodge Ground', with a small rectangular structure at its south-western corner. This is likely to have been the 'very curious Building near a small plantation called the Lodge a kind of Summer House' thought to have been designed, as was the Windmill, by Inigo Jones and built in 1630.[34] This was obviously used as a place for entertainment during the hunt and also for banquets, one of the wainscoted rooms having a cupboard decorated with a *trompe l'oeil* painting of bread, cheese, an onion, a cucumber and a knife.[35] At the corners the two-storey building had canted oriel windows, which Howard Colvin likens to Scottish bartizans, offering extensive views.[36] Chesterton House is sited on the ridge of Mot Hill (now known as Image Hill), encircled on all sides except the south by walled enclosures; these include a 'Garden', a 'Rick Yard' and an orchard, just what one would expect from a mid-seventeenth-century layout with the dual emphasis on ornamentation and agriculture. The southern aspect is open to the view beyond three plinths for statues,[37] but framed by regimented tree plantations. In the valley below, the boundary of the stream, which has been substantially canalised, is defined by a row of trees providing a shady walk. To the east there are parallel canals with raised walks divided by a causeway bridge from a further rectangular canal, which develops into a moated island planted with trees. A path crosses this bridge, giving access south through the 'Hop Yard' to the Archway set in the churchyard wall and continuing north uphill via a gate to the New Meadow.

Remains of this water garden, developed no doubt from medieval fishponds, and the stone causeway bridge which crossed it are still visible in the tangle of undergrowth and bushes at the site; so too is the banked terrace by the churchyard wall (*colour plate 6*). This provided views down to the flat expanse of what had become, by the mid-eighteenth century, a productive area. Intriguingly, when a programme of geophysical surveys was carried out at Chesterton between 2002 and 2006, and the survey plots superimposed on an aerial photograph of the site, this sector was shown to have been originally laid out as a rectangular garden of four distinct quadrants.[38] David Adams, who carried out the archaeological investigation, now believes that the moated element alongside is not the original site of the Peytos' medieval manor, pulled down by Sir Edward Peyto in 1655, but an ornamental feature associated with a great water garden laid out at that time to enhance the grounds below the new classical house. If this is the case, then the watery landscape at Chesterton was one of the most spectacular in the country, rivalling Sir Francis Bacon's layout at Gorhambury in Hertfordshire, and John Harbourne's water gardens at Tackley in Oxfordshire, which were illustrated in Gervase Markham's *Cheape and good husbandry* of 1623.[39] Indeed, it is books like Markham's, and also his earlier *English Husbandman* of 1613, which included 'The Plaine Square' garden of four quadrants, that will have informed Peyto, who was, like his father, extremely well read and who had inherited an extensive library.[40]

Almost contemporary with the grid of enclosures that originally surrounded Chesterton House on its hilltop is a sloping walled garden, which has miraculously survived at **Packwood House**. However, there has been some confusion over the dating of the spectacular Yew Garden within its highest sector. In a ground-breaking book on the Renaissance garden in England, Roy Strong's publisher, Thames & Hudson, were determined to feature the great yews at Packwood on the book's cover.

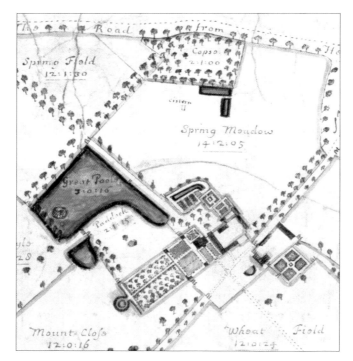

15

This detail of James Fish's 1723 map of Packwood proves that the celebrated topiary garden known as the Sermon on the Mount was a later addition to a homely orchard. *©NTPL/John Hammond*

This implied that they were a recreation of an early seventeenth-century garden and that, together with the spiral Mount in the garden, were symbolic of the Sermon on the Mount. The four yews below are said to represent the Evangelists, with the Twelve Apostles either side of them, and the yews below as the 'Multitude'. While the Mount itself may have been constructed in about 1660,[41] a 1723 map by James Fish shows that this area of the gardens was laid out originally as a fruit orchard (*15*) with rows of trees set either side of a central path.[42] This leads up to the Mount, which is set outside the bounds of the walled enclosure. The Yew Garden is indeed infused with religious symbolism, but the 1723 map proves that it was unlikely, as Strong suggests in his text, to be a 're-creation of a Mannerist garden from before the Civil War'.[43]

Indeed, the current National Trust guidebook, written by Jeffrey Haworth, states that 'the ground was originally set out by John Fether-ston, probably between 1650 and his death in 1670, though there is no evidence of the 'Sermon on the Mount' tradition before the last quarter of the 19th century'.[44] However, earlier on in the guide Haworth writes: 'The Sermon is believed to have been planted by John Fetherston', while later he asserts that 'there is strong evidence suggesting that the present pattern of yew trees replaced an orchard no earlier than the middle of the 19th century', further remarking that the yews 'look young in early photographs'.[45] The 1902 *Country Life* article on Packwood quotes Reginald Blomfield's remarks about the topiary and its symbolism, made in his 1892 *Formal Garden in England*, but neither Blomfield nor the magazine writer give an indication as to who exactly had 'given us the Sermon on the Mount as a wondrous and moving garden creation'.[46] This horticultural hare is likely to have been set running by the landscape architect Geoffrey Jellicoe when he made a plan of the grounds in 1927 for Graham 'Baron' Ash, who had inherited the house on his father's death in 1925. Jellicoe also wrote evocatively about Packwood:

> The garden mainly lies south-east of the house, and is a direct throw-back to earlier days....The small raised terrace so reminiscent of earlier days, separates this [the South Garden] from what lies behind: yews and mysticism. It is the story of the Sermon on the Mount. Step into this medley and its idea takes us back to the days when the teaching of the Church held its sway over the human mind. The lawyer [Fetherston] who planted these yews must have been a disciple of Milton.[47]

In the midst of all this uncertainty, what can be reasonably assumed is that the brick walls enclosing all the gardens to the south of the house were built by Fetherston, and that the whole complex is a horticultural celebration of the Commonwealth obsession, not so much with religiosity, but more with husbandry and productivity for the national good.

The original orchard is a typical indicator of this obsession with improvement, productivity and profit, common themes in the many garden books published in the 1650s and 1660s. The spider at the centre of the correspondence web connecting all these writers was Samuel Hartlib, arch proselytiser of Pansophism, urging that 'perfection was attainable in this world and could be achieved by the universal sharing of every scientific advance, generously and without reserve, between all nations'.[48] Not surprisingly, several books of the period are either dedicated to Hartlib or mention his influence on their ideas. One such is Ralph Austen's *A Treatise of Fruit-Trees*, published in 1653. Austen was a divine, a nurseryman and, as the frontispiece to his book declares, a 'Practiser in ye Art of Planting'. John Goddard's engraving (*16*) shows a walled orchard, not unlike the enclosure at Packwood, with fruit trees planted in quadrants and also grown as espaliers against the walls. Like most of the book's text, the image is underpinned by a biblical quotation: 'A Garden inclosed is my sister my Spouse'. Austen's main aim in researching and writing the book was to answer Hartlib's call for the agricultural improvement of lands: 'It is agreed on all hands, That this worke of *Planting-Fruit-trees* (through the blessing of God) is of vast Profit, where it is diligently, and skilfully undertaken'.[49] But he is also aware of the aesthetic pleasures of these sylvan spaces:

> The sence of Touch may have Pleasure in an Orchard from the coole fruits, and leaves of Trees, smoothing and brushing the face therewith, which is refreshing and cooling in heat of Sommer. But this sense receaves Pleasure chiefly by the shade of Trees in sommer time. Coole refreshing Ayres are found in close Walkes, Seats and Arbours under and about the Trees...Here Profit and Pleasure meet and imbrace each other....Likewise, the sight is delighted with pleasant and delicate Colours of the Leaves, Blossomes, and Fruits, that shew themselves in great variety.[50]

Finally, Austen offers a separate essay – 'The Spirituall Use, of an Orchard; or Garden of Fruit-Trees' – which is an analysis of 'Similtudes' between the physical elements of an orchard and universal spiritual meanings. This perception of the orchard as a place conducive of spirituality, and of God's bounty to Man, is close in spirit to what John Fetherston must have originally devised for the walled garden at Packwood. The overtly religious symbolism of the present topiary in the Yew Garden is, in spite of its earlier Mount, far more typical of nineteenth-century religiosity.

A further indication that this south-facing garden was a place of profit and pleasure is the presence of gazebos in the South Garden. Of the four that overlook the South Garden, that to the north-east (*17*) with its port-

16

The frontispiece of
Ralph Austen's 1653
treatise on fruit trees is
representative of the
Commonwealth's
obsession with practical
husbandry and
productive gardens.
*University of Bristol,
Special Collections*

hole window and diaperwork is known to date from Fetherston's period,
and the others may well have been rebuilt later on earlier bases.[51] It originally functioned as a place of comfort and retreat, offering views out over
the grounds, but its fireplace also heated the adjacent south-facing wall on
which peaches were grown.[52] These pavilions may also have doubled as
'elaboratories', like the one at John Evelyn's Sayes Court at Deptford,
where he carried out his horticultural experiments in grafting and propa-
gating. But the most telling indication that this is a productive garden
synonymous with the earnest spirit of the Commonwealth years are the
series of thirty Bee-boles set in pairs on the south side of the Terrace
Walk wall (*18*). These are symptomatic of the Commonwealth govern-

17

One of several
Gazebos at
Packwood House,
raised by John
Fetherston between
1650 and his death
in 1670

ment's 'stimulation of economic and social reform',[53] and were, no doubt, inspired by contemporary books such as Hartlib's *The Reformed Commonwealth of Bees* (1655), and Thomas Mouffet's *The Theater of Insects,* published slightly later in 1658. While Hartlib's book has one of the earliest architectural designs for a beehive by Christopher Wren no less, Mouffet's frontispiece is enlivened by a bee skep set on a low platform. As with Austen's treatise, Hartlib's aim is stated clearly on the frontispiece, which describes the contents: 'Many Excellent and Choice Secrets, Experiments, and Discoveries for attaining of National and Private Profits and Riches'. This spirit of enquiry and forward thinking is a recurrent theme in the publications of the period; it is not for nothing that Hartlib's chosen title includes the words 'Reformed' and 'Commonwealth'.

One last element of this seventeenth-century garden, with its emphasis on scientific experiment and good agricultural and horticultural practice, deserves a mention. This is the Cold Bath, which is sited in the

18 Some of the thirty Bee-boles set into a retaining wall at Packwood House – another instance of mid-seventeenth-century interest in husbandry

Fountain Court in a yew enclosure to the north-west of the house. The 1723 map of Packwood marks it next to a dog-legged canal that was connected, under a tree-lined walk, to the Great Pool. John Fetherston's son Thomas built it in 1680 long before Dr John Floyer of Lichfield made cold bathing universally popular as a physical regimen. Floyer published his seminal work, *An Enquiry into the Right Use and Abuses of the Hot, Cold and Temperate Baths in England*, in 1697 and constructed his own small bathing spa just outside Lichfield in the 1690s.[54] The Bath at Packwood retains its fine wellhead, which is decorated with the Fetherston coat of arms, while steps still lead down to the flagstoned bath four feet below. A tall Sundial, dated 1667, is close by, providing another point of focus for the gravelled Fountain Court.

There are two further gardens to be considered before the introduction of more insistently formal French and Dutch garden design, which was ushered into Warwickshire in the 1670s at Charlecote by Captain Thomas Lucy. One of these – at Weston in the south of the county – has gone entirely; both the house and its gardens have been swept away leaving barely a trace. The other – at Blyth Hall at the opposite end of

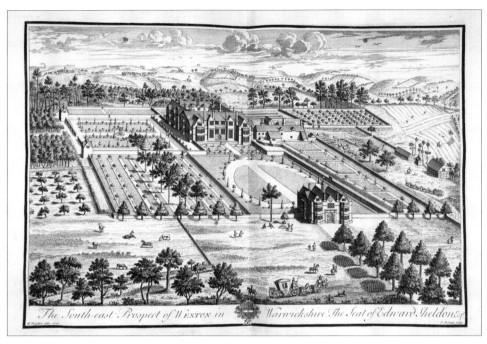

19 Henry Beighton's 1716 bird's-eye view of the house and gardens at Weston records all
the elements, both practical and ornamental, associated with mid-seventeenth-century
layouts. *University of Bristol, Special Collections*

Warwickshire – survives relatively intact and, remarkably, the house is
still lived in by members of the original family.

One of the great treasures of Warwick Museum is the Sheldon
Tapestry Map of Warwickshire, whose brown worsted, shot through with
threads of red and green, marks in charmingly naïve embroidery all the
major country seats and their deer parks, including **Weston House**.
William Sheldon had set up his woollen manufactory in Barcheston, a
hamlet on the outskirts of Shipston-on-Stour, in the mid-sixteenth
century. Although he hailed from Beoley in Worcestershire and lived in
Skilts, in the parish of Studley, by 1545 he had created a significant park at
Weston, south of Shipston on the border with Oxfordshire.[55] His son
Ralph succeeded him in 1570 and by 1589 had built a new brick house on
a commanding site in the park at Weston. This was a symmetrical E-
shaped Elizabethan building with an entrance forecourt guarded by an
imposing bow-windowed gatehouse. The famous series of Sheldon
tapestry maps, based on Christopher Saxton's maps of England, hung in

the Great Parlour of Ralph's new house. They were still hanging there in 1747 when John Loveday visited Weston: 'In the great Parlour are the celebrated Tapestry-Hangings, being spatious and very distinct Maps of several Counties in England',[56] but were auctioned off in the 1781 furniture sale. Three, including the Warwickshire map, were purchased for 30 guineas by Horace Walpole for Strawberry Hill.[57] While the tapestries are well documented, there is no record of the Elizabethan garden at Weston, as it is likely to have been destroyed in the Civil War. Ralph had married into a Catholic family and his descendants were staunch Royalists, Edward Sheldon entertaining Charles I at Weston in 1636.[58] His son William wrote in 1653 that, as well as his house at Beoley being burnt to the ground, 'in September 1643 my house at Weston in Warwickshire was ransacked, and my cattle and goods taken away by souldiers, to a great vallew'.[59]

William Sheldon died in 1659 and his son Ralph inherited the estate. Ralph was known as 'The Great Sheldon' because he was an important antiquary, close friends with Anthony à Wood of Oxford, and was charitable and hospitable. Together with his wife Henrietta Maria, whom he had married in 1647, Sheldon went abroad for his health in 1661. They returned in 1663, but before they could start a family, remodel the house and improve the gardens, Henrietta died. Sheldon never married again. He spent his time thereafter collecting and travelling, though he often entertained his cousin, Frances Sheldon, at Weston. He met Wood in 1771 and engaged him to carry out research and to catalogue his extensive library. Wood became fixated with Sheldon and was resentful of his friend's attachment to Frances, particularly when money promised by Sheldon for Wood's projected book, *Athenae Oxoniensis*, was not forthcoming: 'he is able to throw money away – two or three hundred pounds – to alter his house for the sake of M. of H. [Frances had been Maid of Honour to Catherine of Braganza] and gives her and her brothers what they please'.[60] That was written in 1682, by which time the gardens around the house at Weston had presumably been reshaped.

These are shown in an engraving of 1716, subsequently published in Dugdale's *Antiquities*, by the important cartographer Henry Beighton (*19*). The entrance forecourt to the Elizabethan house was retained but given an additional formal area with raised steps to the south front. In true

Commonwealth practice, the service areas, which included hay barns and a saw-pit, were kept close to the walled areas, while other enclosures contained vegetables and fruit trees. The main ornamental gardens were laid out to the west, possibly within existing walls. The most southerly was a series of grass walks shaded by trees; that to the west front was a formal lawned garden punctuated by evergreens and commanded by two gabled summerhouses, perhaps surviving from the Elizabethan period. There is no sense in the engraved view that the contemporary fashion for axial formality derived from France has had any impact on this corner of Warwickshire, even given Ralph's extensive travels abroad in both France and Italy. The effect is homely with just a touch of grandeur in the approach from the gatehouse and the topiary of the western garden. Sadly, all this has disappeared, the gardens reverting to grazing pasture for horses in the eighteenth century and the house rebuilt in the late 1820s by Edward Blore. Weston House was finally demolished in 1934; only the 1820s stables and some lodges on the Oxford-Stratford road survive.

A similar garden treatment at the house of another Warwickshire antiquary reveals the mid-century conservatism of the county. The historian Sir William Dugdale bought **Blyth Hall** in 1625 and died there in 1686. So the question arises, when did he create the 'stews', which were constructed to cope with flooding from the river Blyth running alongside the gardens? There is a date of 1629 on one of the stone buttresses of the house, which might mark the completion of the initial remodelling of the house and construction of the garden works at Blyth. Sluices were built to divert the river, and the medieval moat was developed into two linear canals that irrigated a productive area of fruit and vegetables to the north of the house. In 1639 Dugdale had acquired a lodging in the College of Arms and thereafter spent most of his time in London. He was on the Royalist side in the Civil War, witnessing the battle of Edgehill, the site of which he mapped, and surrendered with King Charles at the siege of Oxford in 1646. After a short visit to France he returned to London in 1648 and continued his antiquarian researches. These culminated in the publication of his *Antiquities of Warwickshire* in 1656 and his *Monasticum Anglicanum* (1655-73). Given that he was rarely at Blyth after 1639, it is doubtful that he carried out further work on the grounds after the initial remodelling.

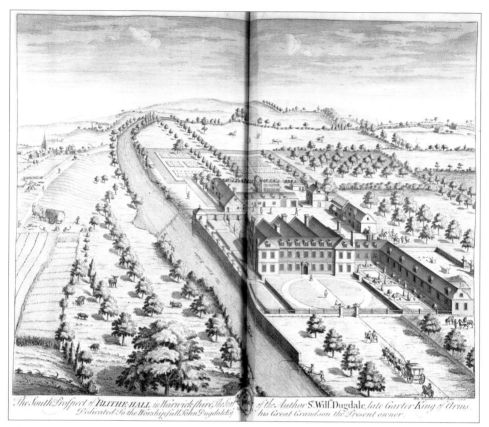

20 This 1728 Beighton engraving of Blyth Hall from Sir William Dugdale's *Antiquities of Warwickshire* records the canal-like 'stews' developed by the author from the adjacent river. *University of Bristol, Special Collections*

It is highly likely, therefore, that the formal gardens depicted on Henry Beighton's 1728 engraving (*20*) are essentially the late-seventeenth-century layout created by his son, Sir John Dugdale, set within Sir William's water-managed enclosure. Sir John, who inherited on his father's death in 1686, had ample funds to develop the grounds, having married two heiresses. He began by building the imposing eleven-bay brick façade in 1692 and continued with the Dutch-gabled service ranges to the east. There is a date of 1704 on the stable block, and the pyramidal-roofed Dovecote shown on Beighton's engraving also survives. Sir John's new layout encompassed the canalised river and fish stews created by his father on the moated north side of the house, which were retained but cut across by a fashionable tree avenue extending into the parkland beyond. However,

21 The retaining wall of the river walk at Blyth was originally topped by urns and
terminated by a summerhouse. Sadly, the summerhouse has disappeared and the
present urns are replacements

his main aim was to produce a grandiose approach to the new south front.
An axial entrance drive was laid out, which led through gate piers and railings to a turning circle for carriages. To the side of this walled area there
was a small parterre garden and to the river a gravel walk, walled and
topped by urns, which terminated in a summerhouse. The summerhouse
has gone, the walk is now grassed over and the urns are replacements (*21*).

With its early seventeenth-century emphasis on productivity – there
are animal feeders and a hay mound behind the service range; along the
banks of the river several men are fishing – and late-century interest in
ornamental parterres, Blyth is a perfect encapsulation of seventeenth-
century horticultural practice. The present owners – Sir William and
Lady Dugdale, together with their gardener Cathy Hurst – are continuing
the productive tradition on the 'Peninsula Garden' with an apple avenue,
a hazel walk and walnut trees. But that original gravel walk alongside the
Blyth, with its urns and summerhouse for riverine views, is a pointer to
the gardens of the next formal phase, their paths bordered by flowerbeds,
their walls commanded by outward-looking viewing pavilions.

endnotes on pages 266-267

3

Canals, walled enclosures and the coming of geometry

Arbury Hall, Charlecote Park, Newnham Paddox,
Honington Hall, Ragley Hall, Castle Bromwich Hall,
Umberslade Hall, Malvern Hall, Honiley Hall, Edgbaston
Hall, Four Oaks Hall, Warwick Priory

THE FASHION FOR FRANCO-DUTCH FORMAL GARDENS THAT BEGAN WITH
the restoration of the monarchy in 1660 and continued until the accession of the Hanoverians in 1714, and a little beyond, seems hardly to have
affected Warwickshire squires. There is just one formal landscape garden
of national significance in the county – Charlecote – the rest being adap-
tations of existing enclosures that had been laid out in the years before
the Civil War. This is a disappointing tally, but it reflects the nature of
Warwickshire's gentry and aristocracy. In other counties of this series
earls and dukes have given the lead. However, in Warwickshire, where
there was only one significant earldom, that of Warwick, owners were
content to reshape rather than design afresh. This conservatism is seen
most markedly in the several bird's eye views drawn by Henry Beighton
and later published as engravings in Dugdale's *Warwickshire*. Beighton has
a family connection with the first of these gardens at **Arbury Hall**. Sir
Richard Newdigate, who we have seen bought Astley Castle in 1674, gave
the neighbouring Arbury estate to his son, another Richard, on his
marriage in 1666 to Mary Bagot of Blithfield in Staffordshire. Soon afterwards Newdigate began a major building campaign and improvement of
the grounds of the Elizabethan house, which had been built in 1567 on the
site of an Augustinian priory by Sir Edmund Anderson. Newdigate
constructed a chapel in the house and added the vast stable block, in
which Christopher Wren might have had a hand, that survives today to

the north-west of the Hall.[1] This appears in a 1708 drawing by Beighton (*22*), which records the completion of Newdigate's extensive remodelling of the gardens around the house two years before his death in 1710. Newdigate must have chosen the artist to produce the drawing because Beighton's father was one of the Arbury estate bailiffs. Quite what survived of the Elizabethan gardens is unknown, but a tantalising glimpse of a formal garden in a painting of Lettice Newdegate might offer some clues.[2] The painting is dated 1606 and the compartmented garden depicted is typical of that period, with an intricate interlocking knot, identical to the patterning on Lettice's bodice, and a fountain surmounted by a statue urinating into the basin, which is surrounded by quartered flowerbeds. Most intriguingly, there is a domed arbour or herber at one corner of the garden. Thomas Hull's 1577 *Gardener's Labyrinth* gives instructions as to how to build and plant up such a feature: 'The herber in a garden may be framed with Juniper poles, or the willow, either to stretch, or to be bound together with Osiers, after a square forme, or in arch manner winded, that the branches of the Vine, Melone, or Cucumber, running and spreading all over might so shadow and keepe both the heat & sun from the walkers and sitters there under'.[3] If this garden ever existed it is likely to have been located in the walled enclosure shown on the Beighton drawing, which survives today, though reconstructed in the late seventeenth century, to the north-east of the Hall.

Apart from the imposing stable block with its separate courtyard, Newdigate concentrated the visual impact on the approach to the house, dramatising the forecourt with twin gazebos topped by the concave pyramidal roofs so characteristic of late-seventeenth-century design. While these have disappeared, a run of openwork balustrading, shown in the drawing attached to the east gazebo, survives alongside the main house. Clipped topiary enlivened the forecourt and the walled gardens to the east, but there were no intricate ornamental parterres, merely grass lawns. However, there is a substantial garden building in the first walled enclosure, which Eileen Gooder believes to have been the 'old' greenhouse for overwintering citrus fruits.[4] This was supplanted by a 'new' greenhouse, built in 1694, in the rear boundary wall that was unheated, but fitted with curtains of blanketing to retain the heat.[5] The complex

22 Arbury Hall in its formal phase from a 1708 drawing by Beighton. The gazebos have gone, but the walled enclosure survives, along with a run of balustrading by the house. *Reproduced with the permission of Birmingham Libraries & Archives*

around the house comprised the Great Garden, the Flower Garden, the Square Garden planted with 'striped' plants, the Birdcage Garden, a Bowling Green, a vineyard, an orchard and the Kitchen Garden.[6] Several garden books belonging to Newdigate have survived, one in which he records in 1682 walking in the garden and looking 'with delight upon my Orange trees and Lemons and Mirtles and Kitchen Garden'.[7] The following year the boundary walls were being planned and flower borders were being planted.

Earlier, in 1678, John Evelyn had visited Arbury and, in advance of his arrival, Newdigate had sent out to Jacob Boart at the Oxford Botanic Garden for striped plants, particularly spurge and phillyrea, to impress him. Newdigate also bought plants, fruit trees and shrubs from the Brompton Park Nurseries; his gardens must have been a riot of colour. This is not shown in the monochrome Beighton view, but it is known that the beds in the Flower Garden were edged with 600 yards of painted boards and that some earthenware plant pots were gilded, while other larger ones were speckled with blue paint. This colourful theme continued in the Best Garden, where the great gates were painted.[8] The Kitchen Garden had hotbeds for cultivating melons and cucumbers and

23 Sir Richard Newdigate produced a series of waterways after 1700, developed from the
Hall Pool in front of the house, to connect the Arbury estate with family-owned
coalmines at Collycroft.

also for sowing annual flower seeds. Gooder believes these were set out
'in parterre fashion in the simple geometric beds' in the easternmost
section of the Beighton view.[9]

Newdigate's most important garden project was the construction of
the Grotto, completed by 1680, with a decorative frontispiece carved by
Robert Mason, a craftsman from London, at a cost of £16. The interior
had a marble pedestal through which flowed water from a cistern above.
It is not known where this was sited in the grounds, but it was a rarity of
its period and of special interest to visitors.[10] Grottoes were a typical
feature of the Mannerist gardens of the first quarter of the century, but
they feature hardly at all in the great formal period after the Restoration.
Might Newdigate also have been responsible for the cave-like Cold Bath
(*colour plate 7*) on the east of the present north drive? It is known that,
with Evelyn's *Sylva* in hand, he added Norway Firs to the existing North
Walk, now the drive, which stretched from the Hall as far as the North
Lodge. If so, the Cold Bath would be contemporary with the one at Packwood, but Arbury's is a far more powerfully numinous structure.[11] Out in

1　The Warwick Earls' armorial symbol, now synonymous with the county –
Rachel Higgins' 1998 memorial sculpture to David Mycroft in the Knot
Garden at the Lord Leycester Hospital, Warwick

2 This lost painting of Kenilworth Castle in about 1620 shows the great Atlas Fountain standing i[n] splendid isolation in what was once the Queen's Privy Garden. *Image J910072, ©English Heritage Photo Library*

3

Princess Elizabeth, daughter of James I – a 1603 portrait by Robert Peake, which may include as its backdrop the Wilderness Garden that she laid out at Combe Abbey. *National Maritime Museum*

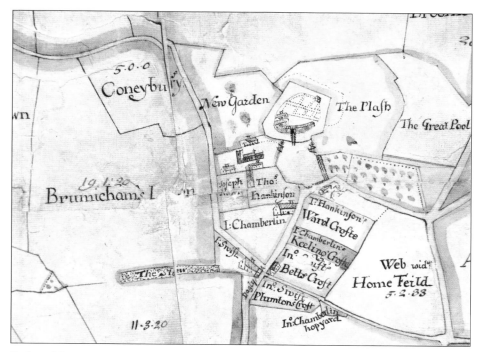

4 Robert Hewitt's 1696 map of Astley shows a compartmented formal garden by the
Castle and the 'New Garden' across the moat. *Warwickshire County Record Office,
CR136/M/9*

5 This mid-eighteenth-century map of Chesterton records the regimented plantations
of trees around the house, the Windmill on the other side of the Mill Pool and the
outlying 'New Plantation' with its Lodge at the south-western corner. *Shakespeare
Centre Library & Archive, DR98/1823*

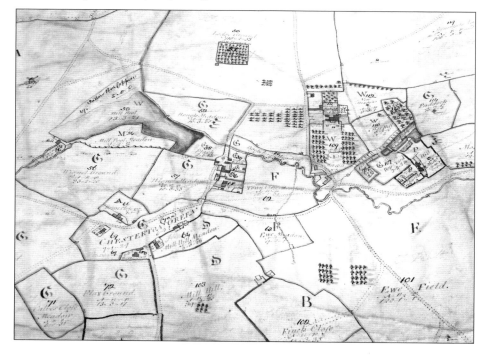

6   The site of the seventeenth-century water garden at Chesterton, with its raised terrace walk and classical Archway giving access to the churchyard

7   Arbury's troglodytic Cold Bath might be part of Sir Richard Newdigate's campaign of the 1670s and 1680s, but could conceivably date from the mid-eighteenth century

8 Charlecote in the 1690s, after Colonel George Lucy had completed Captain Thomas' great water garden. The siting of the canals, which terminate in a tall banqueting house, has forced the artist to include the house off-centre. *View of Charlecote Park c.1696, English. Charlecote Park, The Fairfax-Lucy Collection. The National Trust ©NTPL/Derrick E Witty*

9

James Fish's 1736 map of Charlecote records the survival of the great water garden to that date. Thereafter, George Lucy was to sweep the formality away in a remodelling of the landscape with advice from Lancelot 'Capability' Brown. *Warwickshire County Record Office, L6/1035*

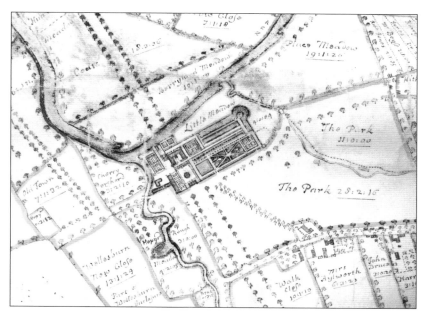

10 Is this languid Philosopher, book in hand, a refugee from the formal gardens at Honington, or a mid-eighteenth-century sculpture carved especially for the Cascade in the Rococo garden of the 1750s?

11 This Soldier, more sleeping funerary than active mercenary, was once paired with the Philosopher on the Cascade piers in the eighteenth-century garden at Honington

12 The polychromatic Orangery at Castle Bromwich reveals an early deployment of the Serlian motif in its fenestration. This classical air is somewhat undermined by the charmingly naïve statue busts

13 A rare summerhouse supported by stilts in the centre of a rectangular pool is shown on this 1726 survey of Malvern Hall by George Crowther. Together with the canals and moated site to the north-west of the main house, it must have formed the centrepiece of an important seventeenth-century garden. *Warwickshire County Record Office, CR299/577*

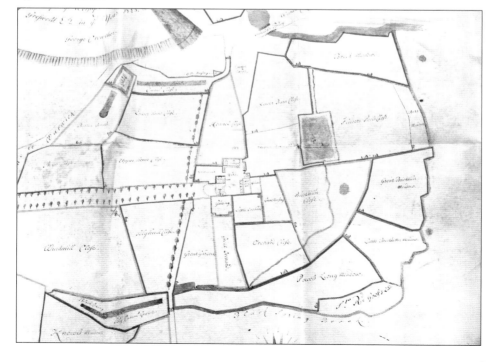

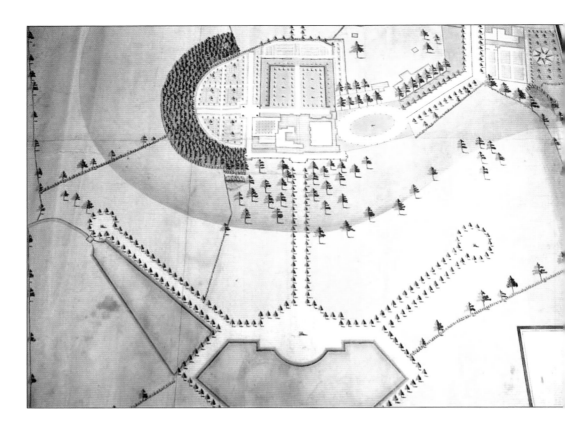

14

This plan of the proposed early-eighteenth-century layout at
Warwick Priory might have been drawn up after 1709 by Henry
Wise, who owned the property, or possibly by Charles
Bridgeman. It reveals a move away from the fussy formality of
the late seventeenth century to a more open, simplified
geometry of tree avenues and walks.
Warwickshire County Record Office, CR56

the park Newdigate also planted silver firs in Fir Grove and Scotch firs near one of his bailiff's houses. In March 1703 he bought 250 yews and 250 silver firs from London and Wise, followed by 250 more of each a week later.[12] He took their planting most seriously and was well versed in the preparation of the ground:

> First raise the ground higher than the rest by half a yard, then make as good as possibly and clear from weedes, but let no green dung be in it. Then set the Fir, only the roots within the ground, not too deep. Set some kitchen stuff viz Turneps or Peas or Beanes or the like about each tree. Let no sobbing wet ly upon them for that was the destruction of the last.[13]

As well as garden making and tree planting, Newdigate was also involved in canalising the water courses around his house to provide 'boatways' both for pleasure and for profit.[14] He began enlarging streams fed by the Hall Pool (*23*) to the south of the house in about 1700, to produce waterways on which small boats would transport timber from his woods. This timber was to be used underground in the coalmines at Collycroft to the east of Arbury; the final part of the journey was made along horse-drawn tramways. This private canal system was further developed by Sir Roger Newdigate after his succession in 1734 and will be considered in detail in a later chapter.

While Sir Richard Newdigate's canals were intended mainly for commerce, those laid out by Captain Thomas Lucy in the late 1670s at **Charlecote** were dug purely for pleasure. They signal the first, very early instance of the impact of Dutch garden fashion on the county and, indeed, the country as a whole, for the best surviving example of Dutch practice, at Westbury Court in Gloucestershire, was not begun until well after the accession of William and Mary at the Glorious Revolution of 1688. This early intervention at Charlecote must have been the result of Captain Thomas' military campaigns abroad, particularly in Holland, where he captained a troop of horse in the Dutch Wars of the 1670s.[15] Godfrey Kneller painted a full-length portrait of him dressed in his Household Guards uniform; it hangs in the Great Hall at Charlecote. As

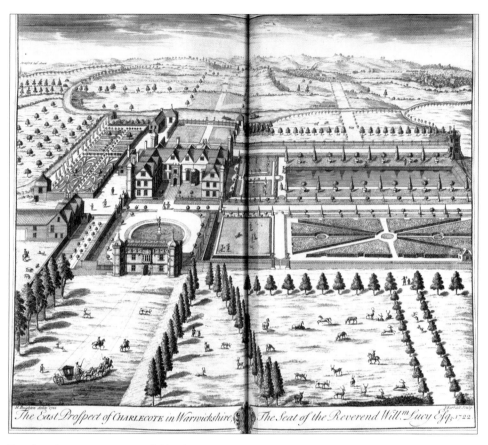

The East Prospect of CHARLECOTE in Warwickshire. The Seat of the Reverend Will.ᵐ Lucy Esq.ʳ.¹⁷²²

24 Beighton's 1722 prospect of Charlecote matches in most respects the oil painting commissioned in the 1690s by Colonel George Lucy to record the completion of Captain Thomas Lucy's great water garden. *University of Bristol, Special Collections*

at Arbury, an early seventeenth-century family portrait gives a fascinating glimpse of a garden that might have existed at Charlecote before the Captain's improvements.[16] Thomas Lucy III and his family are seated in a carpeted garden pavilion which his son and heir Spencer approaches, up a flight of steps, bearing a bowl of apples. The garden allusion is reinforced by Lady Lucy, who is helping herself to some ripe cherries from a bowl held by one of her daughters. The garden is laid out in the contemporary fashion of cut turf compartments bounded by a crenellated hedge.

Captain Thomas owned Charlecote for only seven years before he died from smallpox, aged 40, in 1684. But during that brief period he began the extensive gardens around the house, which are recorded in a beautiful oil painting of the late 1690s, an engraving made from a Beighton drawing of 1722, subsequently published in Dugdale's *Warwickshire*, and a map of the estate drawn up by James Fish in 1736.[17] Charlecote's intensely bucolic site is defined by the River Avon, which flows past the west front, and its tributary the Dene, which borders the south. It must have seemed both practically and aesthetically advantageous, therefore, to utilise this abundance of water on productive and ornamental grounds.

The painting (*colour plate 8*) is oddly composed, with the house set at the right-hand of the canvas rather than centrally, so as to allow for the full length of the canals to be depicted. These stride out from the north front of the house and terminate in a double-lobed pool, the centre of which is dramatised by a tall octagonal brick banqueting house of two storeys with a rooftop cupola. This is accessed from the house via a turf causeway between the two canals, which are separated from the ornamental parterre and a bowling green by a broad gravel walk. The parterre garden has a small gabled pavilion at its north-east corner, and there are further gazebos, this time acting as twin architectural accents, to the parterres in the west garden overlooking the Avon. Finally, there is another riverine pavilion at the south-west corner, where the Dene meets the Avon, in a further walled enclosure, this time planted formally with vegetables. To the east front there was a turning circle and, alongside it behind a brick wall, another quartered vegetable garden close by the stables. Tree avenues radiate to east and west, while another leads directly to the church in the deer park. It is not known just how much of the layout was achieved in Captain Thomas' lifetime, but records state that he made brick-lined ponds for breeding carp, and he built a strawberry house and an orangery.[18] His cousin, Colonel George Lucy, completed the garden and, no doubt, commissioned the bird's eye painting to celebrate the achievement.

The gardens and canals were swept away in the eighteenth century by George Lucy, the bachelor squire who inherited in 1744 and later commissioned Lancelot Brown to reshape the grounds. But the formal gardens had already undergone some changes before they fell into decay. The Beighton view (*24*) records the layout much as it is in the oil painting, but the elaborate parterre garden to the north-east has been simplified into a wilderness with gravel paths radiating from a central *rond point*. The west garden overlooking the river has also lost its parterres, while the kitchen garden has been divided into two, with its easternmost sector laid out as a *parterre de broderie,* overlooked by a new pavilion at the south-east corner. The carriage sweep lawn to the entrance front has become a circular pool centred by a statue. This layout survived at least until 1736 when it was faithfully recorded by James Fish on his map of the estate (*colour plate 9*).

There is little trace of these seminal Dutch canals at Charlecote today, though slight depressions in the ground, each ten paces wide extending from the north front, are still discernible. They terminate in a circular area that is now planted with four oaks and a horse chestnut. This must be the site of the banqueting house, which George Lucy is known to have pulled down. He replaced it in 1745 with a new summerhouse, built closer to the house on the former bowling green. The rectangular site of the bowling green still survives, with roughly the same extent as shown on the views and the map. It is now known as the Cedar Lawn, and is fronted by the 1857 Orangery, which replaced Lucy's summerhouse; it functions as a restaurant. Although the Dutch-inspired parterres did not last long, they were revived, at least on the west front, when Charlecote was re-invented after 1823 as an Elizabethan Revival house by George Hammond and Mary Elizabeth Lucy. Their rebuilding and garden remodelling will be the central focus of a later chapter on Warwickshire's nineteenth-century gardens.

A garden of lesser stature, though one constructed on a marshy site to take advantage of the water, was created at **Newnham Paddox** by the 4th Earl of Denbigh after he inherited in 1685. The layout, or perhaps its owner, was deemed significant enough to warrant inclusion in Leonard Knyff and Jan Kip's *Britannia Illustrata* of 1707. The design (25) was, however, predictable, with twin banqueting houses on the approach to the forecourt and flanking formal enclosures of simple parterres set to one side. On the other side, the water source was developed into a series of canals, mostly rectangular in shape, apart from one of triangular form, all edged with trees. Evidence of some of these is present on the site today, after a 1740s reshaping by Capability Brown, as too is the larger double pool feature to the rear, which was naturalised into a lake. As this commission is Brown's first work in the county and, indeed, one of his

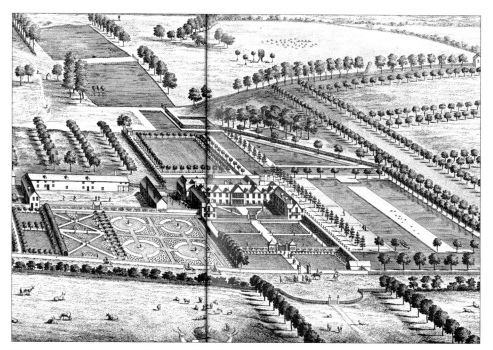

25 Newnham Paddox from Kip and Knyff's 1707 *Britannia Illustrata*, showing the canals
around the house that were later naturalised by Lancelot 'Capability' Brown.
University of Bristol, Special Collections

first design ventures before he had left his position as Head Gardener at
Stowe, it will feature again in chapter 5 of this study.

The landscape at **Honington Hall**, near Shipston-on-Stour, had a
similar make-over in the mid-eighteenth century, though not with the
crushing minimalism of Brown, but rather the conjuring up of intensely
poetic and beautiful pleasure grounds bright with eclectic garden buildings. These were sited either side of the Stour which, like the Avon at
Charlecote, flows directly below the garden front of the house. While
fragments of these ephemeral structures survive at Honington, the great
formal water gardens laid out by Sir Henry Parker in the 1680s have disappeared completely, though the road bridge over the Stour was built in his
time. Fortunately, Honington is well served with visual images, both for
the formal period and the eclectic or Rococo phase. The formal gardens
are shown in a 1731 engraving by Samuel and Nathaniel Buck, while two
paintings of the house and its eclectic landscape were done by Thomas
Robins in 1759.[19]

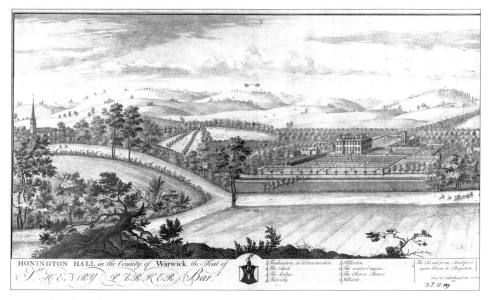

HONINGTON HALL *in the County of* Warwick*, the Seat of*
Sr HENRY PARKER, Bar.^t

26   Samuel and Nathaniel Buck's 1731 engraving of the gazebo-commanded formal gardens
around Honington Hall. *The Bodleian Library, University of Oxford, Gough Maps 32, f.29*

The Bucks' engraving (26) is not easy to decipher, as it is essentially of
the house set within its wider landscape and consequently the detail of
the gardens is lost. But the structure of the walled enclosures around the
house is visible; so too is the river with its parallel canal, later called the
'back water'.[20] A pyramidal-roofed summerhouse overlooks the Stour at
the south-west corner and there is a twin at the opposite corner of the
enclosure which is centred by a circular pool. There is a further pavilion
at the other end of a long walk giving views back along the river. The main
compartments appear to be laid out with vegetables, there is a tunnel
arbour between the gardens and the service area, and at the south-east
corner another enclosure has a small summerhouse as its focal point.
Clipped topiary lines the grand entrance drive from the east and this axis
is continued in a dense tree avenue stretching out into the landscape.
There is a further tree avenue to the west that crosses the canal on a
bridge, while out to the north in a separate field another avenue leads to a
small building labelled in the key as the 'Lodge'; the field is grazed by deer.

Almost all of these improvements, which must date from around 1682
when the house was built, have gone, though there are some intriguing

27

This etiolated statue of
Joseph lurks in the
overgrown shrubberies at
Honington. Is it a forlorn
survivor of the formal
landscape or part of the
Rococo phase of the 1750s?

survivors at Honington which might be of this period. The first is an incongruously placed statue in a niche above the entrance archway to the stable block. This itself has an unlikely frame of giant Ionic fluted pilasters topped by tall entablatures crowned with obelisk finials. All these elements would seem to accord more closely with the parent house, its predecessor, or perhaps a garden structure; in stark contrast the stable ranges either side are of homely vernacular architecture. Could the pilasters have been re-sited, along with the statue, in the eighteenth century? The same might be said for the two recumbent figures (*colour plates 10 & 11*) in the garden Portico that could once be viewed lounging on the piers of the Cascade, a focal point of the mid-eighteenth-century pleasure grounds. These are strange etiolated forms – a Philosopher and a Soldier – more Donatelline than Georgian; they are certainly seventeenth-century in feeling. So too is the statue purporting to be of Joseph, paired with a headless female, across the river, the two aligned on the later Grotto. Struggling to break free of box hedging, Joseph cradles a cup (27),

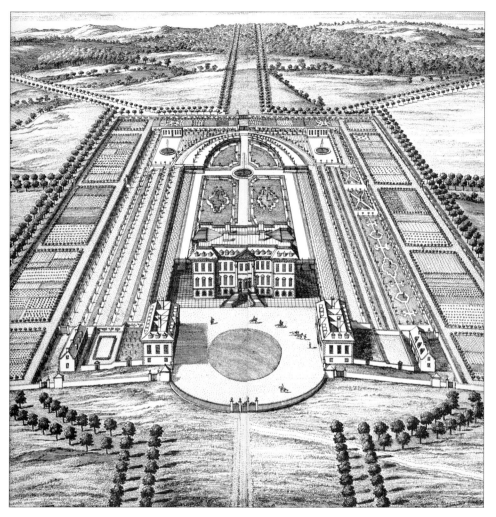

28 A bird's-eye view of Ragley Hall from *Britannia Illustrata*. Robert Marnock's 1870s Rose
Garden followed the lines of the exedral-ended parterre. *University of Bristol, Special
Collections*

which suggests he might be Joseph of Arimathea, who is often portrayed
with the Holy Grail, rather than Christ's Joseph, while the woman has a
vase at her feet draped with a floral spray signifying Flora. Joseph's
anguished lines look seventeenth-century in feel, whereas Flora is softly
moulded in an eighteenth-century manner. The most telling survivor of
all is the marble water stoop set in the wall of the Portico, with its
riotously Mannerist splashback decorated with a grotesque mask, two
bearded fishes and rustic stalactitic drops. Henry Parker is known to have

been an avid collector of curiosities, displaying them in a cabinet inside the house, seen by the antiquary Anthony à Wood in 1678.[21] This stoop, which is decidedly Italian in style and character, could be one of his rarities.[22] It must have been re-sited in the Portico, which was moved from the west front of the Hall to its present position in the late nineteenth century. Given the decorative fish, might it have originally been housed in one of the seventeenth-century riverine pavilions?

A less haphazard and more regular, symmetrical formal garden was laid out around the impressive house begun in 1680 by the 3rd Viscount Conway at **Ragley**. Kip and Knyff later depicted the house and grounds in their 1707 *Britannia Illustrata* (28). Quite when the gardens were constructed is open to question, as Lord Conway died in 1683 with the house incomplete and the gardens unfinished. He was succeeded by his second cousin Popham Seymour, who was killed in a duel in 1699, when Ragley passed to his brother Francis. It is likely, therefore, that the gardens developed over several generations, though they were planted to a unified design with a central formal area of parterres and pools flanked by productive vegetable gardens. The focus was an exedral-ended section with two matching summerhouses, possibly orangeries. No trace of these survives today, as the grounds were extensively altered in the mid-eighteenth century and again in the 1870s by Robert Marnock, whose great circular Rose Garden takes the line of the former exedra as its outer arc.

No such mysteries shroud the extensive formal gardens at **Castle Bromwich Hall**. They have been lovingly restored by the Castle Bromwich Hall Gardens Trust and are well documented in archives and in a 1726 view by Beighton. The gardens were developed by several generations of the Bridgeman family, later earls of Bradford, but the formal seventeenth-century enclosure was laid out by Sir John Bridgeman after 1685 with advice from his cousin, the gentleman architect Captain William Winde. Fortunately, correspondence between Winde and Sir John's wife Mary, Lady Bridgeman, concerning the remodelling of the Hall and the creation of the gardens, survives and has been transcribed by Robin Chaplin and Dianne Barre.[23] This records the progress of the works and reveals Winde to have been as well versed in architectural design as he was in garden making. The gardens continued to be developed, after Sir John's death in 1710 and his wife's in 1713, by the 3rd baronet, another Sir John. He added the church in 1726 when Beighton drew the view, and commissioned more statuary, planted the Holly Walk (1721) and built the Orangery (originally the 'Summer House') and Music Room (mentioned in an 1747 inventory as the 'Pavillion'). The last architectural feature to be added to the complex in 1733 was the Cold Bath, which is sited in the Best Garden west of the Hall.

All this activity over a forty-year period resulted in an accretive garden rather than one designed at a specific moment and then laid out. Consequently, there is no overall vision within the walls, though this does not detract from the variety of the garden spaces, the insistence upon symmetry within the enclosure, and the visual impact of the garden buildings on the perimeter, which act as focal points of the long Holly Walk. What is important to stress at the outset is that the Beighton view shows only half of the garden enclosures – those around the Hall – whereas most of the main features open to the public today are down the slope beyond the Best Garden to the west of the Hall.

The Winde-Bridgeman correspondence gives a fascinating insight into the architect's deft handling of Lady Bridgeman, who had sketched out 'drauffs' of her ideas for his consideration. When the North Garden between the Hall and the later church was being planned in July 1690, Winde wrote:

> I have also returned yr Ladps drauffs & have as near as I can sent my thoughts their on as well as this distance will aforde mee: (viz) yt ye Ground of ye partare befor ye with-drawing Roome bee sunck (if possible) 20 Inches from ye stoole of ye windowes, If a doore bee made out of ye Great parlour & if ye thicknes of ye walle will aforde it, let ye stepps bee made in ye thickness of ye wall, other-wyse ye stepps must be layed outward & to come down in ye partare (or Garden) wch maye bee ornamented with a statue in ye middle & flower pottes on ye sides, or Else Cypres Trees or as yr Ladp shall beste please yr selfe, I approve of ye maeking an open arbor where it is desined on ye drauft wch first ought to bee made of Timber worke, layed in oyle of a white Color & afterwards to bee adorned with Feuilleroy [phillyrea] & other lasting Greens.[24]

Between 1685 and 1703 Winde advised on the planting of an orchard and the laying out of walks, as well as sketching parterres for the North Garden and the Best Garden, the latter known as the 'Dolphin' design.[25] He also recommended suitable flowers, shrubs and garden buildings, and gave directions for the planting of a wilderness: 'I presume to send yr Ladpe my opinion as to the wildernes your Ladp sent me the drauft of to make it compleat, that peece of ground were ye 7 appell Trees are must of necessity bee layed to ye ground for with out it, it will be much to little'.[26] In addition, he recommended important designers and practitioners, including the landscape gardeners George London and Captain Charles Hatton, 'a very great vertueso in gardening',[27] brother of Christopher Hatton of Kirby Hall in Northamptonshire, and statuary masons and sculptors Richard Osgood, John Nost and Caius Gabriel Cibber.[28] Nost supplied statues for the North Garden in 1699, which can be seen in the Beighton view; there are other statues, including the famous Gladiator, sited in the south forecourt. In 1701 London provided two simpler alternative designs of cut turf for the parterres in the Best Garden which, judging by the Beighton view, were carried out.

A letter of 7 March 1699 focuses on the Wilderness, for which Hatton was to provided a detailed planting list,[29] and reveals Winde's sensitivity about sight-lines and the subtleties of keeping certain areas of the garden contained and separate:

> What yr Ladp is pleased to mention of ye firre walk wch as yr Ladp describe, makes a visto from yr Greate Gatte to ye chapel I should bee very Inclynable to have it stand, and so mak ye rest of ye werke conformidable to it, and to keepe the orchard intyerly of itselfe (will be ye beste waye) & not to have any of ye least comunication with ye wildern. they being two distinkt things.[30]

Hatton's specifications for the planting of the Wilderness, of which there are now four, set either side of the Archery Ground and Holly Walk, correspond with advice given in gardening manuals of the period. Apart from the 'Wild Cluster Cherry' or 'Hag-Berry' and the 'Ruicken or Rune Tree', Hatton advised the use of evergreens: holly, yew, fir, pine, bay trees, laurel, wisteria, 'Alaternus, Pyracantha, Laurus Tinus, Spanish Broome, The Cypress, wch I wou'd never advise to sheere or try up, but only strip up ye Lower Branches and they will grow to be Stately, Tall, Spreading Trees'. In amongst these he advocated planting flowering shrubs such as laburnum, lilac, jasmine and 'all ye varieties of Roses', as well as spindle-berry, woodbines, 'Ladies Bower, Althea, Dwarf Almond Trees', and the 'shrubb Hypericum Samach'.

The gardens were featured in a 1904 *Country Life* article when they were still being carefully maintained,[31] but after the death in 1936 of Lady Ida Bridgeman, Countess of Bradford, the gardens fell into decay and were not rediscovered until 1982, after which restoration work began to open them to the public. What is so satisfying about this venture is the Trust's determination to effect a scholarly restoration, choosing plants that would have been available in the 1740s from Kew Gardens and specialist nurseries and, for example, recreating the South Kitchen Garden after a design in Batty Langley's 1728 *New Principles of Gardening*. In spite of the somewhat kitsch collection of temporary-looking structures on the approach, the walled enclosure beyond is a delight to walk in. There is a succession of garden rooms, each with a different horticultural theme, and centring the whole complex is the broad axis of the Holly Walk. The two garden buildings – the Orangery (*colour plate 12*) and the Music Room – give visual emphasis and shelter from the weather; best of all, the two Gazebo-Piers (*29*) at the west end of the gardens offer expansive views down to the North Orchard outside the walls and out over the surrounding fields, and then back into the garden across the complex of leafy sectors. It is hard to imagine, surveying the scene, that the gardens lie within sight of the M6 motorway, though planes on the flight path to Birmingham airport disrupt the tranquillity intermittently.

There were other formal landscapes at Umberslade Hall, Honiley Hall, Edgbaston Hall, Four Oaks Hall and Warwick Priory. Compared to the great gardens at Charlecote, Arbury and Castle Bromwich these were unambitious, toying with formality rather than adopting it with gusto. But the development of the Priory gardens under Henry Wise ushered in the new geometric style of the early eighteenth century and so must be considered at the end of this chapter.

29

The walled garden at Castle Bromwich is punctuated by Gazebo-Piers. These allowed seated views across the garden and also offered a standing prospect of the wider landscape outside the walls

Umberslade, near Tanworth-in-Arden, was built as a grand Baroque house with forecourt pavilions, now gone, by Andrew Archer between 1693 and 1698.[32] A 1725 architectural drawing shows it to have had simple grass parterres centred by obelisks on the entrance forecourt and ornate gate piers 'at ye end of ye Garden'.[33] After Andrew Archer's death in 1741, Thomas Archer inherited and, as well as spending lavishly on the house, he made significant improvements to the estate, where he built several garden buildings including a summerhouse, an obelisk and a portico.[34] The grounds of the Hall, which has now been divided into flats, are fairly desultory, with some vestigial Victorian additions – steps and a pool – within great expanses of lawn.[35] However, a vast central axis to the west still extends through gate piers, across a minor road, and out into the fields beyond towards Tanworth.[36] Sadly, the eighteenth-century Summerhouse and Portico have gone, but the Obelisk (*30*), built in 1749 and designed by William Hiorn, survives on a hill at Nuthurst to the east, overlooking junction 3A where the M40 meets the M42.[37] A similar axial

30

This 1749 Obelisk has been severed from its landscape at Umberslade by the M40 motorway. It is a lone survivor of the eclectic layout achieved by Thomas Archer

avenue was planted at **Malvern Hall**, now subsumed within the Birmingham suburb of Solihull, which is shown on a 1726 survey of the estate (*colour plate 13*) made for Marshall Greswold by George Crowther.[38] Unlike at Umberslade, there was no significant park at Malvern, where the house remained surrounded by fields. However, canals had been developed from a moated site to the north-west of the main house and, in the fields to the north-east, there was a rectangular pool centred by a summerhouse on stilts. A much later sale particulars map of 1915 marks this as 'Maze Pool', but the summerhouse has gone.[39]

Honiley Hall, north of Kenilworth, was the subject of another Henry Beighton view (*31*), published in 1726, three years after the death of John Sanders, who built the church and laid out the gardens around the Hall. It is a strangely evocative site, with two brick service ranges, guarding the entrance gates to the church, the only survivors of the domestic complex. The gatepiers have cartouches carved with elephant heads, one of

Sanders' armorial devices, while their round-headed niches are echoed by the arched windows of the church beyond, which was built by Sanders as a final pious gesture in 1723. The Beighton view records another homely arrangement of areas around the Hall, including simple grass lawns, a canal and an orchard, but there are two ornamental touches. At the north-east corner of the gardens is a gabled summerhouse terminating a raised walk, while out in the field, due east of the church, is a delightful tree house accessed via a ladder.

Edgbaston Hall in Birmingham had a similar layout, with the stable range and church in close proximity to the rather bald, four-square house, which was built in 1717. Another Beighton view records simple avenues and block plantations but also a planned wilderness in the foreground, similar to those laid out at Castle Bromwich. **Four Oaks Hall**, also in the Birmingham suburbs at Sutton Coldfield, was a much more impressive house with an interesting compartmented layout. Beighton's bird's eye view (32) shows the tall nine-bay house of the Foliotts commanding its entrance forecourt, which is flanked by two service ranges with similarly shaped gables to the rooflines. There are grand gates set within a run of ironwork railings, while a statue bearing a staff centres the forecourt. Walled formal gardens enlivened with clipped topiary and espalier fruit trees are sited to the side of the house, while behind the left-hand service range there is a kitchen garden with regular vegetable beds. *Claire-voies* in the form of gatepiers and railings punctuate the walls on each side, offering views out to the fields beyond and the deer park to the rear of the Hall. Sadly, all of this has gone, the Hall having been rebuilt as a towered Palladian house in 1760 and the estate sold in 1870 to make a racecourse, which failed soon after.[40] It is now a leafy private estate with several fine Arts & Crafts houses by the local firm of Bateman and Butler, one of which is almost on the site of the original Hall.

The Warwickshire grounds that provide a link, albeit one that would appear to have been planned rather than executed, between the formality of the late seventeenth century and the emerging informality of the first half of the eighteenth, are those around **Warwick Priory**. As we have seen, the major feature of this landscape was the raised viewing terrace, or 'causey', which commanded a wide prospect of the town. It is now clear

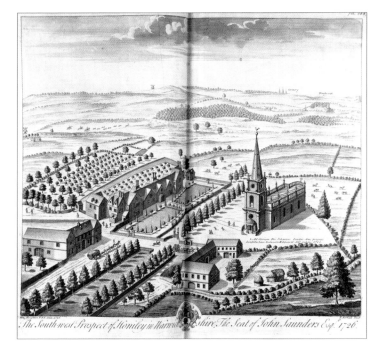

31

Another Beighton view recording the lost formal layout around Honiley Hall, which included a tree house in the field beyond the churchyard. *University of Bristol, Special Collections*

that, rather than the landscape gardener Henry Wise, Sir Thomas Puck-ering constructed it before his death in 1637. This misconception has arisen because Wise bought the estate in 1709 and was, therefore, the most likely owner to have taken advantage of the view to the south. Wise did indeed open up the house to the landscape by demolishing the west range and replacing it with iron gates, as well as laying out a new parterre on the south front of the house. The south parterre is shown in the Canaletto drawing (*33*) mentioned earlier in Chapter 2. The view is of a simple affair of sharply defined gravel paths set in cut grass, enlivened by two urns on plinths and a statue sited on the terrace. This simplification of the existing parterre must have been achieved after Wise drew up a plan for remodelling the grounds, presumably after his purchase of the Priory, and before Canaletto visited in the 1750s.[41] The plan (*colour plate 14*) was discovered by Christopher Hussey in the 1940s and subsequently published in *Country Life*.[42] It shows the parterre to have been laid out with two simple grass plats with clipped topiary, centred by a gravel walk up to the slope of the terrace; buildings are indicated at the north ends of the slope and on axis with the central walk. Most intriguingly, the land-

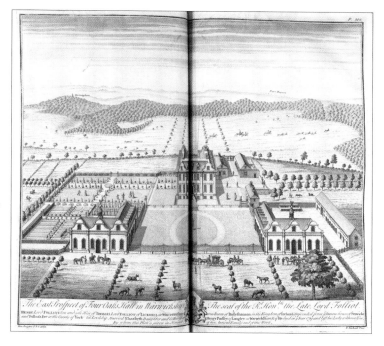

32

The vast formal
gardens around
Four Oaks Hall in
Sutton Coldfield,
now subsumed
within an elegant
private estate.
*University of
Bristol, Special
Collections*

scape treatment to the north of the house, towards the pools, reveals a
move from flowery formality to the more severe geometry in the later
work of Wise and, in particular, Charles Bridgeman, who succeeded Wise
as Royal Gardener. Significantly, the 1711 Warwick town survey was
prepared jointly by James Fish and Charles Bridgeman.

   Whether Bridgeman had a hand in the Priory plan is unclear. What is
significant, however, is that it shows Wise (or Bridgeman if he drew the
plan) moving away from the rigid symmetry of the late seventeenth-
century to a more creative asymmetry, particularly in the handling of the
oblique entrance drive to the Priory from the west and the thick belt of
trees sheltering the fruit and flower garden on the east. While the axis to
the north branched out, at a central clearing, into two symmetrical radiating tree avenues extending into the grounds obliquely and ending in
rond points, it was flanked by randomly spaced trees closer to the house.
The geometric basin beyond, presumably a proposed reshaping of one of
Puckering's pools, is close in style to others by Bridgeman, as too are the
oblique avenues; he laid out similar arms at Amesbury Abbey in Wiltshire.[43] There can be no certainty of Bridgeman's involvement, or, indeed,

33 This 1750s Canaletto view of the Warwick skyline was taken from the south parterre
    garden at Warwick Priory and shows the viewing terrace raised by Sir Thomas
    Puckering before his death in 1637. *Yale Center for British Art, Paul Mellon Collection*

any proof that the scheme was ever carried out. However, the plan charts
the slow shift from the busy formality of the seventeenth century to the
sharp-edged geometry of Bridgeman and John Vanbrugh that would,
under the softening influence of William Kent, result ultimately in the
informal Arcadias of the mid-century.

endnotes on pages 268-269

4

Rococo eclecticism and the Great Master of Gothick

Radway Grange, Idlicote House, Walton Hall, Alscot Park
Honington Hall, Ansley Hall, Barrells Hall, Farnborough Hall
Upton House, Arbury Hall, Soho House

WARWICKSHIRE, A COUNTY OF MINOR SQUIRES RATHER THAN GREAT aristocrats, lags behind the other English counties in almost all the garden fashions. But for one of the county's squires at least, an antiquarian obsession with medieval architecture was the catalyst for a series of remarkable landscapes of that brief 'Rococo', or eclectic, phase of the mid-eighteenth century.[1] Sanderson Miller's passion for revived Gothic in both buildings and gardens secured him the soubriquet 'The Great Master of Gothick', and he spent most of a privileged and leisurely life, until he went mad, living below his mock medieval castle-lodge, which rises from the scarp of Edgehill at Radway. Miller had a large circle of friends, for whom he designed garden buildings and gave advice on landscape. It was a fertile exchange of ideas that were realised on the ground after convivial lunches and satisfying suppers, and in wood and stone by his trusted mason, William Hitchcox. His network of friendship extended across the county, from Honington in the south to Arbury in the north, but his landscape influence in particular is confined to the south-eastern sector close to **Radway Grange** where he lived.[2]

Nothing sums up Miller's gift for friendship and his seminal influence on landscape design at this period than a letter written from Bath in February 1749 and sent to him by John Oswald and Robert Vansittart, friends since their time together at Oxford:

I reckon myself greatly obliged to you for the trouble you took in going to Honington, and Mr Townsend desires me to give you assurances upon his part, he is pleased with your approbation of his schemes, and no less so with your hints of throwing the Eye over the Kitchen garden wall by evergreen shrubs upon the bank of the fence....he disapproved of the way the water falls at present and intended to have it altered, but did not think of filling up the back water in the manner you propose. My idea for the rock was somewhat different from yours. Yours perhaps is better if it can be done with as natural an appearance, mine is not that of the water coming from a cavern....but as I have not seen Ookey [Wookey] hole....that perhaps will make the other seem more natural to me...I fancy [Mr Townsend] will steal a day to see you at Radway.[3]

The letter encapsulates Miller's easy relations with his neighbours and the way in which they were happy to defer to him in matters of landscape aesthetics. As we have seen, Joseph Townsend was to create an archetypal eclectic landscape at Honington, retaining the 'back water' and dramatising it with a grotto. So, while he was happy to ask for Miller's advice, he had his own view of how the water should be handled in his grounds. Townsend inherited in 1739, just after Miller began his own improvements to the landscape at Radway.[4]

Miller took over the running of the estate at Radway Grange when he was twenty-four. The site had the obvious advantage of shelter under the lee of the Edgehill, but for Miller its aesthetic potential lay in its historical associations. Charles I had raised his standard on the brow of the hill, while the house itself was originally a twelfth-century grange belonging to Stoneleigh Abbey. Miller's landscaping, which would encompass the slope of the land up to the hill some 300 feet above, was to culminate in the Edgehill Tower, a 'ruined' castle based loosely on Guy's Tower at Warwick Castle. This was to act as a lodge and viewing tower at the entrance to the park, from which a drive would wind its way down the hillside to the Grange below. On the way the visitors' carriage ride would be enlivened by views across the plantations with optional stopping-off points from which to enjoy the landscape. The most prominent of these was a viewing platform high up the hill commanding the field of battle; several tree clumps were sited to represent the battle stations. William Shenstone, another amateur landscaper, writes of Miller staying with him at The Leasowes when he would rather have been at Radway directing a surveyor 'employed in taking plans of the field of battle near Edge-hill. This he purposes to enrich with a number of anecdotes, gleaned from his neighbourhood; which must probably render it extremely entertaining: and surely Edge-hill fight was never more unfortunate to the nation, than it was lucky for Mr. Miller!'[5] Below and slightly to the west of this terrace Miller contrived a cascade, which fell through rustic arches down to a fountain.

As one walks the site today, the Edgehill Tower is almost obscured by the belt of trees planted just below the brow of the hill, while most of the landscape features have disappeared. So too have the flowering shrubs that the accounts prove he was purchasing from a nurseryman in Faringdon, Oxfordshire, at least as early as 1743.[6] Payments occur from 1748 onwards and include deciduous and evergreen trees and shrubs: cypress, New England firs and Weymouth pines, as well as mezereum, laurel and lauristinus. But the line of the drive can still be made out in the fields, which are dotted with oaks, and between the trees an ironstone Obelisk rises on a natural outcrop. This is not of Miller's period, having been set up in 1854 by Charles Chambers to commemorate the battle of Waterloo. Nearby there are stones defining a rectangular basin, which must be the reservoir Miller constructed to feed the cascade and the pool below it.

In 1743 Miller turned his attention to the hamlet on the top of the hill.[7] He had, no doubt, spoken of this new architectural initiative to Shenstone, who recorded: 'He prints, together with this plan [for the landscape], another sheet of Radway Castle. I approve his design. He will, by this means, turn every bank and hillock of his estate there, if not into *classical*, at least into *historical* ground'.[8] This historical complex was begun with the Thatched House, or Egge Cottage, which had military touches in the rounded corner bastions and was roofed to pick up the vernacular of the area. Miller filled it with books and later let it out to the distinguished Anglo-Saxon scholar George Ballard. In conjunction with the Gothicising of the Grange below, which was supervised by Hitchcox, Miller then began, on the anniversary of the battle on 23 October 1745, to

THE HISTORIC GARDENS OF ENGLAND: WARWICKSHIRE

build his Edgehill Tower (*34*). This was to provide a trumpet blast of anti-quarian scholarship at the approach to his estate and to serve as a retreat for tea and supper parties. Indeed, Miller was already using the Tower for tea on 17 June 1750: 'Walked with Mr Jago, Buckler, Talbot and Lyttleton to the Castle. Drank tea', and later in the month for more exotic confections: 'Haymaking weather. Camera Obscura. Syllabub in Castle. Fine. Walked'.[9]

The plasterer Robert Moore, of Warwick, was brought in to decorate the interior with the coats of arms of Miller's friends and, if the wandering bishop Richard Pococke is to be believed, a niche was made to hold a statue of Caractacus in chains.[10] Sadly, either the niche was too small, or more likely the statue was too tall. James Lovell's eroded stone figure (*colour plate 15*) of the ancient British chieftain languishes by the entrance drive to the Grange; it is 9 feet tall. Miller added a drawbridge to the Tower and a ruined wall and archway across the road to screen some cottages. All of this is shown on an 1862 print,[11] and in later post-cards (*35*). Miller opened the Tower ceremoniously in September 1750, inviting close friends who shared his scholarly enthusiasm for antiquity. Others, like Henrietta Knight, Lady Luxborough, who were not present but heard about the celebrations, poked fun at him. In a letter to Shen-stone she wrote: 'Were you at Mr. Miller's Ball in his Gothic Room? He is sending to Birmingham for cannon-balls, and such like military store, to defend his Castle'.[12] Richard Jago's poem *Edge-Hill*, so dire it should remain forever mostly unquoted, gives a surprisingly accurate, if unctuous, description of the impact of the grounds:

> Thanks, MILLER! To thy Paths,
> That ease our winding Steps! Thanks to the Rill,
> The Banks, the Trees, the Shrubs, th'enraptur'd Sense
> Regaling, or with Fragrance, Shape or Sound,
> And stilling ev'ry Tumult in the Breast!
> And oft the stately Tower's that overtop
> The rising Wood, and oft the broken Arch,
> Or mould'ring Wall, well taught to counterfeit
> The Waste of Time, to solemn Thought excite,
> And crown with graceful Pomp the shaggy Hill.[13]

34

Sanderson Miller's
Edgehill Tower
was begun in 1745
to act
iconographically,
as a symbol of the
Civil War battle,
and practically, as
an entrance lodge
to Radway Grange
in the fields below

In another letter to Shenstone, sent on Valentine's Day 1750, Lady Luxborough gives a fascinating contemporary view of the difference between
classical and medieval approaches to landscape and architectural design
and aesthetics. She is in no doubt that classicism is the more refined taste
and urges Shenstone to give Miller the benefit of his superior advice:

> You are so far from being censorious, as to Mr. Miller's place, that
> your description gives me an infinitely more advantageous idea of it,
> than any I had conceived before from what others have said to me
> of it. Undoubtedly advantages might be taken from the view he has
> on the spot where Edgehill battle was fought; but the memoran-
> dums raised there must proceed from a genius something more
> sublime than that which seems merely turned to Gothic architec-
> ture. Many a man can sketch out a bow-window or heavy castle,

THE ROUND TOWER, EDGE HILL.   2.

35 As part of his medievalising on the approach to Radway, Miller set up a small complex
of Gothick structures on Edgehill, which included the Tower, a ruined archway and the
thatched Egge Cottage, all visible in this early-twentieth-century postcard

who is unacquainted with the beauties of a genteel urn: but many
more people could do the one and the other more easily than dedi-
cate it properly, and impress such ideas as the history and the place
might suggest to those of a more refined though less mechanical
genius than I conceive him to be of.[14]

This is a snide evaluation, between close friends and confidants, about
Miller's thoroughgoing Gothick iconography at Radway and Edgehill.
However, it highlights the mid-century dichotomy in landscape aesthetics
between associations with the classical past and Britain's medieval
heritage. On his friends' estates, where there was no inherent historical
association as at his own Edgehill, Miller was content to advise and even
sketch out classical temples, as well as Gothick castles.

An intriguing garden building, which incorporates both Gothick and
classical elements, and may well have been designed by Miller, is the
Dovecote (36) at **Idlicote House**, a few miles south-west of Radway. This
has cruciform arrow slits and ogee-arched windows, similar to those on

36

Might Miller have
designed this Gothick
Dovecote at Idlicote,
which is close to
Radway Grange, as a
favour for one of his
Warwickshire friends?

the dovecote at Wroxton Abbey, over the border in Oxfordshire, which
Miller designed for Lord North. It combines these with a Diocletian
window on the bottom storey. The octagonal form of the Dovecote is
reminiscent of the Edgehill Tower, though authorities suggest that it is an
original monastic tower surviving from a grange of Kenilworth Priory,
once on the site.[15] Another possible Miller essay in Gothick was Spiers
Lodge in the park at Warwick Castle, built in 1748 in conjunction with
medieval reshaping inside the Castle, which included a Gothick bedroom
for Lord Brooke's wife with a chimneypiece taken from Batty Langley's
contemporary *Gothick Architecture*. As the Lodge is a focal point in the
remodelled landscape by Lancelot Brown, who may have been introduced
to Lord Brooke by Miller, it will be reserved for a later chapter.

With classical temples, such as that at Sir Charles Mordaunt's **Walton
Hall**, a few miles north-west of Radway towards Stratford, we are on
safer ground.[16] This is the octagonal Bath House, set on a wooded ridge
overlooking the park to the north-east of Walton Hall (37). On 29
October 1749 Miller's diary entry reads: 'Settling accounts with Hitchcox

37 A Rococo banqueting room set within a Palladian façade rising above the rusticated
cavern of a vaulted plunge pool – Miller's eclectic 1749 Bath House at Walton Hall

about Sir Charles's bath etc."[17] The simple, ashlar-faced summerhouse is
supported by a cyclopean arch of rough masonry, giving the façade to the
park a rustic appearance. This archway leads to the grotto-like bath below
(*colour plate 16*), which is almost Druidic in feel, with menhir-like stone
seats set within crude niches, while randomly-hewn stone columns carry
arches of jagged stonework. As a complete contrast, the room above is
politely decorated with plasterwork icicle bands by Robert Moore, below
which are swags of shells. These shell ornaments were created by that
inveterate maker of grottoes and shell houses, Mary Granville, Mrs
Delany.[18] On 6 July 1754 Delany wrote from Delville near Dublin to her
sister Anne Dewes, who lived at nearby Wellesbourne House, where there
are similar shell swags on chimneypieces: 'I have not yet got shells large
enough for the festoons and fear it will be in vain to make them here, but
I will send a barrel of shells to Sir Charles Mordaunt's, and hope to give
myself the pleasure of making it there'.[19]

The Bath House is the perfect mid-century Rococo conceit: a playful
building for leisure conceived in a happy combination of architectural
styles. As well as functioning as a health spa for men as part of a physical

regimen – Sir Charles suffered from gout – the upper room was used for dining. Another Miller diary entry of August 1756 records that he 'break-fasted at the bath with Sir Charles',[20] while in October of the same year he was 'Walking with Sir Charles, Mr Mordaunt and Dr Niblet and Mr Palmer at the bath etc.'[21] The building was originally backed and enclosed by Miller's characteristic planting of yews, while the hillside environs are threaded with rock-lined serpentine paths.[22]

Miller was obviously in demand as an advisor on landscape design in the 1750s, particularly in his own neighbourhood. Another park associated with him, but where there is no proof that his views were acted upon, surrounds **Alscot Park**, near Preston-on-Stour. Its entrance hall is the county's most evocative Rococo-Gothick interior, displaying a light-hearted exuberance that is entirely absent from the more celebrated, though far more earnestly archaeological, interiors at Sir Roger Newdi-gate's Arbury Hall. James West, an antiquary like Miller and a fervent bibliophile, remodelled his riverside house in two distinct building campaigns, the first Gothick of 1750-2 and the second more overtly Rococo of 1762-65. Miller's diary for 20 April 1750 reads:

> Went with Bower and Mrs Bower to Sir Charles Mordaunt's in landau at 8 in one hour and fifty minutes. Very wet. Road bad. Went after breakfast with Bower to Mr West's in one and a half hours on horseback......Walking at Mr West's about the park. Seeing painted glass. Drawing plan for Mr West. Stayed all night.[23]

William Hawkes believes that the plan referred to was a preliminary design for the Gothick reshaping of the house, while Jennifer Meir is fairly confident that Miller influenced the layout of the park for a close friend with interests in common. Whatever the truth, access was not allowed to the estate for this survey, so Meir's account of the grounds must suffice.[24]

Fortunately, West's memorandum book survives and gives precise details on the progress of the improvements in the park. Essentially, he widened the Stour by the house to form a lakelet, contrived a series of garden buildings including a rotunda, an obelisk and a Chinese house on the other side of the water, raising a viewing terrace behind them to offer views back across the park. The memorandum book has a small sketch plan of William Holbech's Terrace Walk at Farnborough, which West is known to have visited in 1760. It is therefore likely that, although Miller may have had some influence during the early Gothick campaign at the house, most of these structures date from the second phase, once West had retired from politics. A contemporary map in the house has small vignettes of the Rotunda and the Chinese House, and there is also a plan for a hexagonal Chinese House dated 1757. All the garden buildings have disappeared, but a late nineteenth-century rector recorded that the 'Chinese temple, surmounted by an acorn...stood at the top of a flight of steps leading up from the river', and that this was 'not far south of the rotunda...a lofty erection erected on a mound of earth...It had an octagon tower with domed roof; the alternate sides of the octagon were pierced with arches, the other four being filled in'.[25] It is not surprising that West's landscaping had affinities with Holbech's layout at Farnborough and Joseph Townsend's park at Honington. All lie within a few miles of each other, close to Miller's Radway Grange, in this Rococo-Gothick corner of eighteenth-century Warwickshire.

Mention of the Chinese House at Alscot brings to mind the county's most significant and delightful 'Rococo' landscape of this period. This was laid out below the commanding bay window of the Saloon of **Honington Hall**, the interior of which is a nationally important master-piece of Rococo decoration.[26] As we have seen, Sir Henry Parker rebuilt Honington in the early 1680s, and the house was subsequently sold to Joseph Townsend in 1737. During the 1740s Townsend added screen walls to the entrance façade and the canted loggia to the south front. He further emphasised the link between house and its riverine grounds by building the Saloon between 1751 and 1752 and projecting it out in a tripar-tite bay to the west. This gave views out across the lawns down to the water where, with helpful advice from Miller, Townsend made a cascade. A grotto was sited on the far side of the 'back water', which was essen-tially the original course of the Stour; the river course had been diverted and opened out to form a wider, lake-like stretch of water below the Hall.

The Bath artist Thomas Robins the Elder recorded all these changes, which were complete by 1759, in two beautiful gouache paintings bordered by tendrils of accurately observed wild flowers.[27] The west view (*colour plate 17*) shows the house in its grounds with the tall steeple of St Gregory's church at nearby Tredington and the medieval tower of All Saints, which was retained in the 1680s rebuilding. There are precisely manicured lawns around the south front of the house, contrasted with more densely wooded areas, planted with flowering shrubs, around the northern sector by the Chinese Seat and the Cascade across the river. The back water is edged with more leggy trees and shrubs; it was the culmin-ation of a gravel walk leading through Ray Wood on the western perimeter. While a couple take centre stage discussing the scene, further animation is provided by a group of three walking towards a sundial on the south lawn and a party of three women and two men being rowed in a boat on the water. One man is playing a horn, the other an oboe; wind and brass instruments were always preferred for outdoor music at this period.[28]

The companion view (*colour plate 18*), looking west along the river, shows all the garden buildings in more detail. This focuses on a group of men and women seated beneath the Chinese Seat. They are attended by a servant who has just dropped a basket of flowers, while one of the women places a bay wreath on the head of one of the men: a clever tribute perhaps by Robins to Townsend as creator of the scene? With its Chinese Chippendale benches, tented canopy and dangling bells, the Seat is strik-ingly similar in design to one at Lord North's estate at Wroxton, where Miller also gave advice.[29] From this vantage point the winding course of the river towards the arched bridge can be seen, so too the classical temple backed by Ray Wood. In the centre of the picture the rockwork Grotto with its tiered waterfall fronting the back water is seen behind the Cascade in the foreground, its stepped waters flanked by sculpture piers. The lounging figures of the soldier and philosopher are set above arches of frosty rustication. The three sculptures on the Grotto are harder to discern, though the central figure is likely to be Joseph, which has since been re-sited closer to the riverbank.

Vestiges of this idyllically pastoral and decidedly French scene survive today. As we have seen, the Cascade sculptures now decorate the nine-teenth-century Portico, Joseph and Flora shelter in dense undergrowth,

38 In the 1740s and 1750s Joseph Townsend remodelled the grounds at Honington, adding
a series of stylistically diverse garden buildings and realigning the river Stour to create
this Cascade

and the Cascade still dashes its water (*38*). There are even the rockwork
remains of the Grotto, and chunks of ashlar stonework on the ground
around the site of the classical Temple. Finally, just below the Portico on
the west terrace, there is a rustic Seat formed of large rough blocks
surmounted by a tree-trunk lintel, which must date from Townsend's brilliant evocation of a Warwickshire scene by Watteau or Fragonard. In
strikingly grotesque contrast, his 1763 monument in the church, though
set on a Rococo plinth, is of an ugly putto with a misshapen head.

The presence of the Chinese Seat at Honington calls for a short digres-
sion from the county's mid-century landscapes associated with Sanderson
Miller to one where a major architect inspired a Chinese temple, which is
likely to have been more stylistically accurate than Miller's delightful
confection. John Ludford, who had inherited the estate in 1727, built this
at **Ansley Hall** in the coalmining area around Nuneaton. By 1732 he had
bought the neighbouring manor of Brett's Hall, and much later, in 1767,
built the temple within an island formed by the old moat of the Hall. Not
content to run up a gimcrack building of vague oriental reference, he took

his design from a plate in Sir William Chambers' *Designs for Chinese Buildings,* which were based on the architect's first-hand experience in China. Ludford also built a summerhouse and pavilion, which are mentioned in his son's diaries. Sadly, all trace of these buildings has gone, but close to the surviving fragments of the demolished Ansley Hall, beside a cricket pavilion, there are the remains of a hermitage. This is presumably the hermitage, complete with hermit's parlour, that Ludford is known to have raised in about 1750. The poet laureate, Thomas Warton, is thought to have written a poem about the contemplative life in this building:

> Beneath this stony roof reclin'd
> I sooth to peace my pensive mind:
> And while, to shade my lowly cave,
> Embow'ring elms their umbrage wave;
> ...I scorn the gay licentious crowd,
> Nor heed the toys that deck the proud.[30]

Warton's syrupy verse brings to mind Worcestershire's self-styled laureate, William Shenstone of The Leasowes who, as we have seen, was a friend of Miller and one of this coterie of Midlands garden enthusiasts. His relationship with Miller was obviously important in the development of the gardens below Edgehill, but his influence on a lost Warwickshire garden laid out by an exiled adulteress was perhaps more significant.

Barrells Hall, near Henley-in-Arden, was the estate of Henrietta, Lady Luxborough. Even though all trace of its Rococo layout has disappeared, copious correspondence between Lady Luxborough and Shenstone survives which charts the progress of her pleasure grounds. She was confined at Barrells between 1739 and 1756 by her husband Robert Knight, following a legal battle that effectively placed her under house arrest. Cosy in her chimney corner, she surrounded herself with literary figures including Richard Graves, Richard Jago and Shenstone, and spent her time creating the garden that she referred to in 1748 as a '*Ferme negligée*' rather than a *ferme ornée*, due to its present unkempt state.[31] She had had so much company in the house, and the hay harvest had kept her servants so busy, that 'the gardens were neglected just when they ought to have been put in order', and the dry season had 'prevented the new-laid turf from joining'.[32] Furthermore, her 'pavilion, when almost finished, was pulled down again in part, to add to it a shrine for Venus: so that it is still uncovered; and the roses, &c. are all faded, and gives an ugly aspect to my shrubbery', which awaited Shenstone's 'directions to be new modelled'.[33]

Luxborough's layout and the importance she gave to her ornamental Shrubbery is evoked so beautifully in a later letter to Shenstone of 4 June 1749 that it deserves to be quoted at length:

> The bowling-green begins to look tolerably green since this late rain, which I hope will join the turfs perfectly. The Abele Walk, and that which was gravel, will be filled in the planting season, and the Serpentines altered to lead to the Coppice; but the manner of it I shall leave to your direction, hoping to see you long before that time here, especially as Mr. Dolman does me the favour to propose making me a visit whilst my Shrubbery is in beauty; which ought to be now but it is still winter here! It is true, there are various shrubs well blown, but it is so cold and wet, one cannot walk to see them; and on the dry days the winds are so high, that it is equably disagree-able, and the flowers droop towards the ground when scarcely full blown – You seem destined never to see the embroidery Nature bestows upon my Coppice in Spring; where we had even this year great variety of cowslips, primroses, ragged-robins, wild hyacinths both white and blue, violets &c. &c. In the Shrubbery, I think the finest ornament is the large bushes of Whitsun-roses, which are still in blow, and give one an idea of snow-balls this cold weather. The lilac is already over, and has given place to the syringa; of which I have enough to perfume the place with the help of the sweet-briar.[34]

The letter encapsulates perfectly that combination of winding walks through leafy and scent-laden shrubberies that characterises the paintings of Thomas Robins, and which has been written about so eloquently by Mark Laird.[35]

In addition to the advice given to the 'hermitess' of Barrells,[36] about inscriptions for urns, planting up pathways and adapting Batty Langley's serpentine walks published in his *New Principles*, Shenstone also advised upon the proposed site for Luxborough's Hermitage: 'I doubt whether I understand in what manner you would have *the Hermitage become part of the shrubbery, by means of about three yards of shrubbery on the outside of my lime walk*'.[37] For her part, she sent him progress accounts of her other garden buildings, including the interior decoration of her Summerhouse: 'Mr. Wright of Worcester stucco'd my Summer-house; which is well done, as to workmanship. Where more elegance is required, he employs an Italian under him. They did the new work at Warwick Castle, at the Priory, and the inside of the Temple at Lord Archer's'.[38] The reference to Lord Archer relates to the mid-century landscape laid out at Umberslade Hall, whose garden buildings, like those at Barrells, except the Obelisk by the M40, have all disappeared.[39] The letters make it clear that Luxborough completely transformed the grounds around the former farmhouse by adding both formal and informal features. The 'Abele Walk' and the 'Service Walk' were threaded with winding, shrub-shadowed paths leading to seats for contrived views: 'I propose coming in to the Coppice from the Service-Walk at the farthest end between the Chairs that overlook the Pit, and farther corner of the Wood beyond what answers to the top of the Hermitage Pit'.[40] Barrells was a typical product of its time, created by a gifted amateur who, although she deferred to Shenstone in many matters of landscape taste, had a sure eye for the capabilities of her small domain.[41]

If the grounds around Honington Hall are the county's most important of these mid-century Rococo landscapes, then the eighteenth-century park at **Farnborough** is the most innovative. It represents that aesthetic shift from an inward-looking, shrubbery-shaded eclecticism around the skirts of a house to a visual embracing of the wider landscape. Perhaps because of the close proximity of William Kent's Rousham, Miller had realised the potential of far-reaching views long before the Brownian revolution of ideal, open parkscapes hit the country in the 1750s. The great viewing terrace at Farnborough has obvious affinities with earlier examples, such as that at Duncombe Park in Yorkshire, with its twin Doric and Ionic temples overlooking Rievaulx Abbey. At Farnborough there are also two temples, though their view outwards is focused on Edgehill and the patchwork of hedged fields below it. Bishop Pococke was an early visitor in September 1756 and gave a topographically informed account of what Miller had achieved for William Holbech:

> I went to see Farnborough, Mr Holbeche's, a good house in a narrow valley; there is in it several ancient busts and very beautiful fineer'd ancient marble tables; he has made a very grand grass terrace, winding round the hill for half a mile; there is an obelisk at the end which may be 80 feet high, and in another part an oval open summer house, with a room over the colonnade. This terrace commands a fine view of the rich country, which is called the Vale of the Red Horse, from a red horse, near Tysoe, cut in the hill.[42]

Pococke's mention of the 'ancient busts' and marble tables suggests that he got no further than the entrance hall of the house, where these spoils of Holbech's decade-long stay in Italy, as a result of a failed love affair, are still preserved. Pococke would surely have mentioned the beautiful Rococo plasterwork in the Saloon and the Staircase Hall, work by William Perritt, and perhaps Francesco Vassalli.[43] It is a foretaste of what the visitor will experience, on a much more modest scale, at the Oval Pavilion on the Terrace Walk. Perritt also decorated the Rotunda at Ranelagh Pleasure Gardens in London, so he had already had useful experience of Rococo garden buildings before his commission at Farnborough.

William Holbech returned from Italy in 1734 and, surprisingly, began work on his gardens slightly before the remodelling of the house, which he had inherited in 1717. The earliest proof of the completion of the Terrace Walk is a record in John Loveday's journal for July 1742, which reads: 'rode on Mr W. Holbech's Terrace'.[44] Whether the Terrace was of Holbech's design, or a feature inspired by Miller, is unclear. The Holbechs still live at Farnborough, and family tradition has it that Miller was instrumental in creating the feature; much later, in 1900, Miller's own great-grandson, the Revd George Miller, wrote: 'In these works Mr Holbech was assisted by the advice and taste of his friend and neighbour Sanderson Miller of Radway'.[45] Whoever was responsible, the elevated site lends itself to such a treatment. The house is fairly austere, though the honey-coloured Hornton stone, offset with paler Warwick Grey,

39 Miller's top-heavy Oval Pavilion on the great viewing terrace at Farnborough Hall gives
views across the fields to the Edgehill escarpment

produces a warm polychromatic effect, a perfect prelude for the richness
within. Sweeping lawns below the west and south fronts are shadowed by
a great cedar, while a lone sundial leads the eye off to the east and the
start of the Terrace Walk, which is arched over by deciduous trees. The
first views out are of a charmingly unkempt serpentine river made from
two rectangular pools, which winds along the valley bottom in the foreground, with enclosed fields beyond rising to the escarpment of Edgehill
in the far distance. Then the Walk becomes steeper, flanked by laurels on
each side and beech, yews, hollies and chestnuts in the mature woodland
on the north-east edge. The Terrace Walk itself is also serpentine and
snakes along the ridge towards the Obelisk at the far end.

The first architectural feature is the Ionic Temple of cool Grey ashlar,
set above a projecting bastion of rough Hornton stone. This is no more
than an open alcove with benches and an ochre-washed back wall to
provide a visual contrast with the portico when seen from the river below.
Then there is a straight stretch of grass before the Terrace kinks back to
the south-east, at which point, set back within the woodland, the Oval
Pavilion comes into view (39). This is a charming, if amateur, structure

with an open Doric loggia on the ground floor and a closed circular room above, decorated on the outside with Ionic pilasters. The effect is one of oddly proportioned attenuation, while the columns of the loggia appear too flimsy to support the weight of the room above. These faults are forgiven by the beautiful plasterwork ceiling in the upstairs room and the spectacular elevated views it offers out towards Warmington and Edgehill. The Terrace is terminated by a sharply-pointed Obelisk, which was described by a visitor in 1746, so the date of 1751 on its base may refer to the completion of the Terrace rather than merely the feature. There was another summerhouse that has disappeared, further out on a hill 'in the form of a pentagon, two stories high, with a balcony on the top',[46] and, much closer to the Hall, a delightful loggia-cum-Game Larder, which overlooks paddocks and some of the original seventeenth-century stew ponds. Holbech's landscape was recorded in a map of 1772, commissioned by his nephew, who inherited after his uncle's death a year before.[47]

Farnborough represents a cautious step towards the ideal parkscapes of Capability Brown. Although the great Terrace Walk reaches out into the wider landscape, and the river below it provides that enlivening touch of reflected waters in the middle distance, the land beyond, to east and west, was kept as agricultural fields. This was, and remains, an agrarian landscape, not a landscaped park. However, at **Upton House**, on the other side of the Edgehill scarp beyond Radway, a combination of natural advantages – a steep-sided combe and a plentiful water source – produced a park that was closer in feel to the late-century Picturesque aesthetic of Richard Payne Knight and Uvedale Price than to that of Brown himself. Again, Miller's involvement is conjectural but, given its close proximity to Radway and his diary entries that record visits to Upton, it is likely that he was called in to advise. Whether he had anything to do with the wandering temple is debatable, but it makes for an intriguing detective story.

The National Trust now owns Upton House, where the visitor experience focuses on the important collection of oil paintings and the recently refurbished bedroom and Art Deco bathroom created for Lady Bearsted in the 1930s. Indeed, the current National Trust guidebook begins with an account of Percy Morley Horder's remodelling of the house and gardens for Lord Bearsted, while the eighteenth-century landscape rates barely a page. Unless the visitor is agile and active enough to reach the valley below the spectacular walled gardens on the hilltop, these Georgian improvements hardly register. Fortunately, the landscape is recorded in a beautiful plan (*colour plate 19*) of the estate drawn up by Thomas Richardson in 1774 for Robert Child.[48] It was Child's predecessor Francis Child, head of the important banking dynasty and patron of the architect Robert Adam, who carried out the landscaping after he bought the house from William Bumstead in 1757. Miller's correspondence with Dean Swift, nephew of Jonathan, reveals that he was not on friendly terms with his near neighbour and would not, therefore, have been responsible for any of Bumstead's garden ventures at Upton. The walled enclosures surrounding the house are likely to date from either the late 1690s, when Sir Rushout Cullen owned the estate, or from Bumstead's ownership; he classicised the house in 1735. Whether Miller advised Child is also in question, though a diary entry for 20 July 1750, long before Child bought the estate, reads: 'Went to the workmen and with Mr Willes to Upton, and to Lord North's to breakfast. Drawing floor for the building and Mr Child's plan'.[49] William Hawkes suggests that this plan may relate to an alcove Miller was designing for Child, but if so it must relate to another house, rather than to Upton.

When Francis Child took over he retained the complex of enclosures on the hilltop and concentrated his landscaping efforts on the valley, where the stream had been harnessed to provide a rectangular pool with a semicircular end towards the house. This was flanked by a series of stepped pools with cascade bridges to the east and another, much smaller, canal to the west, which mirrored the larger feature. At the head of the pool a temple was built to command the water, with a small finger of the pool providing a water source for the building; it may, therefore, have had a cold bath in the basement. Temple Pool, as it came to be known, was painted in about 1784 by Anthony Devis.[50] His view is taken from the south, with the Temple backed by trees in the middle distance and the house on the ridge above it. Oddly, when the site is walked today, the Temple (*40*) is sited at the other end of the Pool, where the ground falls away steeply to the south; a rivulet issuing from under the building snakes down the bank to the rear. Quite when the building was moved is unclear,

40

The case of the moving temple – a banqueting house-cum-changing room at the Temple Pool below Upton House. A contemporary painting shows it to have been built at the other end of the lake

but the portico of two pairs of coupled Doric columns and single columns defining the corners looks to be an afterthought and bears little physical relationship with the room behind. The portico is most likely to have been dismantled at some point and attached to a new building. Miller's diary entries in September 1750 and again in October 1756 record visits to Upton to see 'Mr Bumstead's Pool',[51] so it may be that Child merely utilised an existing feature and then dramatised it with the cascades and a new temple. Devis' painting, which may well be inaccurate, shows the Temple with a five-columned portico, an architectural solecism of which even Miller would not have been guilty. Jennifer Meir rightly argues that the temple in the Devis looks remarkably like the Ionic Temple at Farnborough and may, therefore, have been designed by Miller.

At the other end of the Pool are the remains of the stepped pools and their stone bridges, now lost in dense undergrowth. On one of the lower levels the causeway bridge is faced by a small Grotto of petrified stone, sprouting harts-tongue ferns and dripping with water. This, and the clumps of mixed pine and oaks shown on the 1774 plan, similar to ones Miller advised for Farnborough and Honington, suggest to Meir his designing hand, even if he did not supply one of his quick architectural sketches for the Pool Temple for Hitchcox to flesh out.

The Temple Pool and its flanking canal lead us satisfyingly back to the system of pools and canals that Sir Roger Newdigate developed around his estate at **Arbury**, yet another site where Miller is thought to have had design influence. As we have seen, Newdigate, another of Miller's Oxford friends, inherited Arbury in 1733 and began a long life transforming it into one of the most important revived medieval houses in the country, as well as making extensive improvements to the grounds.[52] These included the network of canals that his father had begun earlier in the century. Miller was a regular visitor to Sir Roger and his wife Sophia, who herself took a keen interest in the landscape projects. However, while the Newdigate archive has Miller sketches of architectural features for the house, there is no record of any landscape work. Indeed, the first references to garden buildings at Arbury, in 1748, are to structures designed by the Warwick mason-contractor, David Hiorn.[53] These included an orangery, a tea house and a rotunda, while in 1751 a new cascade for the lake in front of the house was under construction. The orangery and the rotunda have disappeared, but the tea house – a circular, Pantheon-like domed summerhouse fronting a pool, which was built especially for Sophia – survives to the north-east. Closer in there are four classical busts of Roman emperors set on terms arranged in a semicircle and backed by a Doric-pilastered alcove set in the service court wall. These were moved here in the early twentieth century but must be features that Sir Roger arranged around the pleasure grounds. There are also drawings by him for sham ruins, which seem not to have been built, though the North Lodge, which survives, looks to be in a similar rough style. Like Miller, Newdigate fancied himself as an architect, so it is unlikely that he had need for anything other than friendly advice.[54]

Miller was ready to give this when he was visiting Arbury in early December 1750. In a letter to Miller of 2 December from Packington, Lord Guernsey wrote: 'On Saturday Lord and Lady Andover leave us

41 A commercial landscape at the heart of an eighteenth-century estate – Arbury's pools and canals. ©*English Heritage. NMR*

which may possibly prevent my seeing you at Arbury...if I can I have some intention of riding over on Wednesday to breakfast, as I shall be glad to see the cascade and Bow window whilst you are there...I want sadly the joynt opinion of yourself and Sir Roger for placing the Cascade here, as my plantations depend upon it'.[55] The letter is a perfect record of how close friends and acquaintances worked together on their landscape improvements. Lord Guernsey's Cascade at Packington will feature in the following chapter on Lancelot Brown's work in the county.

While Miller was advising on the bow window and possibly the Cascade at Arbury, the watercourse of which still survives by the lake, he is unlikely to have had any input in the development of Sir Richard's canal system. An aerial view of the estate (*41*) shows the High Level Canal snaking off towards the family-owned coalmines at Bedworth and Collycroft on the east, while a series of triangular pools – Gardener's Pool, Convent Pool and Bathing Pool, each one lined with shelter plantations – extends west from the Hall Pool by the main house. It is a most unlikely eighteenth-century landscape, one created by commerce rather than by leisure.

42 This Hermitage is a faithful reconstruction of Matthew Boulton's hermit's retreat at Soho House, part of his industrial landscape in the suburbs of Birmingham

A similar landscape, though on a much smaller scale, was laid out by Matthew Boulton around his manufactory at **Soho House**, now mostly subsumed within suburban Handsworth. Indeed the approach could not be less inviting, with the first advertising flagpole rearing up in front of the now derelict Beehive public house on the main street, while close by the 'Supreme Works', an engaging Art Deco engineering factory of 1922 with ramping lions, moulders away. Fortunately, money has been spent wisely on Soho House, which has been beautifully restored and its gardens recreated. Boulton' s earliest landscape work at Soho dates from the 1790s, when he shaped the pleasure grounds with ornamental water and garden buildings. Today the site occupies less than an acre, and it has been landscaped as an eighteenth-century suburban garden with some features, particularly the Hermitage (42), and planting, based directly on pictorial and archival evidence. The Chinese benches are in the oriental spirit of seats with 'Chinese backs' ordered by Boulton in 1799.[56] Originally, Boulton integrated the mill complex and the manufactory into the parkland, threaded the site with walks and planted it up with trees and shrubs (43). The main

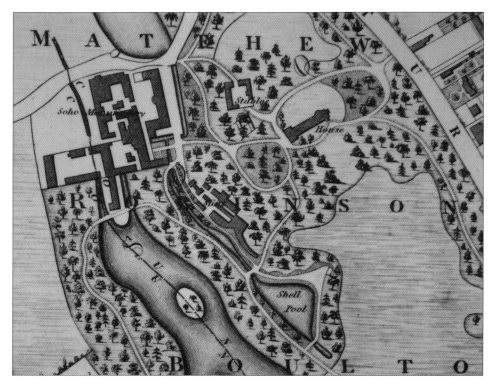

43 The central focus of Boulton's manufactory and gardens at Soho House was the
triangular-shaped Shell Pool commanded by a temple. *Reproduced with the permission of
Birmingham Libraries & Archives*

focus was the Shell Pool, a triangular-shaped piece of water commanded by
a small classical Temple of Flora.[57] A 'Temple of Flora Bed' has been
planted near the car-park which contain plants supplied for the flower
garden around the Shell Pool, while cherry laurels underplanted with early
cream honeysuckle surround the Hermitage, as shown in a 1799 illustration
of the original by John Phillp.[58] It is a most convincing recreation in miniature of what Boulton achieved in his wider landscape and a welcome
breath of culture in an otherwise run-down area of Birmingham.

These semi-industrial landscapes at Soho and Arbury, with their practical emphasis on commerce, are far removed from the preciously
antiquarian and aesthetic interests of the group of Warwickshire friends
who created some of the most engaging Rococo landscapes in the country.

endnotes on pages 269-271

5

The questionable capabilities of Lancelot Brown

Newnham Paddox, Warwick Castle, Packington Hall, Charlecote
Ragley Hall, Combe Abbey, Compton Verney, Coughton Court

WHEN LANCELOT 'CAPABILITY' BROWN DIED IN FEBRUARY 1783, HAVING
collapsed while walking from Lord Coventry's house in Piccadilly to his
son-in-law's house in Hertford Street, he had remodelled no fewer than
170 landscape parks in this country. His achievement had led one witty
contemporary, Richard Owen Cambridge, to remark in conversation with
Brown: 'I very earnestly wish that I may die before you....because I should
like to see heaven before you had improved it'.[1] Cambridge was not to get
his wish, as he outlived Brown by nineteen years, dying in 1802 at the ripe
old age of 85. Brown and his protégés – men like Richard Woods, William
Emes and John Davenport – had literally changed the face of rural
England. In so doing they had effectively killed off those formal gardens
of the preceding century that had survived the early Georgian vogue for
classical Arcadias and Rococo pleasure grounds packed with eclectic
garden buildings. In fact, Brown's vision was far greater than the small
compass of those Arcadias allowed. He worked on vast canvases where a
much more expansive aesthetic was required, and he had the vision to
effect a broad-brush treatment of sentinel tree clumps, snaking stretches
of water that appeared like vast lakes and an enclosing of shelter plantations on the periphery to create majestic landscapes. All he needed to do
was to sow the resultant parks with Dutch clover, construct ha-has to
keep livestock away from the open lawns by the house and, as well as
providing walking and riding routes, satisfy the gentry's passion for
enclosed mobility at speed with carriage drives that swept through the
park. Finally, to encourage the breeding of game birds for slaughter on the

wing, coverts and coppices were planted on the edges of woodland from which beaters could drive the unfortunate victims.[2]

Brown's working life was one continuous journey to estates where, after his initial 10-guinea visit, trusted foremen like Samuel Lapidge, John Midgely and John Spyers were left to sketch out his designs in a survey and then supervise the work through a series of timed contracts drawn up by Brown with the patron. Brown kept a close eye on the progress of the work, returning to the sites to make extensive notes or 'minutes', which were used to further instruct his foremen and the under-gardeners. With such attention to detail and such consummate professionalism, why then has Brown had such a bad press? Back in 1979 Roy Strong famously dedicated his *Renaissance Garden in England* to the 'memory of all those gardens destroyed by Capability Brown and his successors' and even during his own lifetime Brown was subject to criticism and abuse, most notably from William Chambers.[3] After his death the Picturesque theorists Richard Payne Knight and Sir Uvedale Price set up a war of words against his legacy and the current practice of his self-styled successor, Humphry Repton, calling Brown's parks dull, vapid, smooth and unvaried. Why then was his simple aesthetic so roundly criticised? And how much was he merely a victim of changing fashions and the sporting whims of his patrons? Did he, in fact, initiate a new style of landscape gardening, or were the seeds of his revolution to be found in the impracticalities and expenditure of maintaining vast formal gardens with their complex parterres and flower borders? Were landowners now ready to embrace an agrarian aesthetic, one that put hunting, shooting, boating and carriage riding before floral displays and intellectual iconography?

All these elements went to shape the Brownian park. However, before that ideal was achieved Brown, brought up on the smooth mini-contours of William Kent's Elysian Fields at Stowe, its gentle slopes enlivened by buildings of less than subtle political allegory, had to work with the prevailing fashion for eclecticism. As such, his early layouts of the 1740s, particularly those at Croome Court in Worcestershire and Wotton House in Buckinghamshire, are liberally scattered with temples, grottoes, seats and statuary. These eclectic tendencies are also present in Warwickshire, but to a much lesser degree, his patrons here urging Brown into a far more minimalist approach, one that was to become synonymous with his name. It inevitably made for somewhat uninspired layouts, hence the questionable nature of his achievement in the county. A typical example of this lacklustre treatment is **Newnham Paddox**.

As we have seen, the formal gardens at Newnham illustrated by Kip and Knyff in their *Britannia Illustrata* of 1707 were created by the 4th Earl of Denbigh, who inherited in 1685. The site was to provide a setting for one of Brown's earliest landscape treatments.

It had some advantages, particularly its abundance of water and the survival of seventeenth-century tree avenues and plantations. The topography was, however, not in its favour, and any new landscaping would need to dramatise the relatively flat terrain with changes in level, and project long vistas over water and out across parkland. It must be said that Brown's early attempt in the emerging 'park style' was hampered at Newnham by this lack of lively contours.[4]

Brown's patronage came, like so many of his early commissions, through his employer at Stowe, Lord Cobham, who had a wide circle of aristocratic acquaintances. William Fielding, 5th Earl of Denbigh, and his wife Isabella were two such close friends. On returning home from abroad in 1741 they began to make major improvements to the formal grounds. Preparation work for the new landscape was carried out, perhaps with advice from Brown, just after he began working for Cobham at Stowe: 'The Lower waters were begun to be altered from their old State in 1741 and were this year [1743] finished viz the Great Canal & the Triangle'.[5] This refers to the double canals to the side of the house and the triangular piece of water above them, which are shown on the *Britannia Illustrata* view. Brown was obviously shaping the angular lines into more pleasingly curvaceous stretches of water, but these have not survived the demolition of the house and the planting of a grove of silver birches on its site. While he was tackling the formal pools, Brown was also creating an ornamental plantation: 'Planted in the Grove at the Back of the Long Stable about 150 trees each being fenced with Post & Rails the chief whereof were Ash raised from the keys of the garden three years growth, the remainder Elm from Lutterworth of ten years growth'.[6] This was, in effect, a thickening out of the existing single rows of trees behind the stable range to give the environs of the house a sense of green enclosure, and to mask open views of the waterscape beyond. The bowling green must have been levelled at this time to produce that easy, gradual and smooth connection between greensward and house that is such a feature of Brown's parks.

This view to the water was altered in 1746, when modifications of the two rectangular pools began: 'carrying it on to ye head of ye Pond in the Park by a Plan and the direction of Mr. Brown, Gardener to Lord Cobham, with other work done in consequence of this'.[7] Brown naturalised the two bodies of water, which can still be seen on site today, commanded by an Edwardian summerhouse and edged with a collection of modern sculpture (44). In April 1746 Brown was 'levelling the End of the Serpentine Water, Cleaning the first Pond in the Park & laying it with hanging slopes on each side', finishing these in April 1748.[8] The two lakes extended from the house with a break in the middle where the level changes. At this point there is a causeway bridge and a brick-arched culvert, which must be of Brown's contrivance. It is surprising that he did not dramatise the difference in height between the two lakes with a cascade, as he was later to project at Packington and to achieve at Longleat in Wiltshire, but perhaps he was still learning how to contrive such effects. Today the lower lake is flanked by ornamental plantations and specimen trees, which were introduced in the nineteenth century and give the grounds the air of an arboretum rather than that of a Brownian park.

In November 1753 work commenced on the upper pool and continued until June 1754. In the same year, Brown was commissioned to rebuild the house, and in the April workmen 'Began to pull down part of the old house'[9] ready for the construction of Brown's new façade. This was a routine Palladian affair, based on Brown's design for the entrance front of Croome Court in Worcestershire, with a central pedimented section and corner towers.[10] The 5th Earl died in 1755 with the house still unfinished, but work continued under his son Basil until 1761. Typically, Brown was not paid his £200 for 'measuring, surveying, planning' in connection with 'the building of the house at Newnham' until 18 May 1768.[11] When completed, the house and grounds at Newnham must have appeared much like Croome on a minute scale, with an expanse of parkland in front

44 A stylistically eclectic range of modern sculptures lines the lake at Newnham Paddox –
Capability Brown's earliest commission in the county for the 5th Earl of Denbigh

and the enlivenment of water to the side and rear. Brown had done what
he could with an unpromising site, but his landscape and house did not
amount to much at Newnham. Bertie Greatheed, the owner of Guy's
Cliffe, noted this in his journal after a visit to the grounds in May 1825:

> I was out by six o clock, rambling abroad, and making myself
> acquainted with whole domain; laid out by Brown and perfectly in
> his manner with a most serpentinary water, expanding from tail to
> head between the smoothest of banks, if mowed, with however
> some fine old trees. But this part is left in wilderness, and the
> dressed pleasure ground is on the approach side & not possessed of
> any character. This water is unsupplied during the summer.[12]

Another early commission in the county was far more propitious and
confirmed Brown's standing as a new and important professional in the
field of landscape design. The progress of landscape developments on the
Temple Park at **Warwick** are extremely well documented in both maps
and Canaletto's several 1748-52 views of the Castle and grounds painted
for Francis Greville, 8th Baron Brooke, later 1st Earl Brooke and 1st Earl

of Warwick. In addition, there is a 1753 drawing of the Mount by Mrs Delany and many later topographical views of the site, such as Thomas Baker's 1842 painting of the Castle from the banks of the Avon.[13] However, any analysis must begin with the beautifully detailed 1690 survey (*colour plate 20*) of the 'Leafields, Temple Grounds, Spiers Lodge' carried out for Fulke, Lord Brooke, Baron Beauchamp.[14] This has a delightful vignette of the Castle, showing the Mount with its spiral walk topped by a pyramidal tree and the formal gardens laid out below it. The Avon flows past the Castle and is then diverted close to the causeway bridge into the 'Temple ditch', which effectively creates the Castle Meadow. Further out, a tree avenue strides across hedged fields; there is no deer park, merely enclosed fields and meadows for pasture.

By the time the 8th Baron Brooke came of age in 1740, after a five-year Grand Tour in Italy, the Castle grounds were in decay, his trustees having neglected their responsibility to maintain the Castle and collect rents from his estates. Consequently, after an advantageous marriage in 1742 to Elizabeth Hamilton, Lord Brooke set about restoring both the Castle and the grounds. Work began in earnest in 1744 with land purchases to extend the Castle estate, and in 1748 the recently ennobled Earl Brooke employed Brown as both architect and landscape gardener, a commission that covered thirteen years. It is likely that Sanderson Miller introduced Brown to Earl Brooke; they may both have had a hand in the Gothick rebuilding of Spiers Lodge in the park.

Brown began by dismantling the formal gardens by the Mount and replacing them with open lawns, single trees and tree clumps of conifers, cedars and Scots pine, which are shown in Mrs Delany's 1753 sketch. One of Canaletto's 1748 paintings shows the work in progress and even includes a temporary lean-to shed for Brown's labourers.[15] Brown also planted tree clumps on the Castle Meadow. This first phase of work was an attempt to connect the Castle with its grounds and to soften the angularity of the earlier formality; in Horace Walpole's words, 'to let his garden and park be natural'.[16] At this time Brown was still relatively unknown, for Walpole described him as having 'set up, on a few ideas of Kent and Mr Southcote. One sees what the prevalence of taste does'.[17] Earl Brooke was certainly pleased with this new landscape taste, as work continued

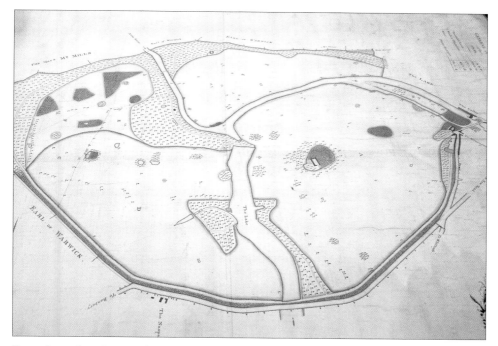

45 Brown's work at Warwick Castle has almost all disappeared in later campaigns, but this map of 1791 shows his signature tree clumps and shelterbelt plantations. *Warwickshire County Record Office, CR1886/M22*

until 1753, when he entered into a more formal contract with Brown for architectural work on the Castle and further improvements in the park. By 1755 the regular payments from Earl Brooke's bank account show that Brown was working on the creation of Temple Park by removing hedgerows and the earlier tree avenue, and planting a shelterbelt alongside the turnpike road. Brown's other signature feature was a carriage drive that began at the medieval bridge across the Avon, crossed the park towards Temple Hill, ran on to the valley of the Ram Brook, which Brown canalised, and continued up to Spiers Lodge, where visitors could enjoy an expansive panorama back to the Castle across Temple Park, a view painted in 1776 by Paul Sandby.[18] The way back to the Castle gardens was via a bridge over the river near Spiers Lodge, which was built for that purpose in 1757. Much of Brown's work is shown on a 1791 estate map (*45*) of the park by E Sale.[19]

Many of Brown's features have been subsumed within later improvements, particularly those carried out by the second Earl, but one charming sketch survives from Brown's last work at Warwick on the enclosure of Barford Common by the southern boundary of the park. It is known as the 'Family Clump' and is a drawing for a regular planting of trees within a circular paling named after members of Earl Brooke's family. It is likely that Brown never got to plant it out as Earl Brooke was sceptical of such features, and was busy modifying Brown's planting ten years later: 'I have undone many things he left me as I thought looking Formal in the planting way, ever making Round Clumps that merit nothing but being very tame indeed'.[20] The remark is prescient, suggesting that, as early as the 1770s, Brown's formulaic planting was found wanting.

In tandem with his work at Warwick Castle in the late 1740s and early 1750s, Brown was also advising Lord Guernsey at Great Packington in the Forest of Arden. This may well have been through another introduction by Miller, as Guernsey was in regular correspondence with Miller in 1746-50 about proposed alterations to the landscape.[21] While no plan survives of the proposals for Warwick, there is a beautiful 1751 Brown survey in the archives at **Packington Hall**. The Rococo cartouche has his signature and the legend: 'A Plan for the Disposition of the grounds at great Packington the Seat of the Rt. Honourable the Lord Guernsey'.[22] The plan is extremely long and thin and decorated at the foot with an evocative sketch of a cavernous grotto-cascade sprouting conifers flanked by rockwork caves within the shadows of which are Arcadian figures (46). At the other end are two more architectural vignettes of 'My Lady's Lodge' and an entrance archway, which were never built. These are both classical in style; the former with its portico *in antis* reminiscent of the garden front of the Queen's House at Greenwich, while the other is a fairly tame affair with a pedimented arch and columned side screens. The landscape between them centres on the two lakes, to be developed from fishponds, below the house that Matthew Brettingham was later to subsume within a new Hall. The junction of the two lakes – the Great Pool bulbous in shape, the Hall Pool serpentine with a narrow stretch arcing out of view in a plantation – was to be the site of the proposed Cascade. While this seems to have disappeared, if it was ever built, there is a classical wellhead

46 This remarkable vignette of the proposed Grotto-Cascade for Packington Hall is closer in style to the work of Thomas Wright of Durham than to that of Brown. *Reproduced by permission of the Earl of Aylesford*

in boggy ground at the east end of the Hall Pool, which might have fed a cold bath. Its waterspout is in the form of a lion and is marked 'Lion's Head' on the 1887 Ordnance Survey map. The southern boundary of the estate was to have a shelterbelt of undulating lines on the park side, while screen plantations and individual clumps were planned to dramatise the Great Pool. Finally, to provide mobility within the park, walks and rides were to edge the lakes and the southern shelterbelt, while further walks were to be threaded through the plantations. Brown drew the map early in his professional career, only two years after Lord Cobham's death, yet it has all the hallmarks of his mature style.

There is a calm serenity about the contoured lawns and Brown's vast sheet of water below the Hall (*colour plate 21*). Further out in the park to the north-east Joseph Bonomi's St James' church crouches low like a brooding fragment of the Baths of Caracalla, while the Old Hall nearby has a more sprightly profile of gables and pediments. The Hall is part-moated, with a small brick pyramidal-roofed garden pavilion, which looks like a Bonomi refugee. He is also known to have designed, in 1788, Forest Hall, to the south-east towards Meriden. This is still the headquarters of the Woodmen of Arden; successive earls of Aylesford have been keen archers and have acted as Wardens of the Forest.

At Brown's next commission in the county he faced a similar problem to that at Newnham Paddox. When he was brought in, in about 1750, to remodel the grounds at **Charlecote**, Captain Thomas and Colonel George Lucy's Dutch-style water gardens must have been in sad decay. George Lucy, who inherited Charlecote in 1744, had already removed the tall octagonal summerhouse from its peninsula, shifting the leisure focus closer to the house. After the obligatory visit to Italy, Lucy set about improving the gardens and park, making contact with Brown, possibly through his friend Lady Coventry of Snitterfield, who had family connections with Croome. Instead of initially reshaping the existing canals running parallel to the Avon, which would have been a huge undertaking, Lucy commissioned Brown to manage the confluence of the Avon and its tributary the Dene, or Wellesbourne Brook, that flows into it at the south-east corner of the site. Brown first drew a rough plan of Charlecote and then made a visit to advise on the widening of the Dene. However, Lucy did not formally engage him until 1757, when a Cascade was built where the Dene meets the Avon. It was completed by March 1761, when Lucy wrote from Bath: 'pray how doth the Cascade look now it is finished?'[23] The Cascade (*colour plate 22*) is not as impressive as Brown's later waterfall at Bowood in Wiltshire, as the change in level is relatively minimal, but the crashing waters cleverly mask the merging of the two rivers and dramatise an otherwise uninspired landscape.

In 1760 Lucy entered into a contract with Brown for works that included the final destruction of the unfashionable water gardens. The third article of Brown's contract states: 'To fill up all the ponds on the north front of the house, to alter the slopes and give the whole a natural, easy, and corresponding level with the house on every side'.[24] In place of the walled gardens Brown created a wilderness, separated from the open meadow by a ha-ha wall, while a raised Cedar Lawn (*47*), set six feet above the level of the entrance forecourt, replaced the bowling green and parterres by the house. The Avon was widened and its banks smoothed to give them a 'natural and easy level'.[25] Brown agreed to source all the trees, replant any that might die, and sow all the improved ground with grass-seed and Dutch clover. However, he was in such demand that work at

Charlecote did not run smoothly, Lucy reporting from Bath in March 1761 that 'Mr. Browne, who everyone wants, hath not yet made his appearance here'.[26] In April of the same year Lucy was waiting for his Thomas Gainsborough painting to be delivered and also waiting for a further visit from his landscape gardener: 'Mr. Brown was here [in Bath] on Sunday last, and staid till Tuesday, when he called upon me... and told me he should not be at Charlecote till May, which I suppose will be June at the soonest'.[27] In fact, Lucy had to wait until the following year when Brown sent him a letter reporting that the additional trees would be planted, and that all

47 Brown's tranquil Cedar Lawn at Charlecote replaced the busy formality of Captain Thomas Lucy's seventeenth-century bowling green and parterres

corrections to the work would be completed: 'you may depend that everything shall be put to right'.[28] All this was supervised by Brown's foreman, John Midgely, at a total cost of £525.

Brown's work at Charlecote is now overshadowed by the early nineteenth-century medieval revivalism of George Hammond Lucy and his wife Mary. It was never a significant contribution to what remains a somewhat desultory landscape, particularly those fields across the Avon from the house. The 'easy, and corresponding level' of the greensward slopes that obliterated the seventeenth-century canals is hardly 'natural', but the cedars of Lebanon which dramatise the lawn above the forecourt add an air of shadowy majesty to an otherwise disconnected pleasure ground.

Brown's work at **Ragley Hall** is also difficult to disentangle from the spectacular formal terraces and Rose Garden designed in 1871-2 by Robert Marnock, or the Jerwood Foundation Sculpture Trail which threads its way through the grounds, both of which will find their respective places in later chapters of this study. And, while there are no surviving accounts, Horace Walpole remarked on a visit in 1758 that Ragley had had 'a great deal done to it since I was here last'.[29] His earlier visit had been in July 1751, so Brown's reshaping must date from that period: 'Browne has improved both the ground and the water, though not quite to perfection'.[30] The 1886 Ordnance Survey map marks tree clumps in the park alongside the Arrow to Wixford road, which may be of Brown's planting, and there is a shelterbelt plantation containing 'Ladies Wood' on the southern perimeter, but the centrepiece lake is a dull trapezoid with none of Brown's usual graceful curves. However, Ragley found favour with Bishop Pococke, who passed by in September 1756 and noted that: 'There is a fine lawn, woods, and water like a serpentine river, behind the house, and it commands a view of small hills from the front either finely cultivated or diversified with wood'.[31] It may be that the banks of Brown's lake were later remodelled.

The same is true of Brown's contribution to **Combe Abbey**, where the grounds have been so altered in the nineteenth and twentieth centuries as to render his interventions almost invisible. But his lake has survived these depredations, and its original character and that of several garden buildings on the estate were captured in a series of beautiful watercolours painted by Maria Johnson between December 1797 and February 1798.[32] These, together with Matthias Baker's 1778 survey of the estate, mentioned in an earlier chapter, make it possible to judge Brown's contribution to the landscape.

William Harrington, 6th Baron Craven, who had inherited Combe in 1769, commissioned Brown in about 1770 to remodel the formal gardens by the house, shown in the *Britannia Illustrata* view, and to construct buildings in the park including lodges, kennels, and a menagerie to

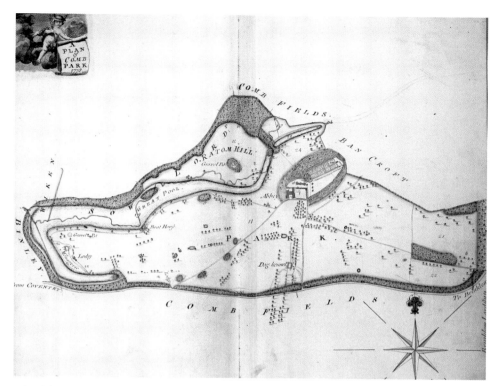

48 The full extent of Brown's remodelling of the grounds at Combe Abbey, with its shelterbelts and serpentine lake, is recorded on this 1778 map by Thomas Baker. *Warwickshire County Record Office, CR8/184*

Brown's design or to that of his son-in-law, Henry Holland junior. Lord Craven wrote to Brown in about August 1770 that, although he was detained in London, he was keen that Brown should go to Combe without him and consider possible alterations: 'All that I have further to observe, is that you to exert yr. utmost abilities to improve the place....I hope you will not leave Combe till you have made a plan and estimate'.[33] Work subsequently began in September 1771, with payments being made until May 1774.

The Baker survey (*48*) is a fascinating document that records with precision Brown's adaptation of an existing formal landscape. Most of the walled enclosures around the house have been removed, though Brown retained the practical kitchen gardens to the north-east of the house, wrapping them with a shelter plantation. Further out in the park he made allowances for the flat landscape, planting only one major clump amidst

49 The sharp outlines of Brown's lakes have often been lost in encroaching vegetation. Maria Johnson's 1798 watercolour of the water at Combe Abbey records his original conception. *The Herbert Art Gallery and Museum, Coventry*

the scattering of trees, some of which were remnants of the formal tree avenues, which he broke up, seemingly at random intervals, to produce a more picturesque effect. New planting connected the two existing blocks of woodland behind Oratom Hill and a shelterbelt was extended almost around the entire estate. The canals were developed into a serpentine lake, which was praised by Samuel Ireland, a contemporary landscape watercolourist and Picturesque fancier: 'the easy winding of a spacious sheet of water, upwards of two miles in length, that runs at a proper distance from the front of the abbey, highly enriches the scenery of the very extensive park'.[34] Baker's survey shows clearly the smooth banks of the lake, as does Johnson's *View of the Water*, with the edges of the lake undulating into the distance (49), painted on 24 February 1798.

Where the lake doubled back at the western extremity a Menagerie was sited. This was built in the 1770s to a design, either by Brown or by his son-in-law Henry Holland Junior, inspired by the Royal Menagerie at Versailles. It is Palladian in style, as one would expect from Brown, with

James Lovell's statue of Caractacus was found to be too tall for its prepared niche in the Edgehill Tower. It now languishes in the herbaceous border on the approach to Radway Grange

116

The cavernous plunge pool under the Rococo banqueting room at the Walton Bath House – Sanderson Miller's 1749 design for the gout-stricken Sir Charles Mordaunt

17 The perfect Rococo conceit – Thomas Robins' view of the pleasure grounds at Honington, take from across the 'back water'. The Chinese Seat and the Cascade with its attendant sculptures ar clearly visible. *Reproduced by kind permission of Bristol Reference Library*

18 Robins' companion view of Honington, painted by the Chinese Seat, shows the Cascade, the Grotto and the Temple – all essential components of a mid-eighteenth-century eclectic landsca *Reproduced by kind permission of Bristol Reference Library*

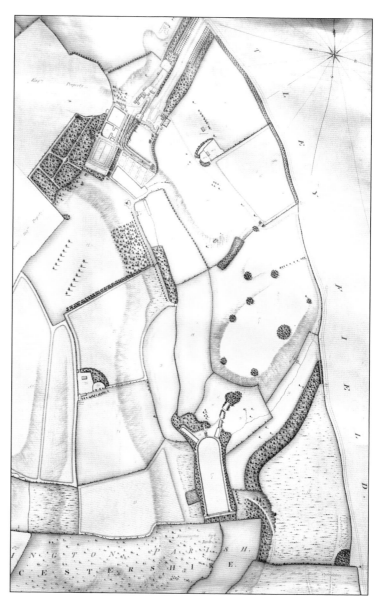

19

Thomas Richardson's 1774 estate map of Upton House and its landscape includes the Temple Pool in the valley below the house with the temple sited at the northern end. The building has now moved mysteriously to the southern dam. *Oxfordshire History Centre, J/IV/5*

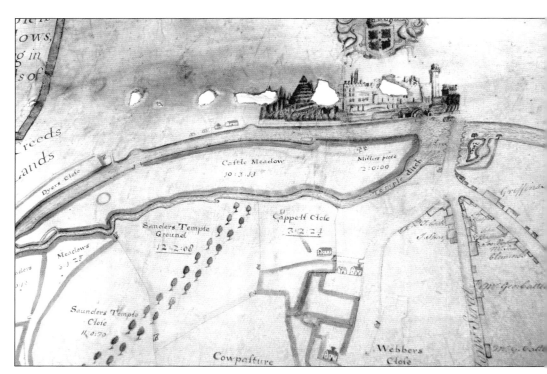

20 The Temple Grounds, Warwick Castle where Capability Brown was to create a new landscape park for Earl Brooke after 1744, are recorded as homely fields on this 1690 survey. It includes a vignette of the Castle and the Mount with its spiral path. *Warwickshire County Record Office, CR1886/M6*

21 Capability Brown's lake at Packington follows fairly precisely the lines drawn out on his 1751 plan, prepared for Lord Guernsey

22 Brown's 1761 Cascade is an ingenious and dramatic way of masking the confluence of two rivers at Charlecote – the Avon and the Dene, or Wellesbourne Brook

23 Henry Holland Junior's 1770s Menagerie at Combe Abbey was based on the Royal Menagerie at Versailles

24 Brown often favoured the Gothick style for ancillary buildings in the park, as here in the lost Kennels at Combe Abbey, seen in one of Maria Johnson's exquisite 1790s watercolours. *The Herbert Art Gallery and Museum, Coventry*

25 Paul Padley's 1818 estate map of Compton Verney shows Brown's naturalised Wilderness across the water from the house and the western, Regency extension of the lake. *Shakespeare Centre Library & Archive, DR98/1832*

6 Moseley Hall with Birmingham on the horizon in Humphry Repton's watercolour before his proposed improvement of the view. *Courtesy of the Frances Loeb Library, Harvard Graduate School of Design*

7 Repton's improved sketch shows how he plans to appropriate the industrial city into a private landscape, by carrying the eye in the middle distance, via a Boathouse on the lake, to the smoking chimneys of Birmingham. *Courtesy of the Frances Loeb Library, Harvard Graduate School of Design*

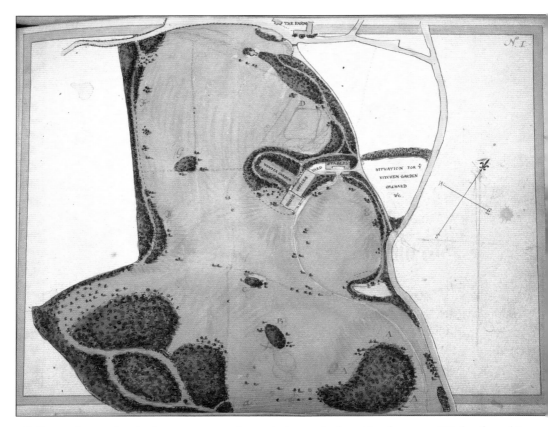

28 Repton's map for the improvement of an existing agricultural landscape at Warley from his 179
Red Book. *Sandwell Community History & Archives Service*

two pyramidal-roofed towers at one end and a domed octagon at the other (*colour plate 23*). Maria Johnson's watercolour is taken from across the lake, showing it to have been framed by deciduous trees and some evergreens. The building is currently undergoing a sensitive restoration. The site is enclosed on the north-west by tall brick walls that may once have provided the structure for cages which housed exotic birds and other creatures; these may well be the remains of the horseshoe-shaped feature on the survey. Other ornamental buildings with practical functions were the Dog Kennels, due south of the house, which were demolished by 1886, and the East Lodge, which survives, much altered. Johnson's watercolours of these show them both to have been in Gothick style, like several other park buildings designed by Brown, particularly for Blenheim. The Kennels (*colour plate 24*) was a castellated quadrangular building with a spired turret, while the East Lodge was originally a pretty Gothick conceit decorated with quatrefoils and arrowslits.[35] In stylistic contrast, the West Lodge was designed as a classical triumphal arch.

Brown's working relationship with several architects, including the two Henry Hollands, junior and senior, James Paine and Robert Adam, often makes it difficult to identify his architectural work. At Combe he may have been responsible for the Gothick buildings and perhaps the Menagerie, but the West Lodge looks decidedly like Holland's later work with its touches of Adamesque neo-Classicism. This architectural conundrum is also apparent at **Compton Verney**, just off the Fosse Way near Kineton. Here, there are documented buildings by both Brown and Adam, though the author of the serene sphinx-guarded Bridge, which conveys the drive across the lake to the house, is a tantalising matter for conjecture. But then so is the landscape itself, which may not have been extensively reshaped by Brown, as many of the so-called 'Brownian' features were in place long before he arrived in 1768. It is highly likely that he eased an existing landscape into the perfect parkscape by judicious planting and the merest reshaping of the seventeenth-century wilderness.

The seventeenth-century landscape at Compton Verney is shown in Hollar's 1656 engraving published in Dugdale's *Warwickshire*. It is a typical scene with the house and its medieval church overlooking an extensive mill pool, and the Stratford to Kineton road bordering the site to the south. Parkland, fields and orchards surround the site, while there is a possible viewing mount set in the middle of a field east of the road. So the landscape already had some natural advantages before the great remodellings of the early eighteenth century. These might have found a more logical place in this study in the chapter on formal gardens, but they are so crucial to an understanding of what Brown did, or did not, achieve at Compton Verney, that they must feature here. The first improvements were carried out by George, 12th Baron Willoughby de Broke, who inherited in 1711; they were recorded in surveys of 1736 and 1738, commissioned by Richard Verney, 13th Baron Broke.

George reconstructed the house with an additional west range, laid out formal gardens close to the house, and transformed the mill pool into a lake crossed at three points. James Fish's 1736 survey (50) records all these features. An ornamental canal was built on the west lawn, while across the lake a shrubbery was planted, intersected by geometric paths. South of the lake tree avenues radiated out into the wider landscape. Interestingly, the survey title refers to a proposed 'New Park', suggesting that further improvements were under consideration. John Loveday visited Compton Verney in 1735 and described the grounds: 'The Gardens rise up an hill, and are well-contrived for Use and Convenience. There are Views down to a Pond; of these Ponds there are 4 in a string, which make a mile in length'.[36]

These were the pleasure grounds that John Peyto Verney, the 14th Baron, inherited in 1752. By 1760 he had received two inheritances that enabled him to make plans for sweeping changes to both the house and the landscape. These ambitious designs coincided with his proposed marriage in 1761 to Louisa, the sister of Lord North of nearby Wroxton Abbey in Oxfordshire. For the house Verney engaged Robert Adam to add new wings and a Corinthian portico between 1762 and 1768, the work being supervised by a local mason-architect, William Hiorn. For the landscape he commissioned Brown, who is known to have started work in 1768, soon after the reconstruction of the house was completed. Brown's account book records that he was paid £120 on 19 November 1768 after he had visited Compton Verney and provided plans.[37] By May 1770, landscape work priced at £1,000 had been completed and a new contract begun, which by 1774 totalled £2,830.[38]

50 The pre-Brown landscape at Compton Verney, with its formal enclosures around the house and geometric Wilderness Garden across the lake, is shown on this 1736 map of the estate by James Fish. *Shakespeare Centre Library & Archive, DR98/1820*

The early payments were for buildings including a five-bay Orangery (*51*) with Doric columns supporting a central pediment, which was sited north-west of the house and offered views across the pleasure grounds and lake.[39] In 1772 the medieval church was demolished, opening up views from the house across the lake, and in 1776-9 a plain Palladian Chapel was built to Brown's design to the north of the house. The Chapel survives, but it has a grim look, with shuttered windows, the re-used stained glass from the medieval church having been sold at auction in 1931. Around the house itself, Brown replaced the formal gardens with greensward and trees, principally cedars of Lebanon, and incorporated existing tree avenues into his newly formed landscape. However, there were no huge waterworks to complete, as the pools were already in existence. He merely planted the banks around the upper reaches of the lakes to smooth their outline and removed a small dam between the two upper pools, linking them into a single sheet of water, at the same time making

51

Brown's Doric
Orangery at
Compton Verney, yet
another of his
recycled architectural
designs, was sited to
the north-west of the
house; it has since
been demolished.
*Country Life Picture
Library*

way for a bridge. A new south drive, dramatising the approach to the
house that came into view just as the Bridge was reached, was constructed
by altering an early eighteenth-century formal walk into a more serpentine route. The nearby road was moved a short distance for a ha-ha to be
created west of the house, and views from the house to the south and the
west were opened up.

The Icehouse was built in 1772, near the Wilderness, and was almost
certainly to Brown's design. The final payments in November of that year
included 15s 2d to William Harris for thatching the roof.[40] It has recently
undergone a scholarly and sensitive restoration. The Wilderness, which
once featured geometric walks, became an ornamental Shrubbery
threaded with serpentine paths. The later Paul Padley estate map (*colour
plate 25*) of 1818 shows the new feature quite clearly. A section of Compton
Verney's accounts in 1772, entitled 'Mr Brown's Work', records payments
for gravel brought to the estate, no doubt for the winding paths.[41] In 2008

52 The Upper Bridge at Compton Verney may have been designed by Robert Adam when
    he was remodelling the house for the 14th Baron Broke between 1762 and 1768

an outer circuit of paths attributed to Brown was found in the Icehouse
Coppice, with gravel lying on a base of limestone fragments.

Adam and Brown worked at Compton Verney at roughly the same
time, so it is difficult to decide which of them provided the designs for
the two bridges, the foundations of which were laid in 1770. The Upper
Bridge with sphinxes (52), built on the site of the dam that divided the
Middle Pool from the Upper Long Pool, has been attributed to Adam.
Certainly it is very close in style and sophistication to a design he
prepared for Kedleston Hall in Derbyshire.[42] However, it might be that
Brown designed the Bridge himself or had it constructed to a design by
Adam. Designs for the Lower Bridge, over which the Banbury to Strat-
ford road passes, survive but they are undated and unsigned.[43] In the
Compton Verney accounts, again under 'Mr Brown's Work', the carpenter
John Maunton was paid for work on the Lower Bridge, suggesting a
possible Brown attribution.[44]

There is evidence on the 1818 survey of large-scale tree planting,
including one clump on Combrook Field, and serpentine belts at the
western edge of the estate. Thorn, elm, ash, oak, and sycamore were

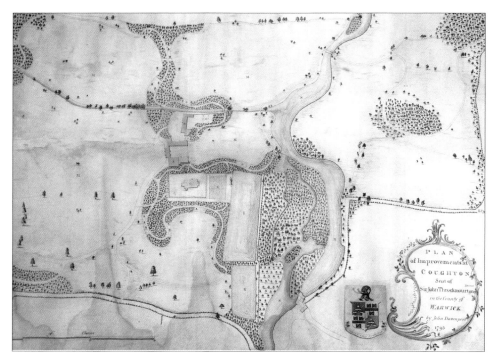

53 A landscape too far – John Davenport's outdated 1794 plan for reshaping the grounds at Coughton Court. By that time Brownian minimalism had been rejected in favour of a more savage Picturesque style. *Warwickshire County Record Office, CR1998/M21*

planted, while payments were made in 1769 and 1772 to Robert Patterson for 'trees and shrubs', and in 1772 to John Maunton for 'Paling the Plantation'.[45] Payments for trees and shrubs continued throughout the 1770s, with 200 elms purchased on 23 December 1776, the accounts also recording work 'mounding the clump'.[46]

Compton Verney appears to have been Brown's last work in the county, but there is one more estate where a plan in his style was offered and then rejected. Ten years after he had died, Sir John Throckmorton went abroad for a year upon inheriting **Coughton Court**. He returned in July 1793, having visited France and Italy. He was keenly interested in landscape, as in the following year he made trips to parks and gardens in England, including Stourhead, Longleat and Bowood. Before setting out on his English garden tour he had already commissioned a plan for landscape improvements at Coughton by John Davenport, one of Brown's protégés (53). This is a typical Brownian treatment with expanses of open parkland, a serpentine lake, shelterbelt plantations and winding walks threaded through woodland wrapped around the house, but it was never executed.[47] There is an obvious reason why. 1794 marked the publication of the two polemic tracts – Richard Payne Knight's didactic poem *The Landscape* and Uvedale Price's *Essay on the Picturesque* – which amounted to thinly veiled character assassinations of Brown and his landscape aesthetic. Davenport's proposal was, therefore, ill-timed and ill-judged. In future, patrons would require designs that brought out the dramatic, romantic capabilities of a landscape rather than its smooth beauty, something that Humphry Repton, self-styled successor to Brown, was to learn to his cost.

endnotes on pages 271-272

6

Repton and the 'modern days of upstart Innovation'

Moseley Hall, Warley Hall, Stoneleigh Abbey

THERE ARE SO MANY IRONIES IN HUMPHRY REPTON'S CAREER AS A landscape gardener; none more so than his assertion in the Red Book for Stoneleigh Abbey that he was living in an age of 'upstart Innovation'. He was, of course, referring to the current vogue for revived classical architecture, rather than landscaping, but his stricture might well apply to his own improvements, which were frankly modern and, more often than not, carried out for the new moneyed professional classes rather than the established gentry or aristocracy. Repton had the misfortune to begin his new career just before war broke out with France, thereby limiting his client base to the *nouveaux riches*, businessmen who, unlike the landed gentry, were making money out of the conflict. Consequently, many of his early commissions in the 1790s were for men engaged in banking and trade in the big cities like Bristol, where he designed no fewer than five landscapes, and Birmingham, where he produced Red Books for **Moseley Hall** and Warley Hall, and possibly gave advice at Great Barr. Typically, given his penchant for social interaction with the upper classes, 'the flattering patronage with which I have been honoured by the first characters of the living age', as he put it in the Moseley Red Book, Repton despised such parvenus.[1] Indeed, he felt that the subject of landscape gardening would be 'very little understood in the neighbourhood of large manufacturing towns, where each individual feels that he has a right to follow his *own taste*, however absurd or ridiculous'.

How then was he to justify working for John Taylor of Moseley, who was a button manufacturer and banker, busy building a brash new hall after the 'Priestley Riots' of 1791 had reduced the former building to rubble and ashes?[2] Ever the obsequious counterfeiter, Repton side-stepped this by claiming that Taylor's request for Repton's 'opinion respecting the improvements of Mosely' was the 'strongest proof that *you* are excepted from this general censure'. With his inimitable verbosity, Repton continued: 'I shall therefore without fear of offending some of your neighbours, boldly deliver my opinion, that it may occasionally glance at the bad taste of Birmingham'. Perhaps this explains why Repton was to receive only one further commission near the city, three years later in 1795, from Samuel Galton of Warley. Money talks, and perhaps the word got around that Repton was two-faced.

The Moseley Hall Red Book is dated 19 September 1792 and concerns the appropriation of landscape not belonging to Taylor in order to extend 'the appearance of the property'. The first before-and-after sketches (*colour plates 26 & 27*) cleverly bring the industrialised landscape of Birmingham, seen on the horizon across the Rea Valley, into a private parkscape, where the smoking chimneys of the conurbation become part of a picturesque view. Repton proposed enlarging the existing lake to make a sheet of water for reflection and enlivening it with a 'simple cottage...over a boathouse'.[3] Ever mindful of the practical use of such decorative additions, Repton continued: 'and if a decent plain room were preserved here for the use of the Ladies, it would often be pleasant to pass a whole summer's day on the banks of the water, and make a variety in the amusements of the place'.[4] Trees were to be cut down on the banks to open up the view, drawing the eye, first to a spired church and then to the Anglican cathedral, which had been stoutly defended by Taylor.

This view is completely lost now, the two sectors of the estate having been severed by the growth of suburban Moseley. The house survives as Moseley Hall Hospital, surrounded by car-parks where there were once shrubberies, but near the road there is a charming brick Dovecote and small Bothy, which must both date from the Regency period. The lake is accessed via a small cut-way, further down the hill opposite the Fighting Cocks public house. It forms the centrepiece of a tranquil park, edged by select suburban housing. A brick-fronted Icehouse is set within a bank on the once-contoured grass down towards the lake, while on the periphery of the water a small rivulet, brick-lined by the water's edge and with rocky outcrops beyond, threads its way into the woodland. These may well be coeval with the Red Book proposals.

Repton's next Birmingham client was the gun manufacturer Samuel Galton junior, who lived at **Warley Hall**, just off the Hagley Road near Smethwick. No doubt Galton's status as President of the Lunar Society would have given him the intellectual cachet that Repton so longed for in his clients. The landscaper visited the site in July 1794 and produced his Red Book of proposals in March the following year.[5] Warley was a relatively unusual commission for him, as he was asked to create a new landscape rather than improve an existing terrain; the land was still divided into fields when he arrived. These are evident on a 1792 map by T Pinnel.[6] The Warley Red Book, researched in the year that Richard Payne Knight and Uvedale Price published their polemics on the Picturesque, is interesting in that it attempts to address some of the issues raised by them, particularly 'the new doctrine advanced by Mr Price, who supposes the study of *painting* to be the basis of *Landscape Gardening*'.[7] Repton does his best to scotch the idea, arguing at great length that the limited scope of a painter's canvas can never encompass what the eye can see in nature. His text for sketches II and III exposes 'the absurdity of this Gentleman's ideas on the affinity betwixt Painting and Gardening':

> This view from the south front of the proposed house, consists of objects which I believe the laboured finishing of Bruegel or Paul Brill would not be able to render pleasing as a picture, but I assert, that it is capable of becoming in reality, exactly what the view from the windows of a Country Seat ought to be, and yet the principles on which it is to be improved, are not such as any painter's works would suggest, nor can this sketch do more, than explain my ideas, leaving to the mind to compleat that beauty, which Nature and not painting can produce.

The Warley Red Book is also one of the most theoretical, re-using several texts from earlier Red Books, and was to form the basis for sections on 'the sources of pleasure in Landscape Gardening' that were to appear in his *Sketches and Hints on Landscape Gardening* of 1795. Indeed, Repton comments in the Introduction that he is not sure whether the Warley Red Book or the printed copy of the extract from the manuscript would appear first.

Repton's transformation of the unimproved landscape at Warley seems to be driven by a desire to satisfy Price's notion of 'Picturesque Effect', which 'furnishes the gardener with breadth of light and shade; forms of groups, outlines, colouring, balance of composition, and occasional advantage from roughness and decay, the effect of time and age'. After some initial pages of generalised comment about character, situation and the siting of a house within its landscape, Repton gives a map (*colour plate 28*) of his proposed improvements for Warley. This was to be a simple scheme, but one that necessitated the re-routing of a road close to the old hall. The existing field system was to be turned into a park with a few clumps, while the Great Copse to the south-east was to be threaded with paths and given a Doric temple to offer views back up to the house on its new site. A snaking drive was to pass between this and another shelter plantation parallel to the road to produce that 'burst' view of the new house on higher ground which Repton so favoured. The house and its offices were to be laid out in an arc, backed by more plantations, with a Winter Garden, wrapped around with more planting, to the west. Finally, a woodland walk led from the house to an existing summerhouse – the Warley Tor – which pre-dated Galton's purchase of the estate. This 'Prospect building', as Repton calls it, was a circular summerhouse with lower wings sited on a commanding position in the park between what is now Grove Road and Lenwade Road. It offered views out towards Galton's house at Great Barr, seven miles away. Galton's son Hughbert commissioned the architect Robert Lugar to extend it in 1818, but it is not known if this was carried out; it has since been demolished. Remnants of the planting that Repton planned survive today in Warley Park and Woods, which is now council-owned public open space surrounded, as at Moseley, by suburban housing. However, Warley Hall has gone, while part of the parkland is now a golf course.

Before and after views (*54 & 55*) of the field system at Warley, and its replacement with parkland enlivened by clumps and a lake, with Repton proudly pointing to what he would achieve for Galton, who stands by

54 An agricultural landscape at Warley before Humphry Repton's suggested improvements. *Sandwell Community History & Archives Service*

55 With the slide pulled back, an improved landscape is revealed with a carriage drive flanked by plantations and a naturalised lake, all surveyed animatedly by Repton and his client. *Sandwell Community History & Archives Service*

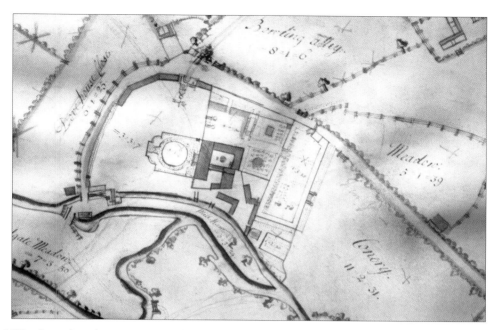

56 The formal enclosures surrounding Stoneleigh Abbey, from Thomas Wilks' survey of 1749. *Stoneleigh Abbey Ltd*

him, completed the Red Book process. Repton features in several of his Red Books, most notably at Endsleigh in Devon, where he is caught directing operations from a sedan chair. He appears again at **Stoneleigh**, where the great hulking bulk of Francis Smith's 1716 Baroque range broods over the landscape. Here Jane Austen once walked, and Repton, his trusty green umbrella at the ready, fidgeted with the improvements. Stoneleigh's great eighteenth-century block must surely be the least appropriate house for its site in the country, as it completely dominates the diminutive river valley to the south and turns its fifteen-bay façade away from the Avon towards the park beyond. This would be understandable if it had once commanded a vast formal garden to the west, but Thomas Wilks' survey (56) of April 1749 shows that the entrance forecourt was closed off from the park by a paled fence, and that most of the formal enclosures, which included a bowling green garden, were sited to the north and east.[8] Repton must have longed for the more humanly-scaled Cistercian abbey and subsequent Elizabethan house that it partially replaced, as his remodelling attempted, but never quite achieved, that unity of house and grounds which he had done so much to effect in landscape design after the vacancies of Brown's revolution. Indeed, Austen herself must have felt the same yearning for such a cosy connection between house and garden, for when she wrote *Mansfield Park*, both Mrs Norris and Edmund Bartram describe Sotherton, which is obviously modelled on Stoneleigh, as 'the noblest old place in the world', and 'built in Elizabeth's time'.[9]

The novelist's connection with Stoneleigh was through her mother, who was born Cassandra Leigh. Stoneleigh was her ancestral home, but she had never set foot in the place until her elderly cousin, the Revd Thomas Leigh, inherited in 1806. As at Combe Abbey, we have a 1798 Maria Johnson watercolour of the house before its improvement,[10] and also an engraving and description by Samuel Ireland, published in his 1795 *Picturesque Views*. These, together with Austen's fictional, though topographically close, descriptions in *Mansfield Park*, and an important diary entry made in October 1810 by Horace Walpole's correspondent and Bertie Greatheed's friend, Mary Berry, give a fairly precise image of the grounds that Repton was to reshape after his first visit to Stoneleigh in 1808. It is apparent that, although he drew up his plans in May 1809, the estate had still not been improved by late 1810. Furthermore, a later letter of May 1811 from Repton to Leigh concerned the bridge over the river, which had still not been built, though it had been marked up on the Red Book plan.[11]

What is so valuable and informative about the connection between Repton's work at Stoneleigh and Austen's fictional account of Regency landscape practice in *Mansfield Park* is that Repton himself appears in the book. Mr Rushworth, who like Thomas Leigh has recently inherited, remarks: 'It wants improvement, ma'am, beyond any thing. I never saw a place that wanted so much improvement in my life; and it is so forlorn, that I do not know what can be done with it'.[12] Of course, in reality, Rushworth's alter ego, Thomas Leigh, had known exactly what to do to remodel the grounds at Stoneleigh, as he had already employed Repton at Adlestrop in Gloucestershire.[13] Miss Bertram is also in no doubt as to who should help with Sotherton's improvement: 'Your best friend upon such an occasion...would be Mr. Repton'. Fortunately, Rushworth has heard of him: 'That is what I was thinking of. As he has done so well by Smith, I think I had better have him at once. His terms are five guineas a day....Smith's place is the admiration of the country; and it was a mere nothing before Repton took it in hand. I think I shall have Repton'. Austen's characters discuss the merits of modern improvement at length with Mary Crawford quoting the poet William Cowper on the demise of one of the formal avenues that Rushworth wants to cut down. She is anxious to see the place before anything is done, so Edmund Bertram describes it to her, giving a perfect account of an estate in want of remodelling:

> The house was built in Elizabeth's time, and is a large, regular, brick building – heavy, but respectable looking, and has many good rooms. It is ill-placed. It stands in one of the lowest spots of the park; in that respect, unfavourable for improvement. But the woods are fine, and there is a stream, which, I dare say, might be made a good deal of. Mr. Rushworth is quite right, I think, in meaning to give it a modern dress, and I have no doubt that it will be done extremely well.

When the party finally reach Sotherton they make a tour of the 'lower part of the house' and, rather than view the upper rooms, Rushworth urges them outside: 'we shall not have time for what is to be done out of doors. It is past two, and we are to dine at five'.[14] Mrs Norris, interfering as ever, tries to organise the group with carriages and horses, but 'the young people, meeting with an outward door, temptingly open on a flight of steps which led immediately to turf and shrubs, and all the sweets of pleasure-grounds, as by one impulse, one wish for air and liberty, all walked out'. They walk towards the lawn to survey the scene:

> Mr Crawford was the first to move forward, to examine the capa- bilities of that end of the house. The lawn, bounded on each side by a high wall, contained beyond the first planted area, a bowling- green, and beyond the bowling-green a long terrace walk, backed by iron palisades, and commanding a view over them into the tops of the trees of the wilderness immediately adjoining. It was a good spot for fault-finding.

With no such concern about Stoneleigh's perceived faults and the need to correct them, Ireland wrote: 'The situation of this abbey is truly beautiful; the Avon, winding before the house at a proper distance, supplies the corn and fulling mills, whose distant sound, aided by the rushing waters falling from the stream, contribute in no small degree to render a complete landscape delicious to a contemplative mind'.[15] Ireland's engraving is taken from across the river and shows the unimproved course of the water and a small rustic bridge, which Repton was later to suggest that Leigh re-use. Johnson's watercolour is of the Abbey Gatehouse only, but shows a greenhouse with tall glazed windows adjoining. These elements are shown on the Wilks survey, to which is appended a view of the house and its immediate environs by J Clark. At this time the greenhouse was unglazed; there is a dovecote, now gone, by the weir, and two further mill buildings in that area. Most significantly, high walls cut the house off from the lawns sloping down to the river. The survey also marks the bowling green garden to the north and two formal gardens to the north-east.

When Bertie Greatheed visited the estate with Mary Berry, Repton had yet to begin work on the improvements: 'Before we entered we met our acquaintance Mrs. Leigh (whose husband is to succeed to this place after the present incumbent), and the old incumbent himself, and Mr. Repton, planning future improvements; very probably, like the Irishman's, for the worse'.[16] This jaundiced view must have been heightened by Repton's typically obsequious behaviour when they met up again after their tour of the grounds: 'Mr. Repton (whom I had never seen before), fired off an exceeding fine complimentary speech to Agnes and me from the window of the carriage'.[17] However, Greatheed's diary for the same day records that Repton's 'manners correspond with his renown'.[18] Their dislike of contemporary landscape practice is not surprising, as both Berry and Greatheed were aficionados of the Savage Picturesque, rather than the closely manicured suburban style of Repton's Gardenesque. Like the party at Sotherton, who thought they needed a key to get into the wilderness, only to find the door unlocked, Berry wrote:

They gave us a key to the park, but we continued on foot, and were led by Greathead to the most beautiful parts of the most beautiful woodland scenery. The Avon, which runs through it, is here in some parts a pretty rippling trout stream, with such magnificent oaks hanging over it as mine eyes never before beheld; and in others it has steep sandy banks, covered by the same magnificent trees, which in this park are in every state and stage of growth, of full vigour, and of natural decay, producing every possible accident of woodland scenery. Many of the oaks measured by Mr. Greathead are twenty-seven and twenty-nine yards round. If this park shows some marks of neglect, it is, at least, unspoiled by improvement.[19]

This account might well have been written by Uvedale Price, who also valued 'natural decay' and the 'accident of woodland scenery' above improvement, even if the parkland showed 'some marks of neglect'. Austen's mother expressed a similar delight in natural scenery when she finally visited Stoneleigh after her cousin inherited:

I had expected to find everything about the place very fine and all that, but I had no idea of it being so beautifull.....The Avon near the house amidst green Meadows bounded by large and beautiful woods full of delightful walks....We walk a great deal, for the Woods are impenetrable to the sun even in the middle of an August day. I do not fail to spend some time every day in the Kitchen Garden where quantities of small fruits exceed anything you can form an idea of.[20]

Repton is perhaps more conspicuous at Stoneleigh than at any other estate where he worked. As we have seen, not only is he mentioned in contemporary accounts and even in contemporary fiction, he makes a point of including a self-portrait in the Red Book (*colour plate 29*). He paints himself dressed in his favourite blue topcoat wearing black wellingtons and with his green umbrella to hand, directing a workman who is digging the new line of the lake, which has been laid out with white stakes. Understandably, given the desultory nature of much of the land around the house, Repton concentrated most of his efforts on the Avon below the south front of the house. But before he could reshape this area of advantage he needed to deal with the approach. In amongst the interminable essays on correct taste in the Red Book text, Repton gives clear and precise directions as to how the drive can be improved and, when the Abbey Gatehouse is reached, how the approach to the main range can be enhanced. Here again, the Red Book has an intimacy that is delightful (*colour plate 30*), with three women 'Sweepers in their Costume, and the Wardour on duty'.[21] There follows a map relating to his general plan for the improvement of the 'Character and Situation' of Stoneleigh: the former relating 'to what is advisable, and the latter to what is practicable'.

Repton's keyed plan summarises neatly his proposals (57). There is to be a new drive from the Coventry to Warwick road signalled by two gate lodges and, across the road from the entrance, a range of timber-framed 'Labourer's Cottages' with gardens (N) set either side of the new bridge across the river. The drive is to sweep across the 'Home Lawn for Cow Pasture' and enter the environs of the house by a new stable range (K) and under the Abbey Gatehouse (G). The line of the tributary is shown as it was in 1808, when the map was drawn, and its proposed alteration in 1809, when the river had been widened into a lake below the south front of the house. This necessitated a new bridge alongside the old stone Abbey Mill Bridge over the weir, which still bears the date 1704. A plantation is proposed as a backing for the tributary and another, parallel to the river, further east. The before-and-after sketches then take up the improving narrative, their slides revealing enhancements to existing scenes. His 'View towards the West' is opened up by the demolition of walls around the skirts of the house revealing a lawn dressed with picturesquely grouped sheep and a tantalising glimpse of the lake backed by its new plantation (*colour plate 31*).

After an analysis of the dysfunction of the interior room layout of the house, where 'little attention seems to have been given either to the Prospect or the Aspect', Repton discusses his plans for the landscape below the south front which, in turn, will necessitate the alteration of the façade itself. Never one to miss an opportunity for securing an architectural commission for either of his sons, John Adey or George Stanley, Repton produces two alternative designs: an extension of the elevation

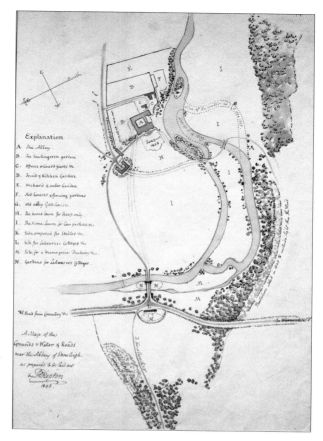

57

Repton's proposed
remodelling of the formal
grounds around Stoneleigh
involved the realignment of
the river and the creation of a
new carriage drive from the
Coventry road.
Stoneleigh Abbey Ltd

from four to seven bays, fronted by an Ionic portico, and an even grander
addition to the existing four bays of a columned loggia set on a round-
arched podium, which leads to an orangery terminating in an Italianate
tower (*58*). This remarkable sketch prefigures similar, but much later,
Italian-style alterations at Trentham in Staffordshire and Chatsworth in
Derbyshire. Not surprisingly, the Abbey Gatehouse can be seen in the
distance, cowering beneath the grandeur of this ducal-scale palace. In true
Gardenesque fashion, the lawns below the house are decorated with
island beds of shrub roses, while an ornamental, latticed fence leads the
eye down to the Cascade and a boathouse beyond topped by a trellised
pergola smothered with climbers, under which a couple enjoy a tryst. Two
before-and-after views taken from the east end of the lake, one of which
has Repton organising workmen, depict this magical transformation. In
the spirit of his determination to bring people back into the landscape,

58 Busy island beds filled with shrub roses – a Repton staple – dress the lawns below a
newly improved Stoneleigh Abbey in one of his atmospheric watercolours from the
1809 Red Book. *Stoneleigh Abbey Ltd*

what he terms 'inhabitancy', Repton's transformed scene (*colour plate 32*)
has gentlefolk viewing the scene from both the loggia and the terrace
below, while on the lake a lady is helped into a small craft by the boatman;
three chairs, artfully placed by the lakeside, await strolling guests.

There are two more atmospheric watercolours in the Red Book. One
is of the old Abbey Mill Bridge and Repton's proposed bridge over the
'new Channel', for which he has been inspired by 'some favourite subject
of Ruysdales pencil in which he has imitated the effect of Twilight'. As a
temporary expedient, Repton recommends 'that the present wooden
bridge be removed to this spot'. The other is a view of the finished landscape from a slightly more oblique view, seen through trees, with the
house above its new lake, the Cascade in the centre and the new bridge
arching over its channel (*colour plate 33*). Repton has not taken the 'Model'
for this view 'from the imaginary scenes of Claude, Watteau and Ruys-
dael', as in his other sketches for this Red Book, but from his own
improvements to Leigh's former estate at Adlestrop: 'I have only to
recommend the same good Taste and management, which has succeeded
so well at Adlestrop, to provide still greater effects at Stoneleigh Abbey'.

It is not easy to read Repton's improvements at Stoneleigh today, as

59 This trellised Arbour set above the weir at Stoneleigh probably dates from Repton's improvements for Thomas Leigh

many of his proposals were ignored, or modified.[22] The Revd Leigh died in 1813, effectively bringing to an end Repton's involvement with the estate. Thereafter, the improvements were carried out by James Henry Leigh and his wife Julia; Repton's outstanding account for fifty guineas was settled in October 1813.[23] The Bridge on the driveway was designed by John Rennie and built between 1812 and 1815, together with Grecian lodges where Repton had planned them, but the stables, built in 1815-20 by the local architect, Charles Samuel Smith, were sited much further away from the house to the north. Repton's elaborate terracing, loggia and conservatory planned for the west front never materialised, though work was in progress on the 'Abbey Gate Terraces' in June 1814, while William Andrews Nesfield would later supply that required Italianate touch with his 'Italian Garden' in the late 1840s and 1850s.[24]

The most poetic of Repton's proposals – the boathouse with its pergola – remained a paper dream, but he may have achieved a similar arbour on the weir to the east of the house at the entrance to the Shrubbery. Here there is a trellised and pedimented Summerhouse, no more than a shelter with a bench seat, which is now in sad decay (59). The cross-hatching of its fence is identical to those on Repton's sketches, suggesting that it is at least of his period, if not designed by him.[25] Oddly, though not surprisingly given the blinkered archival predilections of many historians, particularly when it comes to Red Books, all commentators on the grounds have missed this charming structure. It is the epitome of the Gardenesque, and might have been enjoyed by Mary Crawford, had she been a real person rather than a fictional character. Austen has her pronounce, in an air of typical patrician detachment: 'I would have everything as complete as possible in the country, shrubberies and flower gardens, and rustic seats innumerable; but it must all be done without my care'.[26] Sadly, the dangers of Repton's aesthetic in the dressed landscape and gardens around a house are inherent in Crawford's assertion that everything must be 'as complete as possible'. This holistic approach would lead to the worst excesses of the Victorians, who seem never to have known when to stop designing. In Repton's more considered work, the best elements of Brown's minimalist parkscapes were combined with a new resurgence of interest in flowers and decorative garden furniture. It was a delicate balance that Repton often got wrong, and that the next generation failed dismally to preserve.

endnotes on page 273

7

In the shadow of Guy of Warwick – history recreated at Guy's Cliffe

GLIMPSED THROUGH THE TREES FROM THE SAXON MILL BY THE AVON, ON the Warwick to Kenilworth road, the ruined Gothic mansion of Guy's Cliffe (*colour plate 34*), mouldering and forgotten for almost a century, rises steeply above the broad sweep of the river. Its soaring towers are flecked with wind-borne flowers and its once luxuriant gardens are now a tangle of bamboo and seedling trees. Mysterious caves and hollows surround the site, while waters lap into dark caverns by the dank river meadow below the cliff. These are the forlorn eighteenth-century pleasure grounds, developed later by Bertie Greatheed, Regency gentleman and landowner, who improved their scenic beauty to create a masterpiece of the late Picturesque. The catalyst for this historicist recreation of both house and landscape was Greatheed's obsession with the legend of Sir Guy of Warwick; his new Gothic mansion was, quite literally, built on Guy's cliff.

Not surprisingly, the dry caves in the cliff face once sheltered hermits. Saint Dubritious established an oratory dedicated to St. Mary Magdalene in about 600.[1] Dugdale reports: 'in the Saxon dayes, did a devout Heremite repair; who finding the natural Rock so proper for his Cell, and the pleasant Grove, wherewith it is back'd, yielding entertainment fit for solitude, seated himself here'.[2] John Rous, a medieval historian who lived at Guy's Cliffe in about 1440, wrote that one of the hermits was Sir Guy, Earl of Warwick, once a common man, but great in stature and proficient in warfare.[3] The myths and legends surrounding this Saxon knight were at first handed down through oral history, then recorded in medieval chap-books and poems, which include *Gui de Warewic*, an Anglo-Norman poem of about 1232-1242,[4] and *The Auchinleck Manuscript* of about 1330:

> Guye of Warrewik his name was
> In all the courte nōōn more honoured nas:
> ... Mikell he was, and of grete mighte
> And fairest of all other be sighte.[5]

A version of the tale has Guy falling in love with Felice (Phyllis), the daughter of Rohund, Earl of Warwick: 'Felice la bele Of all faire she was the floure, Nōōn so faire in halle nor boure, As she was'.[6] To gain her hand in marriage Guy had to attain knighthood and complete a variety of tasks including killing the Dun Cow, a beast which had terrorised villages on Dunsmore Heath in the county. Travelling abroad to Byzantium with other knights, Guy destroyed an army of Turks and Saracens before returning to marry Felice. Shortly after their marriage Guy inherited the earldom but, troubled by the deaths he had caused, he made a pilgrimage to the Holy Land, returning to England wearing the robes of a palmer. On his way home Sir Guy fought the Danish champion Colbrand at the request of King Athelstan, afterwards returning to Warwick 'for three days taking alms at the hands of his own lady'.[7] Thereafter he lodged with a hermit at Guy's Cliffe, and made the cave his home. Felice often visited Guy's Cliffe to walk in the grove above the Cave, not knowing that her husband lived beneath. When the hermit died Guy stayed in the cell until, aware that his own death was near, he sent Felice their wedding ring so they could meet once again before he died.

Fourteenth-century chroniclers adopted this story as a true history of Guy of Warwick, and later in the sixteenth-century John Leland, who visited Guy's Cliffe in the 1530s, reported the tale:

> There is a right goodly chapell of St. Mary Magdalene upon Avon river, ripa dextra, scant a myle above Warwike. This place of some is caulyd Gibclif, of some Guy-clif ; and old fame remaynethe with the people there, that Guydo Erle of Warwike in K. Athelstan's dayes had a great devotion to this place, and made an oratory there ... It is a place of pleasure, an howse mete for the muses; there is silence, a praty wood, antra in vivo saxo [grottoes in the living rock], the river rollynge with a praty noyse over the stones.[8]

As a result, Guy's Cliffe became a place of pilgrimage, with so many visiting that there was a need to 'set up a praty house open lyke a cage coveryd, onely to keepe cummers thithar from the rayne'.[9] Leland also recorded that the visitors, in essence medieval spiritual tourists, were guided around the site: 'Men shew a cave there in a rok hard on Avon *ripe*, where they say that he usyd to slepe. Men also yet showe fayr springs in a faire medow thereby, where they say that Erle Guido was wont to drinke'.[10]

Henry V visited Guy's Cliffe in 1421, planning to found a chantry with a living for two priests, but died before anything was done. Subsequently, Richard Beauchamp, 13th Earl of Warwick, applied for a licence to Henry VI in 1422-3 to build the new chapel.[11] This is confirmed by Leland's account:

> This place had fore the tyme of Richard E. of Warwike only a smaul chappelle and a cotage wherein an heremite dwellyd... Erle Richard beringe a greate devotion to the place made there a goodly new chapell, dedicate to St. Mary Magdalen, and foundyd Cantuars prists there [to serve God.] He set up there an ymage of E. Guido great lyke a giant, and enclosyd the silver welles in the medow with pure whit slike stone like marble ... He also made there a praty howse of stone for the Cantuary Prists.[12]

However, no firm evidence exists regarding Sir Guy and his heroic deeds. Rous compiled a pictorial roll celebrating the history of his patrons, the Earls of Warwick, giving Guy an Anglo-Saxon ancestry. Thelma Richmond suggests that Rous, 'an antiquarian in the tradition of romance historiography', was 'the most influential perpetrator of Guy's legend', being loyal to his patrons in enhancing the family's prestige.[13] The names Guy and Felice are more likely to be of Norman derivation, linked to the chivalric romance surrounding the Crusades. The main purpose of the tale was to strengthen the Warwick family status, as, like many other Anglo-Norman families after the Norman Conquest, they lacked a long English family history.

As we have seen, to further enhance the story, oversize relics purporting to belong to Guy were kept in Warwick Castle. The presence of the huge statue in the Chapel at Guy's Cliffe also reinforced the notion

The prospect of GUYES CLIFFE from the meadows on the north-east thereof.

Dugd. p. 184.

A. Guye's Cave.
B. The alley over the Cave.
C. The lower walks.
D. A Cliffe in the rock.
E. The Cellar vnder the Chapell.
F. The Passage into the lower walks.
G. The great Cellar in the Court.
H. Chambers in the rock.
I. The Stillhouse.
K. The Chapell.
L. The house
M. The Springs.
N. The river Avon.

60

Wenceslaus Hollar's engraving of Guy's Cliffe is helpfully keyed and shows Guy's Cave (A) set into the cliff-face to the side of the Chapel (K). *University of Bristol, Special Collections*

of gigantic size. After the Dissolution the Chapel, 'Buildings, and Possessions' were granted to Sir Andrew Flammock on 4 June 1547.[14] Flammock, a rough and uncouth knight and courtier,[15] was given these monastic lands as a reward for services to the Crown.[16] His house and garden grounds would, no doubt, have been designed in the latest fashion. In his Journal, Bertie Greatheed indicates that a bowling green and a mount were in existence in the early nineteenth century. Flammock may well have created these, as well as the *allée* above Guy's Cave, known as Fair Felice's Walk.[17] In his 1662 *History of the Worthies*, Thomas Fuller hints that the improvements made to the site were more for entertainment than sanctity: 'Some say it is too gaudy a place for that purpose, as having more of a paradise than wilderness therein, so that men's thoughts would rather be scattered than collected with such various objects'.[18]

Although there is no pictorial evidence of Flammock's house and grounds, a substantial building appears in a Wenceslaus Hollar engraving of 1656, later published in Dugdale's *Antiquities* (60).[19] This is helpfully keyed and shows that the Elizabethan house, which overlooked the river, had a high-pitched, gabled roof and tall chimneystacks. The Chapel is across the courtyard and appears to have had a thatched roof. There are numerous caves – 'Chambers in the rock' – in the courtyard between the house and the Chapel, and underneath the Chapel is a cellar, which is accessed from the cliff face. The entrance to Guy's Cave is through a side door next to the Chapel. Above it is an 'alley', no doubt a formal walk along the cliff top. To the west of the Still House two lines of trees that descend down the hillside suggest an early formal avenue near the emerging springs at Guy's Well.

Flammock died soon after his mansion was built and Guy's Cliffe remained in the family only until 1580. The estate then passed by marriage to the Beaufoys of nearby Emscote and Milverton.[20] John Evelyn visited Guy's Cliffe in August 1654, while visiting his friends Henry and Elizabeth Puckering at Warwick Priory, and in his description of the site recognised its romantic appeal and potential for what would be seen as a Picturesque landscape in the next century:

> Hence to Sir Guys Grott, where they say he did his penances, & dyed, & 'tis certainely a squalid den made in the rock, croun'd yet with venerable Oakes, & respecting a goodly streame, so as were it improv'd as it might [be], 'twere capable of being render'd one of the most roma[n]tique & pleasant places imaginable.[21]

In 1701 Dame Beaufoy sold the mansion, together with land and the mill, to William Edwards of Kenilworth, who was 'skilled in Chirurgery'.[22] It is likely that the mansion was extended and altered in the 1720s.[23] Thomas Ward suggests that a driveway led from the front door of the house, passing through an avenue of Scotch Firs planted by Edwards, towards an eye-catcher, a small house on the horizon.[24]

In 1748 Guy's Cliffe was let to Samuel Greatheed, who was described unkindly by the poet, Thomas Gray, as 'a fat young Man with a head & face much bigger than they are usually worn'.[25] Greatheed was the eldest of twelve children born to John Greatheed of Yorkshire, who had travelled to St Kitts in the West Indies, to make his fortune by involvement with the slave trade. Inheriting the sugar plantations from his father in 1739,[26] and more 'trade' than nobility, Greatheed quickly enhanced his family's status. He became a Whig MP for Coventry in 1747, and married into the aristocracy. His bride was Lady Mary Bertie, daughter of Peregrine Bertie, 2nd Duke of Ancaster and Lord Chamberlain of England.

Greatheed eventually bought Guy's Cliffe on 9 August 1751 for £2,000,[27] thereby joining the landed gentry, and proceeded to develop the house in the classical taste. A report completed in 1758 by the Master in Chancery describes the improvements, which had cost £6,000: 'A Capital Mansion House built with stone & brick ... in a large commodius & Elegant Mannor with convenient Offices and Stabling for Twenty Horses and Standing for four Carriages all hewn out of Solid Rock'.[28] A 1788 view shows the mansion with a neo-Palladian wing and a columned Ionic entrance façade, possibly designed by William Hiorn between 1751-57, which faced south onto a new courtyard.[29]

In the surrounding pleasure grounds, serpentine walks and shrubberies were laid out, and the entrance to the house was turned away from the Fir Avenue. The carriage drive now passed into the courtyard through a 44-foot high, rusticated stone Triumphal Arch. The lawned garden facing the Fir Avenue, which featured a lead statue of a kneeling slave supporting a sundial, was named Blackamoor Green.[30] Below the cliff by the river, a cave was excavated and called the Cloister. In 1821 Bertie Greatheed wrote that it had 'arcades in it...known by all the masons by the name of Harris's Cave; the man who cut it for my Father, a Warwick mason, now dead. His work will remain by Avonside for age on age after all else is swept away; companion to Guy's venerable cell'.[31] The cavern survives like some fragment of a vast Byzantine basilica (*colour plate 35*), its barrel vault and arched niches looming above the water-borne debris. Its function is unclear, but it is most likely to have been used as a boathouse.

Inside the mansion, the Greatheeds decorated in the fashionable Rococo style, with elegant plasterwork garlands and wreaths of foliage, possibly executed by Robert Moore of Warwick. He had already created exquisite plasterwork for the Archers of Umberslade, who were close friends of the Greatheeds. Lady Mary and Samuel Greatheed decorated a Shell-Room at Guy's Cliffe between 1751-55 using, no doubt, shells from the Caribbean plantations. It was described by one of their friends, Lady Luxborough, in a tetchy 1755 letter to the poet William Shenstone: 'The prettiest thing I ever saw of the kind, is the shell-room at Guy's Clift: Mr Greethead and Lady Mary have executed it all with their own hands: bed-hangings, chimney-boards, pictures over the doors, &c. If you was not lazy you would see it'.[32]

Lady Mary Greatheed, considered to be 'a person of great taste in improvements',[33] supervised the enhancement of the estate without any professional help. The Rococo spirit of the house interiors was continued in the grounds. She decorated several grottoes between 1751 and 1757, including the ancient spring of Guy's Well, 'over which sea shells have been stuck with most happy taste!!!'[34] Horace Walpole, however, in his typically competitive and malicious manner, poured scorn on the design of the garden. In a 1777 letter to the Countess of Ossory he wrote: 'Did you go to Guy's Cliff, and see how Lady Mary Greathead has painted it straw colour, and stuck cockle-shells in its hair?'[35] The pleasure grounds were also criticised by Thomas Gray:

> there was the Cell of Guy, Earl of Warwick, cut in the living stone, where he died a Hermit...there were his fountains bubbling out of the Cliff; there was a Chantry founded to his memory in Henry the 6th's time. but behold the Trees are cut down to make room for flowering shrubs, the rock is cut up, till it is a smooth & as sleek as satin; the river has a gravel-walk by its side; the Cell is a Grotta with cockle-shells and looking-glass; the fountains have an iron-gate before them, and the Chantry is a Barn, or a little House. Even the poorest bits of nature, that remain, are daily threatened, for he says ... he is determined, it shall be all new. These were his words, & they are Fate.[36]

Samuel Greatheed died in 1765 and the development of the landscape continued under his son Bertie, whose improvements are extremely well documented in journals that cover the years from 1782 to 1826. These are in part a spiritually uplifting exercise recording the day's happenings, the weather, reading material and the comings and goings of guests, but also a description of his European travels, work completed on the estate, and a record of the tourists who flocked to Guy's Cliffe to gain a glimpse of Sir Guy's garden.

Bertie, born on 17 October 1759, was the second son of Samuel Greatheed. He inherited Guy's Cliffe and the family's West Indies plantations in 1766 after his elder brother Peregrine died of consumption.[37]

Educated at the University of Göttingen, Greatheed was well read, not only in English, but also in many European languages. He was interested in poetry, the classics and science, having a large circle of friends including Agnes and Mary Berry (the socialite friends of Horace Walpole), the actress Sarah Siddons, the chemist Richard Chenevix, Sir John Herschel the astronomer, and the theorists Uvedale Price, Richard Payne Knight and his brother Andrew Knight. Greatheed married his first cousin Ann (whom he called Nancy), daughter of Marmaduke Greatheed of Basseterre, St Kitts, at Leek Wootton on 31 July 1780.[38] Their son, also called Bertie, referred to here as Greatheed the Younger, was introduced into this rich, creative mix of friends. The family considered travel a necessary part of his education and set out together on a Grand Tour of the continent, travelling between 1782 and 1800 to France, Switzerland, Germany, Austria and Italy.[39] It is at this time that Greatheed began to write of his experiences of the continent and of the Sublime in Nature:

> The day was charming and the air as clear as possible, the dark gloomy woods of Fir with the bright Glaciers descending through them down. As the fields and cottages which skirt the winding course of the Arno whose stream is increased by numbers of Torrents that falling from the pointed and variegated rocks still rising beyond the woods from the most beautiful cascades; above all the pure and dazzling snow separated by an edge sharp & distinct beyond expression from the sky of bleu [sic] exceeding any I had even seen...Our whole party mounted on mules set out after breakfast.[40]

In Florence the Greatheeds became part of a literary circle of friends called *gli Oziosi* ('The Idlers'), contributing to a collection called *Arno Miscellany*, which was published in 1784, and later contributed to the Della Cruscan *Florence Miscellany* with William Parsons, Robert Merry and Mrs Hester Lynch Piozzi.[41] Returning to Guy's Cliffe, Bertie Greatheed produced a verse drama, *The Regent*, which opened (and closed) at Drury Lane in 1788.[42]

Bertie Greatheed the Younger also showed talent, in the style of the

Swiss painter John Henry Fuseli. In 1796 Walpole wrote to express his admiration of four sketches completed by the young Bertie to illustrate his *Castle of Otranto*: 'Such delineation of passions...in boyhood are indubitably indications of real genius'.[43] Walpole's book was one of the earliest Gothic novels, followed by William Beckford's *Vathek* (1786), Ann Radcliffe's *The Mysteries of Udolpho* (1794), and Matthew Gregory Lewis's *The Monk* (1796). In Jane Austen's *Northanger Abbey*, a spoof on the genre, there are descriptive passages which recall the mansion at Guy's Cliffe. However, it is not known whether Austen visited the house and grounds, although she stayed at nearby Stoneleigh Abbey. Her Northanger had 'long, damp passages, its narrow cells, and ruined chapel, were to be within her daily reach, and she could not entirely subdue the hope of some traditional legends'.[44]

The family were in Paris between 1802 and 1803, so that young Bertie could sketch the art treasures that had been brought to the Louvre by Napoleon,[45] and then travelled to Italy after hostilities were renewed between France and England. Unfortunately, Bertie was taken ill, diagnosed with influenza,[46] and died, aged twenty-two, in Vincenza on 8 October 1804.[47] After his death a pregnant young woman, Lisette Nepell from Dresden,[48] claimed that Bertie was the father of her baby, later named Ann Caroline Greatheed and adopted by Bertie and Nancy Greatheed as their granddaughter.

Back in Warwickshire, Greatheed set about improving the house and grounds at Guy's Cliffe, making trips to friends in Lincolnshire, Shropshire and Herefordshire, many of whom had improved their landscapes in the new Picturesque taste. His journals reflect that whenever he had finished one area, he was busy arranging another, as long as there were funds to pay for it. Throughout the development of the estate the theme of linking his family home and landscape with antiquity persisted as he drew attention to specific areas with inscriptions, ensuring that all visitors, both gentry and aristocrats, could appreciate the allusions made.

The improvements were possible due to three injections of capital at different times during the late eighteenth and early nineteenth centuries. Although by 1824 he was a believer in the abolition of slavery,[49] Greatheed's frequent trips to the continent and the first phase of the development of Guy's Cliffe were funded by revenue from the family plantations. However, in 1810, when funds from the West Indies ceased, Greatheed was forced to cut back severely on his expenditure, laying off servants and shunning guests. After 1810 his finances were improved by speculative development in the nearby spa town of Leamington, which developed from a small agricultural town with a population of 315 in the 1801 census,[50] to a health resort catering for the elite of society with a population soaring to 15,724 by 1851.[51] Greatheed sold 65 acres of prime land, which he had inherited from his mother, for development north of the river, on which was built a terrace on the west side of the Parade.[52] Greatheed also discovered a saline spring north of the River Leam, developing the site with a local syndicate to become in 1814 the most fashionable Pump Rooms and baths in Leamington Spa. The clientele of the spa town not only used the baths but also visited Guy's Cliffe as a tourist attraction, entranced by the legend of Guy of Warwick and the romantic and picturesque nature of the place. As Leamington grew, Greatheed's social circle widened and he entertained lavishly at Guy's Cliffe, with the walks and rides around the pleasure grounds arranged as part of the entertainment. A third injection of cash occurred around 1819 when Greatheed was left a very large sum of money by the Duke of Ancaster,[53] together with an important art collection including Dutch landscapes which Jonathan Lovie suggests influenced his work at Guy's Cliffe.[54] The inheritance money enabled Greatheed to enlarge his estate after the enclosure of Leek Wootton in 1821, and again when the Earl of Warwick sold off the Loes Estate in 1824.

By 1814 Greatheed had enough money to embark on the first major reconstruction of the mansion, choosing to draw up the plans himself, but with help from Agnes Berry in sketching designs for new alterations. He transformed the predictable eighteenth-century classical house into a romantic Gothic Revival building, perfectly in tune with the tenor of the times; it would not have looked out of place in a novel by Sir Walter Scott. In the gardens Greatheed worked again alongside Agnes Berry, but with advice from Greatheed's close friend Uvedale Price. The mid-eighteenth-century Rococo landscape was loosened and reshaped to accord more with Price's ideas of the Sublime and the Beautiful.

The house had an irregular profile with projecting bays and oriel windows to the north river front, while the west façade was dramatised by an arcaded verandah with ogee gables and lit by Tudor-style bay windows.[55] Visitors to the house were greeted by casts of classical statues including the *Venus de Medici* and the *Florence Faun* and *Apollo*,[56] with the Gothic represented by Bertie Greatheed the Younger's painting, *The Cave of Despair*, from Edmund Spenser's *Faerie Queene*. Exhibited at the Royal Academy in 1803, it was later displayed behind closed doors in the Music Room at Guy's Cliffe, because the subject of the painting was considered so dreadful. When the family was not at home and visitors were shown around the house the guide would make 'a dramatic gesture opening the doors and "young ladies" were expected to swoon on the spot'.[57] An 1815 account gives a good impression of the view from the oak-floored Elizabethan Great Drawing Room:

> the great depth of the rock strikingly appears. The river winding round it, and washing its foundation – the moving water-mill – the foaming cascade – the wooden bridge – the flourishing plantations, on the one side – and the fertile meads on the other, enlivened with cattle and sheep, feeding or reposing – and, in the more distant view, Gaveston Hill, on the left, where the dissolute favorite of Edward II. was beheaded – the new built church of Wootton in front, and the little recluse village of Milverton, on the right, with its rustic church almost buried in the shade of trees.[58]

There were three main walking routes around the estate. A circular route was developed for tourists from Leamington Spa, while guests of the Greatheeds took pathways into the park, visiting the stables and dairy to the south and Gaveston's Hill, via Como Pit, to the north. Visitors arriving from the Warwick-Kenilworth road walked along the serpentine driveway, with shrubberies hiding the heart of the estate, to the courtyard through the Triumphal Arch. Facing the house to the left of the Arch was the Blackamoor Green, which in 1813 was the starting point of the circular tour. It offered a view of the surrounding countryside from the top of the cliff and also a view through the Fir Avenue. Nancy Greatheed had redeveloped this area as a formal parterre by 1810, retaining the sundial in its commanding position, but surrounding it with a symmetrical design of box-edged beds to produce a charming flower garden suitable for entertaining and taking tea.[59] The garden writer John Claudius Loudon, who coined the term 'Gardenesque', visited Guy's Cliffe in 1831 and commented on the contrast between this garden and the wilder nature of the distant pleasure grounds.[60] The parterre was intended to be seen from the windows of the Elizabethan Drawing Room. Prince Pückler-Muskau reported: 'It overlooks a level plain laid out as a very pretty French garden, in which gay porcelain ornaments and coloured sand mingled their hues with the flowers, and terminates in a beautiful alley overshadowed with ivy cut into a pointed arch'.[61]

The Fir Avenue was given a new viewpoint in 1824 when Greatheed cut down the hedge, which had been planted in the 1770s, thereby opening up the vista. Austen's *Northanger Abbey* heroine, Catherine Morland, describes such a fir avenue: 'It was a narrow winding path through a thick grove of old Scotch firs; and Catherine, struck by its gloomy aspect, and eager to enter it, could not...be kept from stepping forward'.[62] At the end of the Avenue a *claire voie* of tall stone piers topped by ball finials was built, the height of the wall being raised from April to June 1824.[63] This gave privacy to the route through the holly and yew shrubbery, which wound down in walks laid out to Guy's Well in the Well Meadow.

Uvedale Price's design influence in this area of the garden is well documented in Greatheed's journal.[64] Price and his family stayed at Guy's Cliffe for Christmas 1823, when he advised Greatheed on the 'dressing' of the Well Meadow and riverbank. At the beginning of the visit Greatheed was delighted by Price's reaction: 'it is delightful to see Price's enjoyment of this; discovering and making pictures all about', but as time went on Greatheed was bemused by his friend's feverish activity. He wrote on Christmas Eve that he had had 'an interesting walk with Price after two o'clock: there is no getting his mind to new things; he is ever for running to his favourite spots; and dressing them with over minuteness'. On Christmas Day Greatheed went with Price 'around the well meadow in which small space he has I know not how many stations, or picturesque combinations'.

Visitors emerging from these Picturesque stations, or places from which views could be enjoyed, on the Well Meadow would move eastwards to the River Walk, where the caves and cavities in the rock and the Chapel with its subterranean rooms made ideal subjects for sketching. As too did Guy's Cave, which by the 1890s was shrouded by trees and ivy, and entered at its side through a pair of massive oak doors.[65] Back in the early nineteenth century Greatheed had found an eroded inscription cut into the south wall at the back of the Cave, covered in lichen so that the writing was indiscernible.[66] In 1870 an expert who was cleaning the panel found, allegedly, two inscriptions: one in Anglo-Saxon runic characters and another in Roman capitals. Both were meant to read: 'cast out, thou Christ from thy servant this burden, Guy',[67] thus linking the Cave with the legend of Guy of Warwick. In 1815 the upper part of the Cave was said to look like a 'natural cavity', while the lower area showed marks of being dug out of the rock and resembled a grave, presumed to be that of Guy.[68] By this time there was also an oval opening opposite the inscription in the side of the cave, giving views out over the river to Old Milverton.

The River Walk continued, passing the site of an early nineteenth-century Boathouse, whose boat was used for excursions to Leamington or Warwick, or for the entertainment of visitors travelling to Warwick Castle. The Boathouse area may also have been the site of a formal bathing place contrived by Greatheed in May 1822: 'Made a beautiful place for a rude bench & bathing at the end of the lower garden'.[69] The garden walks and rocky cliff walls were described in a 1900 *Country Life* article as providing alternate light and shade: 'From the Cave of Despair we emerge to sunlit spaces, where radiant flower beds glow in the summer. There are spaces of the greenest lawn, shadowed by most handsome trees. Water-lilies add beauty to the lake, and irises and other water-loving plants are thick upon the banks'.[70]

The Walk then climbed, via a serpentine path, up towards Fair Felice's Walk, through a 'shady plantation', passing the Bowling Green to the top of the cliff, where a terrifying drop of sixty feet gave visitors a frightening surprise.[71] The cliff top also offered a new viewpoint over the surrounding landscape. In the area referred to as the Mount, visitors could look towards Sir Guy of Warwick's family home, Warwick Castle, and to the parish church of St Mary, the last resting place of Richard Beauchamp. The Edwardian traveller W Field found the view striking: 'From this spot, passing towards the terrace – the tower of St. Mary's church, first opens strikingly to view – and, next, those of the venerable Castle, and the spire of St. Nicholas, are successively disclosed, ascending above the summit of stately spreading trees and groves'.[72] From the Mount and Terrace there were alternative routes with paths leading back to the entrance gate through an avenue of yews; whilst another walk led north-west towards the stable area, before returning to the end of the circular route by the Triumphal Arch.

In the wider park Greatheed developed new land acquisitions, so that by his death in 1826 there were three distinct areas of parkland within the Guy's Cliffe estate. The first was on land sloping down to the Avon from the village of Old Milverton, where at one time the settlement of Lower Green, now deserted, lay. On what had been developed initially as agricultural land by his father, who acquired areas of Old Milverton in 1747, Greatheed planted a variety of trees, which correspond to hedgerows on the 1886 Ordnance Survey map. The second area of parkland, laid out today as pasture with scattered mature specimen trees, is to the south of the house and includes the stables, pleasure grounds and walks near the Tudor-Gothic buildings, known as the Dairy, at the eastern boundary of the estate. The stables, originally built by Samuel Greatheed in the Gothic style in the 1750s, were re-styled by Bertie Greatheed in April 1822, when he raised the height of the stable roof and gave it an alpine slope.[73] The Dairy was in existence in 1810, but improved around 1820-21.[74] About 500 metres south-east of the mansion was a quarry, accessed from the River Walk. During 1819-20 it supplied stone for the house and other estate buildings. Enclosed to the east by Patten's Grove, the quarry was known as Dick Ward's Hole, after the quarryman who worked for Greatheed. The planting of evergreen shrubs and the introduction of a statue of Dick Ward in 1822 made it into an ornamental feature.[75] An inscription, composed by Greatheed, was carved in stone and erected on the roughly-hewn statue of Dick Ward in November 1823:

Here be I Dick Ward heon eout in the rok
To which I ha ge en full mauny a nok
And a this un shall stond I'll wayger a paund

When ye loggeryeds all lie six feet i'the graund.[76]

Greatheed's use of the local dialect is yet another attempt to project the historical status of the estate, along with the Roman and Anglo-Saxon script in Sir Guy's Cave, and another contemporary inscription on Gaveston's Cross.

West of the Coventry road lay the last area developed as parkland, after Greatheed's 1824-25 land purchase from the Earl of Warwick. Numerous specimen trees were planted, including 100 oaks, three cedars of Lebanon and 60 hollies in the area known as the Knoll.[77] At the northern end of the estate Greatheed created an ornamental plantation, which included hollies, and dammed a stream to form a pond – Como Pit – with a vague resemblance to the shape of Lake Como, Italy.[78] His grand-daughter, Ann Caroline, and her husband, Charles Percy, had been touring the continent, so the development of the pond may have been linked to their homecoming.

The Kitchen Garden was sited opposite the main drive to Guy's Cliffe, on the other side of the Kenilworth road. Originally eighteenth-century in date, there were two later phases of work on the Garden in 1806-07 and 1824-25. In the winter of 1806-07 an orchard was planned, with two rows of espaliers planted 'one to the right the other to the left of the middle walk of the kitchen garden', with new varieties of apple trees, including Ingstree and Dr Downton Pippins, given to Greatheed by his friend Thomas Andrew Knight, who was President of the Horticultural Society of London and brother of the Picturesque theorist Richard Payne Knight.[79] At the side of his Kitchen Garden, on a seven-acre piece of land, Greatheed planned a peachery and a grapery, taking advice from his builders Taylor and Morris, and also from friends and acquaintances, after visiting Mr Charles Mills's peachery at Barford Hill House.[80] By September 1824 Greatheed had embarked upon another project: the construction of an ornamental canal in the Kitchen Garden, which was completed by October 1825. The peachery was at the cutting edge of tech-nology for the period and came complete with lights and trellis, while the canal had a small plank bridge to 'cross the water-course above the pond'.[81] Greatheed also took advice on the walls, hot-houses and planting, finally stocking the peachery and the south aspect of the walls in February 1825, declaring by March that he thought he had more than half a mile of planted walling.[82]

Greatheed's Picturesque plan for the estate relied upon the careful alignment of views to buildings within the landscape. This is apparent at the Saxon Mill, dating from the Norman period, which was turned into an eye-catcher to be viewed from the new apartments of the mansion. It has been suggested that the Mill was remodelled to Greatheed's design in 1813,[83] but in 1810 Agnes Berry and Greatheed discussed designs for a new porch for the building, Berry submitting drawings in October 1810.[84] The revamped Mill is a result of Greatheed's and Berry's European tours, its roof having deep overhanging eaves and a steep pitch reminiscent of alpine chalets. Greatheed's builder Fairfax made alterations to the roof and general structure of the Mill between March and April 1813, culminating in the construction of a Swiss-style balcony.[85] The design was an important early example of the cult of the picturesque Swiss style, which flourished in England in the 1820s. This was led by the architect and pattern-book writer Peter Frederick Robinson, the designer of London's Swiss Cottage, who was a keen follower of Uvedale Price.[86] Other buildings on or near the estate that were given this treatment included the stables, St James' Church at Old Milverton and the Mill Bridge, referred to as the Alpine Bridge. Ann Caroline Greatheed continued this quintessentially Swiss manner later on, adding sloping roofs in 1835 to a new lodge and cottage by John Gibson, and supplying the cows in the local fields with bells in the continental fashion.[87]

Along the east façade of the Mill a terrace with a battlemented parapet, shaded by mature plane trees that had been planted when Bertie Greatheed was born,[88] led to two bridges, shown in a painting of 1795 by Samuel Ireland.[89] One crossed the Cascade to the side of the millpond, while the other traversed the marshy ground of Neatholme to the east of the Avon. It is not known when the Cascade was constructed, but it is likely to date from the Rococo reshaping carried out by Samuel Greatheed, with the bridges replaced several times since.[90] A footpath led over the fields to Old Milverton and St James' church. There is evidence that this Mill Walk was planted around 1806 with stone pines brought back as seed from Florence, and later with laurels.[91] These features are still present today.

Another viewpoint in the wider landscape was Blacklow Hill, the site of the execution of Piers Gaveston, lover and favourite of Edward II. Dugdale records that Gaveston was 'beheaded....without judgement of his Peers, or any courte of Law ...[near the top]...of the hill, in the place where since that time stood a Cross called Gaveston's Cross'.[92] In Dugdale's time the rocky hollow where Gaveston lost his head had an almost illegible inscription: '1311 P. GAVESTON EARL OF CORNWALL BEHEADED HERE'.[93] Anxious, as ever, to connect with the historic past of his estate, Greatheed renamed the outcrop Gaveston's Hill, and erected a new memorial. This was a stone cross, designed by Greatheed himself, to be seen as an eye-catcher from the main windows of the mansion. An inscription composed by Greatheed's friend, Dr Samuel Parr, was recorded in Greatheed's journal in May 1822, though the date of Gaveston's death was incorrect; he died on 13 June 1312:

> In the hollow of this rock
> was beheaded
> On the 1st day of July 1312
> By Barons
> Lawless as himself
> Piers Gaveston Earl of Cornwall
> The Minion
> Of an odious King
> In life and death
> A memorable instance of misrule.[94]

The inscription was on the face of the Cross that could be seen from the mansion, specifically so that it could be read by telescope: 'I [Greatheed] had a good opportunity at last of a good trial of the powers of my Reflector both by day on the inscription on Gaveston's cross and afterwards on the heavenly bodies till a thin haze came over the sky'.[95] Gaveston's Hill was improved with shrubbery planted in August and September 1821. This comprised hollies, cedars and cypresses, together with six cedars of Lebanon by Gaveston's Rock.[96] A walk to the site was established both for the family and for visitors, Greatheed being proud of his achievement: 'Walked with the Percys to see the admirable growth of our Gaveston hill plantation'.[97] A carriage drive was also developed by 1825 to take visitors to Gaveston's Hill, the Knoll and then around by Loes Lane returning to the mansion.[98]

Professional engravings of the house and gardens appeared in numerous books and magazines, the introduction of the lithographic printing process in the 1820s paving the way for mass production of cheap, good quality pictures.[99] In addition, many sightseers liked to make their own record in the form of drawings or paintings. Washington Irving wrote in 1820 that it was 'the fashion for modern tourists to travel pencil in hand, and bring home their portfolios filled with sketches'.[100] Part of the attraction of Guy's Cliffe's Picturesque landscape was that there were so many opportunities for creativity. Several famous poets and artists sought to view the delights of the house and grounds, including William Wordsworth, who arrived early in the morning expecting to be shown around the grounds and the Chapel.[101] The improvements at Guy's Cliffe were an outstanding success. Greatheed's staff charged for showing people around the house and garden whenever the family were not at home.[102] On one day in early summer 1824 over 150 people visited the house and garden,[103] and in August 1824 a three-day exhibition was staged and 380 people visited.[104]

When Bertie Greatheed died in January 1826 after a brief illness, the estate passed to his granddaughter Ann Caroline and her husband, the Hon Charles Percy, later Lord Charles Greatheed-Bertie-Percy. By the end of the nineteenth century the legend of Sir Guy of Warwick began to be re-evaluated. The general public, once enamoured of medieval tales, now wanted realism: 'It is certain that Guy was not only possessed of great wealth and power, but was also the most famous warrior of his time, and his deeds have been celebrated and exaggerated with so much hyperbole, that it is difficult to distinguish clearly the simple facts on which the ornaments are laid.[105] In 1882 John Ashton debunked the myth of the Guy of Warwick relics held in Warwick Castle: 'His breastplate, or helmet, is the "croupe" of a suit of horse armour; another breastplate is a "poitrel".

61 One of the most important historic sites in the county, Guy's Cliffe is on the edge of total ruin

His famous porridge-pot or punch-bowl is a garrison crock of the sixteenth century, and his fork a military fork, *temp.* Henry VIII'.[106]

In 1891 Lord Algernon Percy inherited the estate and made a final addition to Guy's Cliffe in 1898. A polygonal tower was built onto the west wing, facing the courtyard, disguising a lift.[107] *Country Life* magazine photographed the house and pristine grounds, publishing articles in 1897 and 1900 when there was still a plentiful supply of gardening labour before the outbreak of the First World War. Its correspondent wrote in lyrical terms of the house and grounds that Bertie Greatheed had perfected:

> It is a place meet for the Muses, a veritable Castle of Otranto, seeing as if it might be the home of romance. Those were the impressions of a visitor who saw Guy's Cliff, as it were, by surprise, and saw it with such conditions of atmosphere and sunlight as Claude or Turner would have desired.[108]

Although Guy's 'Porridge Pot' and 'Sword' can still be seen in Warwick Castle, the future for Guy's Cliffe looks bleak. The ruined house (*61*) is on the Heritage at Risk Register and only the Chapel, owned by local

Freemasons, remains in use as a Masonic Temple. The wider landscape, including the Fir Avenue and Guy's Well Meadow, is fragmented in private ownership. Today stark, empty windows overlook a deserted car-park where there were once the colourful flowerbeds of the Blackamoor Green. The delightful River Walk is now an impassable tangle of under-growth, its path choked with Japanese knotweed and towering stands of bamboo. Any attempt to reach the caverns and caves in the cliff face requires scythes or machetes. The Friends of Guy's Cliffe have attempted some stabilisation of the house and grounds, but with the division of the wider landscape there will always be the danger of development.

endnotes on pages 273-277

8

Guinea gardens, allotments and a public park

Stoney Road Allotments, Hill Close Gardens
Westbourne Road Leisure Gardens, Birmingham Botanical Gardens
Royal Leamington Spa, Jephson Gardens

AS A RULE, THIS SERIES ON THE HISTORIC GARDENS OF ENGLAND HAS BEEN confined to the exploration of private gardens. However, as with all good rules, there are exceptions, in one case *Cheshire*, which included a dedicated chapter on public parks in recognition of their international historic and cultural significance.[1] However, in any given county there are a number of spaces that hover somewhere on the margins between the public and the private; Warwickshire has several of these. Some of the most overlooked and neglected are the 'guinea gardens' or detached pleasure grounds, which reached a level of popularity in the nineteenth century. According to the garden commentator and designer, John Claudius Loudon, there were upwards of 2,000 such gardens in the neighbourhood of Birmingham alone.[2] Of the four remaining guinea-garden sites placed on the English Heritage Register of Parks and Gardens, three are in Warwickshire: Edgbaston Guinea Gardens, now Westbourne Road Leisure Gardens, on the outskirts of Birmingham; Hill Close Gardens in Warwick; and the town gardens of Coventry, now known as Stoney Road Allotments.[3] It seems important, therefore, to include them here.

Unlike rural allotments, which originated in the eighteenth century as a means for the labourer to provide for himself and his family after the process of enclosure had removed his rights to use common land, the guinea gardens were urban detached pleasure gardens where ornamental design elements were combined with productivity. They were termed 'guinea gardens' in response to the high rents charged for such spaces.

The annual rent for the Edgbaston Guinea Gardens was between 17s 6d and 30s.[4] The high prices reflected the fact that they were in demand with the skilled working classes and respectable shop owners that 'flocked into cities such as Birmingham, Nottingham, Coventry and Sheffield' during the period.[5] Loudon described these gardeners and their use of the plots:

> It is not uncommon for single men, amateurs, clerks, journeymen, &c., to possess such gardens, and to pass a part of their evenings in their culture. In one of these gardens, occupied by Mr. Clarke, chemist and druggist, Birmingham (the inventor of Clarke's Marking Ink), we found a selection of hardy shrubs and plants, which quite astonished us…It were much to be wished that such gardens were general near all towns; as they afford a rational recreation to the sedentary, and a useful and agreeable manner of passing the leisure time of mechanics and workmen of every description.[6]

Apart from the cost of the plots, and the often exotic planting, one of their defining characteristics was that each had a permanent summerhouse:

> Every garden has its summerhouse; and these are of all scales and grades, from the erection of a few tub staves, with an attempt to train a pumpkin or a wild-hop over it, to substantial brick houses, with glass windows, good cellars for a deposit of choice wines, a kitchen, and all necessary apparatus, and a good pump to supply them with water. Many are very picturesque rustic huts, built with great taste, and hidden by tall hedges in a perfect little paradise of lawn and shrubbery – most delightful spots to go and read in of a summer day, or to take a dinner or tea in with a pleasant party of friends.[7]

Whether or not these buildings could always be termed picturesque might be a matter of taste. According to one writer describing Birmingham in 1803, 'The town is, in every direction, bordered by gardens; and, in the language of poetry, invested by a zone of vegetable beauty, in which are stuck, by way of grotesque ornaments, arbours, and summerhouses of all the forms that untutored fancy can devise'.[8] This also

62 One of the surviving Garden Houses on the Stoney Road Allotments in Coventry is in danger of total collapse

suggests that the land was fairly unregulated and that tenants could do with it almost what they pleased, which again differentiates the plots from allotments with their strict rules that might even include compulsory attendance at church.[9]

Warwickshire is particularly fortunate as not only have these plots survived, but so too have the summerhouses. At the **Stoney Road Allotments** outside Coventry, a significant group of seven has survived from the late nineteenth century.[10] One of the more elaborate of these has a fish-scale tiled roof and a stained-glass window, as well as a panelled interior with a fireplace. Another is timber-framed, while a further has Gothick-arched windows and one run of a trefoil-pierced bargeboard. Sadly, most are in a state of extreme disrepair and may soon disintegrate entirely or have to be demolished as unsafe (62). Laid out in the early years of the nineteenth century on land owned by Lord Hertford, originally part of the medieval Cheylesmore Park, the plots are still under cultivation as modern allotments. One plot, number 24, even corresponds closely to the layout shown on the 1889 Ordnance Survey map with its central path, summerhouse and avenue of fruit trees.[11] Each garden is still individually enclosed with a gate and hedges composed of hawthorn, holly, box or privet, giving the occupants a degree of privacy.

Another complex of guinea gardens is in the Warwick suburbs, alongside the racecourse. The **Hill Close Gardens** have been brilliantly restored by a Trust and are now open to the public. The reason so few detached gardens have survived is that they have been built upon as cities have developed and expanded. At Hill Close the site was first identified as prime building land by Warwick District Council in 1947. However, it was only the arrival of a bulldozer crashing through the site in 1993 that alerted local residents to the fact that the Council had been buying up the overgrown land in the intervening years with a view to building 30 houses on the grounds.[12]

These gardens face east on the south side of Linen Street and were originally laid out in 1845 when the then landowner separated the area into individual gardens. Unlike other guinea gardens, which were leased, these detached plots were bought by the tenants when the freehold was put up for sale in the 1860s. It is this divided ownership that has preserved them throughout the twentieth century. As in other cities, the owners were 'mainly shopkeepers: boot and shoe makers, corn dealers, a draper, a grocer, a druggist and so on',[13] who lived in the town centre where infilling was at its greatest. The 1886 OS Map shows that at that time there were already summerhouses, mature trees, complex path systems and terraces.[14] As there has been a continuity of gardening on many of the plots since their inception, there are still collections of mature fruit trees, vines, glasshouses and eight brick-built summerhouses.[15] The Summerhouse on plot 18 is present on the 1851 Board of Health map and four others date from before 1866.[16] They are all located at the eastern end of their plots, to make the most of the views across the adjoining common land (63). On a more utilitarian level there are also the remains of a brick bothy and a brick-built pigsty.

Westbourne Road Leisure Gardens, sited next to the Edgbaston Archery and Lawn Tennis Association and the Birmingham Botanical Gardens, have been less fortunate. Once part of the much larger Edgbaston Guinea Gardens, they fell prey, like many other gardens in the Birmingham area, to a 1970s directive from Birmingham City Council's Allotments Committee. This banned chimneys on plots and removed 'old

63

A restored
Summerhouse at Hill
Close Gardens in
Warwick

and decrepit' structures deemed to be unsightly.[17] According to Sheila
Hughes, 'a convoy of lorries, workmen and a bulldozer came down the
lane and straight through the hedges, proceeding to demolish all the
sheds and summerhouses, many of which dated back to the first tenants,
and now, mellowed and moss-covered, were quite beautiful in their setting
among all the old fruit trees'.[18]

However, the reduced area still retains the basic structure of the earlier
gardens, which were laid out on land given back to the Calthorpe Estate
by the Botanical Gardens for financial reasons in 1844.[19] The third Lord
Calthorpe laid out the area to the north-west of Edgbaston as a set of

gardens that were divided by a track and ran as far south as the Chad Brook, which was used as the water supply for the gardens.[20] Lord Calthorpe may well have had philanthropic intentions when developing the site, as it would have been considered prime housing land. By 1855 the area had been extended to either side of the Brook and the site continued to be expanded into the late nineteenth century, reaching as far as the new railway line. David Lambert describes the site as being exceptional, even in 1887, with a total of 148 plots.[21] In the twentieth century the land was gradually encroached upon and sections were lost to the Edgbaston Girls School and the Archery and Lawn Tennis Association.[22] A later renaissance occurred when 20 of the plots were leased by the Botanical Gardens and six were remodelled and cleared by the BBC who used them for their 1960s Gardening Club series, fronted by Percy Thrower. Today the surviving plots are owned by the City Council and are generally in use as gardens, although in 2009 English Heritage reported that one of the plots was unusable as the Council had used it for tipping, which suggests that their Grade II listed status, awarded in 1997, is still very much needed to ensure their survival.[23]

Adjoining these guinea gardens are the **Birmingham Botanical Gardens**, created by the Birmingham Botanical and Horticultural Society. The Society had been formed in 1829 under the presidency of the Earl of Dartmouth and, following the examples of Manchester, Liverpool, Hull and Glasgow, they charged themselves with a similar venture. A suitable area of meadow land was identified on Lord Calthorpe's Estate adjacent to the villa and pleasure gardens of Mr Aspley, whose villa and grounds were absorbed into the gardens. This land was described as 'a mixture of soil, suitable for Botanical and Horticultural purposes...the site commands a bold southern aspect, well protected from the North-East and North-West winds, has a pleasing view of Edgbaston Hall, and an extensive view of the surrounding country'.[24] The site having been bought and David Cameron, previously the head gardener of Bury Hill near Dorking, appointed as curator, the committee then approached J C Loudon, who already had a strong reputation as a landscape designer, to lay out the site. Following an initial visit in 1831, Loudon published his detailed designs in *The Gardener's Magazine,* of which he was the proprietor, in 1832. He describes clearly the intentions of the committee and the problems of funding such a venture:

> The committee, in mentioning to us the objects they had in view, stated that they wished to combine a scientific with an ornamental garden; and these, to a certain extent, with a nursery and market-garden; so as, by selling superfluous plants, fruits and culinary vegetables to lessen the annual expense of keeping.[25]

From these discussions he created a detailed plan and described how the different horticultural areas should be distributed:

> The contents of the whole are thus disposed of: - Botanic garden, 7 acres; pleasure-grounds, 2¹/₂ acres; American garden, ³/₄ of an acre; flower garden, ¹/₄ acre; orchard and fruit-tree nursery, 1¹/₂ acres; kitchen and agricultural-ground 2 acres; reserve garden and experimental ground, ¹/₄ acre; space on which the hot-houses stand, gravel walks &c., 1 ³/₄ acres: in all 16 acres.[26]

This was all to be achieved over a long period of time, as funding was found piecemeal to pay for the elements to be executed:

> It was further stated, that, whatever plan might be adopted, it could only be executed by degrees; as the funds available for that purpose did not exceed three thousand pounds, though a considerable addition to this sum was expected to be obtained, when the garden should be commenced, and the public had an opportunity of inspecting it.[27]

At this time public parks were rare elements in cities. Subscription botanical gardens, as opposed to academic botanic gardens, such as that at Oxford which was attached to the University, offered both an educational and semi-private garden space for those who could afford it. Like many others, the Birmingham Botanical Gardens were funded by subscribers who paid an annual sum to gain entry for their family and friends. It was not until the 1840s that members of the working classes were allowed to be admitted on Mondays and Tuesdays for a daily entrance fee of a penny.[28] Throughout the garden's history there seems to have been continual negotiation concerning finance and the terms of access, and today the Gardens are still largely maintained through a combination of membership and entrance fees. Similarly, the Society relied on donations of plants from other botanical gardens and private individuals to fill the grounds with interesting specimens. This was extremely successful, as in 1833 alone they received 2,400 plants from forty-two donors and by 1834 they had a collection of over 9,000 species, which at this date made them among the best stocked botanic gardens in Britain.[29] In reciprocation, Cameron also donated duplicates from the Society's growing collection to other interested parties, beginning as early as 1833.

The constraints on the finances available, particularly in the initial phase, seem to have led to the loss of the greatest element in Loudon's plans. His designs for ranges of quite remarkable circular glasshouses were not implemented. As the entrance to the garden was confined, he argued that the hothouses would be approached from behind so that 'the first object that met the eye would be the back sheds', which was also the case at the Liverpool gardens.[30] In order to counteract this and to make them aesthetically attractive from all sides, he designed them on a circular ground plan. He submitted two designs: one basic and the other more ambitious, realising himself that the latter was likely to be too expensive.

Unfortunately for Loudon, the committee decided that they were both too expensive and put the glasshouses up for tender, in the end choosing a design by Messrs J Jones and Co of Birmingham. This consisted of a linear arrangement of hothouse, circular conservatory and storehouse.[31] On seeing the plan Loudon wrote furiously:

> We entirely disapprove of it, and of its position in the garden; and we have no hesitation whatever in saying that the whole of our design is completely spoiled, as the general effect depended on the glass-houses being circular in the plan. We only regret that the committee have adopted our circuitous line of main walk (which, indeed, we staked out when on the spot), because we dislike exceed-

ingly the idea of having our name associated in any degree, however slight with a garden which, though it might have been one of the most perfect in its kind existing anywhere, and although unique in some arrangements is now bungled and never likely to reflect credit on any one connected with it.[32]

Once built, he described the result in no uncertain terms as 'one of the worst in point of taste that we know of. The centre is semicircular in the front part of the plan, with a lofty dome, surmounted by a second small dome, cupola, or glass turret, not unlike in form to those sometimes put up on the roofs for pigeons, and totally unfit for plants'.[33] However, his rage was tempered by this stage and he went on to state that:

> Having found fault with this range of glass, we have nothing but praise to bestow on the management of the rest of the garden, which does highest credit to Mr Cameron...On the whole we were highly gratified with this garden, and especially with the growth of trees and shrubs as a consequence chiefly of the manner in which they have been managed, although partly also of the excellence of the situation.[34]

As Miles Hadfield has written, this was truly a lost opportunity: 'looking back we see that his whole conception centred on those remarkable glasshouses (which is not unreasonable to consider quite practicable) was of astonishing originality, and if carried out would have placed Loudon far ahead of his contemporaries and indeed his successors'.[35] It is worth noting that these designs were made in 1832, before Joseph Paxton created the great conservatory at Chatsworth and well before the erection of the Palm House at Kew Gardens. The original glasshouses, which so upset Loudon, were replaced during the nineteenth century and new buildings were constructed to house the burgeoning collections of plants. In 1852 a Lily House was designed free of charge by Charles Edge, who also designed and installed a fountain, again *gratis*, which fulfilled another element of Loudon's design. The Lily House was built specifically to install a Giant Water Lily specimen that had been donated to the Society by Paxton in his role as Head Gardener at Chatsworth House, Derbyshire.[36] A Palm House was also constructed in 1871 and the Terrace Glasshouses and Exhibition Hall were erected in 1885 on the site of the original glasshouses, to cater for the growing need for covered prome-nades and areas for botanical exhibitions; they were renovated in 1987. All these features and the separate garden areas were recorded on an 1886 map by W Hillhouse.[37] In addition, there is a late-Victorian Bandstand and, across the lawns, the Lawn Aviary and Rose Garden (*colour plate 36*), which were opened in July 1996.

Examples of other semi-public green spaces are to be found in the spa town of **Royal Leamington Spa**. As the town revived its reputation for its healing waters in the 1780s, an increasing number of wells were sunk in response to the number of visitors searching for a cure for various ailments. In 1813 a small syndicate was formed with the intention of building the New Pump Rooms in the rapidly developing New Town area. One of the members was Bertie Greatheed of Guy's Cliffe, and it is no surprise, therefore, that the site eventually chosen for this enterprise was on land already owned by him. The syndicate's stated aim was that a bathing establishment would be built 'on a scale far surpassing anything yet attempted: that would excel, in fact, all that had been built in England'.[38] The building was designed by Charles Samuel Smith of Warwick and opened in 1814; a year later its title was changed to the Royal Baths and Pump Room. Shortly after its opening, the land adjacent to the building was laid out as an enclosed private garden so that patrons of the spa could also take therapeutic walks: 'An orchestra (rotunda) has been erected on the walks, where a military band is in attendance, in the evening during the summer, for the gratification of the subscribers as they walk around the gay and pleasing circular grounds'.[39]

These grounds were to remain closed to the general public until 1889 and, given the growing tourist industry, it is perhaps not surprising that they were not the only example of private gardens for visitors to the many wells. There was also a small garden behind Abbott's Baths in Bath Street and there were the privately owned Ranelagh Gardens in Clemen's Street. This last was originally established as the Leamington Nursery and Pleasure-Grounds in 1811, but was taken over and renamed by John Cullis in 1814, who tried to remodel them along the lines of the famous and highly popular Ranelagh Gardens in London.[40] He charged a single entrance fee, of 10s 6d per person or £1 1s for a whole year, and organised spectacular gala fêtes within his gardens. An 1828 advertisement for one of these stated that the entertainments would include a 'most splendid Display of Fireworks by Mr Crosbee of Sidney Gardens, Bath. The whole to conclude with a splendid Representation of the Diamond Temple of Golconda, extending its fires upwards of Thirty feet high and Twenty wide'.[41] However, this garden was eventually encroached upon by the Eagle Foundry and is now a forlorn factory site.

One garden site established during this period that has survived is the **Jephson Gardens**, which are located opposite the Pump Rooms and run eastwards along the northern bank of the River Leam. This is now a beautifully maintained public park with walks, a modern tropical house and flowerbeds containing national plant collections; it still forms a central focus for the town. At the start of the nineteenth century this land was part of the Newbold Comyn estate, owned by the Willes family, and known variously as Newbold Wood Walks, Newbold Comyn Fields and Newbold Pleasure Gardens or Grounds, which suggests it was laid out in an ornamental fashion even before the park was created. The tenancy was taken over in the 1830s by John George Jackson, a local architect, and it appears that he set about developing the land as private pleasure grounds. From 1831 purchasers who bought building land along the side of the park, known as Newbold Terrace, were to be granted perpetual rights of free entry to the gardens.[42] So, in a similar way to developments around Regent's Park in London and the People's Park in Birkenhead, the desire to turn the land into a park was related to the commercial sale of land in the adjoining area. As Christine Hodgetts has written, it is not clear what the formal arrangements for access were to the gardens, and although there seems to have been some limited free access it is likely to have been a private venture paid for by a combination of subscription and entrance fees, similar to the Birmingham Botanical Gardens.

In 1836 the Willeses of Newbold Comyn Hall leased the ornamental gardens to trustees for a nominal rent with the condition that the grounds were never built upon.[43] In 1845 the area was renamed the Jephson Gardens as a testimonial to Dr Jephson. The townspeople believed that he had helped increase the prosperity of the town through his advocation of its spa waters, as well as acting as a philanthropist and generous benefactor; he was also a keen gardener. Loudon visited his garden at Beech Lawn in 1840 and commented that, 'besides a pleasure-ground planted with a considerable variety of trees and shrubs, there is a small fruit-garden, and an excellent kitchen-garden, with a vinery, peach-house, pine-pits, &c.'[44] Typically, being a critical designer, he could not help but suggest that 'a great improvement to the place would be a terrace and an Italian flower-garden to connect the house with the lawn'.[45]

From 1846 a management committee of trustees, chaired for many years by Dr Jephson himself, ran the Gardens, which were laid out by men employed by the Labourers' Fund. It is possible that Loudon, who seems to have been recording or involved in all the schemes in the area during this period, devised the layout. In 1840, when he visited Dr Jephson's garden, he noted there were 14 acres, 'which is intended to be laid out as a public garden, and for which we have made a plan.'[46] According to Hodgetts, this plan was mentioned as the basis of the new garden layout in *Beck's Guide* of 1845 and in the *Warwick Advertiser* later in the same year.[47] The 1881 first edition Ordnance Survey map shows that the Gardens have retained much of this scheme. Elements such as the Hitchman Fountain, the monument to Dr Jephson and the Willes Obelisk (*64*) are marked on it, as are the perimeter and internal walks. Other features that have since been lost include several arbours and a large maze, based on the one at Hampton Court.[48]

In 1853, the author Nathaniel Hawthorne was resident at No 10 Lansdowne Circus, a stone's throw from the gardens. He published recollections of his time in Leamington in *Our Old Home* in 1863 and described the park in vivid detail in its Victorian heyday:

> The Garden is shadowed with trees of a fine growth, standing alone,
> or in dusky groves and dense entanglements, pervaded by woodland
> paths; and emerging from these pleasant glooms, we come upon a
> breadth of sunshine, where the greensward – so vividly green that it

64 The Jephson Obelisk in Leamington's public park

has a kind of lustre in it – is spotted with beds of gemlike flowers. Rustic chairs and benches are scattered about, some of them ponderously fashioned out of the stumps of obtruncated trees, and others more artfully made with intertwining branches, or perhaps an imitation of such frail handiwork in iron. In a central part of the Garden is an archery-ground...There is space, moreover, within

these precincts, for an artificial lake, with a little green island in the
midst of it...In still another part of the Garden there is a labyrinthine
maze, formed of an intricacy of hedge-bordered walks.[49]

Owing to chronic financial difficulties the Gardens were taken over by the
Leamington Corporation in 1896, and are now owned and managed by
Warwick District Council. After being bought by the Corporation they
were extended by the Mill Gardens on the opposite side of the Leam, which
were laid out predominantly as a children's play area in 1903. A recent
Heritage Lottery Fund grant enabled the Gardens to be both restored and
also developed in keeping with changes in the tastes and needs of the local
population. A new focal point has been provided by a striking modern
building fronted by a beautiful stone seat by Nicholas Dimbleby into which
have been inserted bronzes of elephants, on one of which rides Rudyard
Kipling's Mowgli. The glass-and-steel structure contains a subtropical
glasshouse, restaurant and teaching studio, while the Victorian Buffet,
converted into an aviary in 1965, has since been sensitively transformed into
a café. However, the educational element of the glasshouse, with its collection representing plant evolution from approximately 500 million years ago
to the present day, would have been understood and applauded by Loudon
and other reformers of the Victorian age.

endnotes on pages 277-278

29 Repton on site, directing the expansion of the river at Stoneleigh Abbey into a more picturesque, lake-like watercourse. *Stoneleigh Abbey Ltd*

30 As well as introducing pictures of himself into many of his Red Books, Repton animates his scenes with both workers and owners, as here at Stoneleigh's Gatehouse, where women are sweeping the path and a warder stands on duty at the gate. *Stoneleigh Abbey Ltd*

31 The approach to Stoneleigh from Repton's Red Book, now opened up by the removal of confining walls to offer a glimpse of the river beyond. *Stoneleigh Abbey Ltd*

32 Stoneleigh's improved landscape with latticed fences wreathed in shrub roses, a pergola for trysts set above a boathouse and the addition of a lofty loggia to the house for companionable strolling and landscape enjoyment. *Stoneleigh Abbey Ltd*

33 Repton's idealised view of the improved Stoneleigh landscape as seen through trees on the other side of the river. *Stoneleigh Abbey Ltd*

34 The ruined towers of Guy's Cliffe rising above the Avon, as seen from the Saxon Mill

35 Harris' Cave, which is cut deep into the rock face at Guy's Cliffe, probably functioned as a numinous boathouse

36 The 1996 Lawn Aviary and Rose Garden at Birmingham's Botanic Garden continues the spirit of JC Loudon's original glasshouses

In 1870 this Italianate Loggia was brought to Ettington Park, where it accords uneasily with the Gothic polychromy of the main house

Mary Elizabeth Lucy's vibrant 1840s River Terrace parterre was expertly restored by the National Trust in 1995 with the aid of aerial photography

39 The Flower Garden at Warwick Castle, also known as the Peacock or Italian Garden, was restored between 1984 and 1986

40 William Andrews Nesfield's terraced garden, laid out after 1842, at Merevale Hall contains ur rescued from Drayton Manor in Staffordshire

1 Warwickshire's most elaborate and well-maintained Victorian garden at Welcombe House – another all-encompassing design by WA Nesfield. The Obelisk on the hill beyond was raised in 1874

2 Thought to have been laid out by W A Nesfield, when his son, William Eden Nesfield, was working on the house, these parterres at Combe Abbey are instead the work of the Head Gardener, William Miller

43 David Backhouse's 1973 bronze of the Three Graces is a welcome distraction from the vacant spaces around Ashorne Hill House, which were once covered with topiary and flowerbeds

44 In true Arts & Crafts style, Charles Annesley Voysey's Brooke End connects, via its porch and terrace, with the flower borders and lawns below. At each end of the terrace are archways – 'Inspection Eyes' – giving views beyond

9

Victorian revivals – an uneasy juxtaposition beneath the house

Ettington Park, Bilton Grange, Charlecote Park, Ragley Hall
Warwick Castle, Bitham Hall, Merevale Hall, Stoneleigh Abbey
Welcombe House, Hampton Manor, Wroxall Abbey, Studley Castle
New Hall, Combe Abbey, Ardencote Manor
Highbury Hall, Wootton Court

IT SEEMS APPROPRIATE TO BEGIN THIS CHAPTER ON THE VICTORIANS, essentially style victims in both matters architectural and horticultural, with the landscape architect John Webb, who was often brought in to realise Humphry Repton's later Gardenesque schemes, only to avoid their most kitsch excesses. Webb featured prominently in Cheshire, where he succeeded Repton at sites where owners were not ready or willing to allow Repton to carry out his ambitious proposals. In Warwickshire, as we have seen, Repton's work is limited, so there was little scope for Webb to be drafted in as a trouble shooter. However, he was called in to remodel the grounds at **Ettington Park**, close to the Fosse Way, south-east of Stratford, where the satisfying late-Georgian aesthetic of contoured lawns and undulating plantations is a perfect counterpoint to the polychromatic dress of spiky and inscription-laden revived Gothic conceived by John Pritchard between 1858 and 1863. At Ettington the Georgian mood survived, at least in the pleasure grounds, while closer to the house its calmness was undermined, as in so many other sites in the county, by the return of insistent, yet jejune, formality and the onslaught of regiments of bedding plants.

Proficient in the disciplines of both architecture and landscaping, Webb had produced Tudor-Gothic designs for the house in 1814 for Evelyn John Shirley. These came to nothing, but it is generally thought that Webb was responsible for reshaping the grounds. This involved the retention of the old parish church as a ruin, which now served as a garden feature – the villagers having been re-housed at Upper Ettington in 1795 – and the introduction of Reptonian island beds full of shrubs in the lawns.[1] Today, despite the manicured croquet lawn for the use of spiteful hotel residents, the site is a rare archaeological treat, with ruined garden buildings and features strewn all over the yew-shadowed shrubbery which edges the lawns to the south of the house. These include a scabrous, tufa-like mini Grotto fronted by stone-edged planting beds and a decaying rustic Arbour constructed entirely of wooden staves and bark.[2] Much closer to the house there is a renewed 'country house style' parterre, which is saved from banality by a beautiful Italianate Loggia (*colour plate 37*) that looks to have been constructed of re-assembled stones, much as many 'Elizabethan' four-poster beds are an assemblage of bits of old oak furniture. It was brought here from Coleshill Hall in about 1870, when a more appropriate parterre of stone-edged circular beds and heart-shaped embroidery plantings was laid out as an 'Italian Garden' to complement it.[3] The Loggia and its parterre garden represent precisely the style conundrum that characterises the entire Victorian period until the Arts & Crafts movement established coherent style parameters and reintroduced hard landscaping for structure. Given that most major houses built from the 1850s onwards were confections of continental Gothic like Ettington, what garden style was appropriate for Gothic historicism? When the new design for Ettington was illustrated in *Building News*, the journalist delighted to see the removal of the 'Palladian portico and sundry pseudo-classical excrescences' when Pritchard re-cased the house. Yet the Loggia, though seventeenth-century in date, is unashamedly classical and Italianate and would have accorded with the original house. Now it sits most uneasily in the shadow of Pritchard's vibrant essay in Ruskinian Gothic.

The same stylistic uneasiness is apparent at **Bilton Grange** near Rugby where, after his purchase of the estate in 1846, Captain John Washington Hibbert commissioned AWN Pugin to remodel the house. Hibbert had family connections through his wife with the Talbots of Alton Towers in Staffordshire, where Pugin had worked. Today the house is a preparatory school and the grounds have been significantly altered and simplified, but they retain many mature trees from the original planting, particularly a majestic avenue of monkey puzzles alternating with yews. Another original avenue has Deodar cedars alternating with common yew. Between them are ornamental trees and shrubs.[4] While the grounds are comprised principally of formal tree avenues and lawns, to the east of the house, below the former Library and Drawing Room, there is a flagged terrace giving onto a sunken garden. Here, at least, there has

65 Puginesque attention to scholarly detail in the 'Old Letter' script balustrade of the garden wall at Bilton Grange, where the hard landscaping, at least, accords well with the Gothic revivalism of the parent house

been some attempt to tie the house in with its surrounding gardens. Although the planting has now been replaced by children's play apparatus, the balustrade (65) mentioned in the 1861 sale particulars as a 'noble open-work stone terrace wall, formed by a Register of the date of the house [1846], beautifully and quaintly cut in Old Letter' survives.[5] Its brick podium is decorated with dark blue diaper-work to match that on the house. But what was the planting in the enclosure? A plan attached to an indenture of 1855 shows a 'simple arrangement of parterre beds and a sunken bowling green below the south front', so perhaps the garden had few design pretensions.[6]

The same cannot be said for the new gardens laid out in the 1850s by

Mary Elizabeth Lucy for **Charlecote Park**, which she and her husband George Hammond Lucy had done so much to revive after he inherited in 1823. After his death in 1845, Mary Elizabeth turned her attention to the grounds and commissioned the architect John Gibson, who had worked on the house, to provide a design for the River Terrace. As at Bilton, a retaining wall, this time of Jacobean-style strapwork with corner seats and urns, enclosed a flower garden laid out on the site of the original 1690s parterres. Since the destruction of the seventeenth-century floral parterres in the Brownian restyling of the landscape, flowers had been banished from Charlecote. Mary Elizabeth filled Brown's Wilderness with Solomon's seal, foxgloves, ivy, box and wild flowers, while creating star-shaped beds in the Parterre to take bedding plants. In the 1950s the National Trust grassed over the Parterre for ease of maintenance, but it was restored in 1995 with the aid of aerial photography. The box-edged beds have been filled with annuals – geranium, marigold, berberis, heliotrope, salvia – while the borders contain old varieties of rose (*colour plate 38*). It is not to everyone's taste, but is representative of the constant renewal that Charlecote has undergone since the seventeenth century.

A similar approach was taken at **Ragley Hall** in the 1870s, when Robert Marnock laid out formal terraced gardens to the west of the house where there had been formal parterres in the late seventeenth century, as shown on the Kip & Knyff engraving. Indeed, Marnock took the exedral-ended shape of the former Stuart gardens as the western perimeter of his own design. At Ragley, Marnock was designing for the 5th Marquess of Hertford, probably on the strength of the Rose Garden and Flower Garden he had just created for the 4th Earl of Warwick at Warwick Castle, to which we shall return. Marnock's circular Rose Garden at Ragley is best viewed from the air (*66*), where the cross paths and flowerbeds, laid out like spokes in a wheel, can be clearly seen. The gardens were planted out in 1873 by local builders Clark & Smallwood, under the supervision of William Tasker.[7] Today they are a riot of garish colour, but they epitomise the Victorians' delight in unsubtle polychromy. The green grass and vacant spaces of the Jerwood Sculpture Park, which lie beyond the formal confines of the Rose Garden, are a welcome relief; they will feature in the last chapter of this study.

66 This aerial shot of Ragley Hall shows the circular form of Robert Marnock's 1870s Rose Garden, laid out to the rear of the house on the lines of the earlier formal parterre. ©*English Heritage.NMR*

Marnock's slightly earlier (1868-9) Flower Garden at **Warwick Castle** is more successful in that its backdrop is the eighteenth-century Conservatory, dramatised by the famous Warwick Vase, now replaced by a brilliant copy, and relies more on sharply-delineated design in the form of box hedges and topiary (*colour plate 39*) that encloses the roses, rather than on a brash show of colour purely for visual effect. This may, in part, be due to a sensitive restoration between 1984 and 1986. Known as the Peacock or Italian Garden, it is hexagonal in plan with geometric yew and box-edged beds. Owing to its distance from the Castle, there is no stylistic clash between house and grounds at Warwick, and the Flower Garden works well with the Conservatory, which, despite its Gothick-arched windows, is relatively plain in style. Marnock's lost Rose Garden was recreated in the early 1980s under the supervision of Paul Edwards and planted with David Austin old English roses; it was opened by HRH The Princess of Wales in July 1986.

The often uneasy juxtaposition of house and garden characterises many of the Victorian sites in the county, and also in the country as a whole, unless the parent house is Italian in style, as at **Bitham Hall**, Avon Dassett. The noted horticulturalist Thomas Aloysius Berry built the stuccoed Italianate house there in 1853-55 and engaged Joseph Knight of the Knight & Perry Exotic Nursery, Chelsea, to supply plants for the grounds and design the plantations. At Bitham there was a pleasure ground of lawns and woodland that might have been taken from a painting by Claude to accord harmoniously with the parent house, its advancing wings acting like belvedere towers reminiscent of some north Italian hill town. Most of the interesting trees and shrubs line the two approach drives: one from the south up from the village street, alongside which was a 'Rustic Garden', and the other to the north from which a walk branches off into the fields to a summerhouse, now gone, with a view of groups of monkey puzzles; the Fox Covert further down was also planted with specimen conifers. Knight was the first nurseryman to undertake in 1831 the commercial introduction of the *Araucaria araucaria*. Closer to the house there are stepped terraces decorated appropriately with urns, a Rock Garden planted with more conifers, a Kitchen Garden, now the Coach House, and a Conservatory, which was constructed in 1855. The panelled Gothic podium and arching glass vault give this the air of a mini railway terminus; inside there are some specimen camellias with striped flowers surviving from Knight's original planting.[8] The combination of overshadowed drives, open lawns, specimen conifers displayed in groups rather than singly, ornamental terraces and horticultural technology makes this a most satisfyingly coherent landscape, one perfectly in tune with its parent house.

Sadly, that synergy is rare in other major Victorian sites in the county, though the gardens at **Merevale Hall** in the north of the county near

Atherstone succeed admirably because they are tied into the main house by hard landscaping. The Hall is in towered and turreted 'Jacobethan', designed initially by Edward Blore and later completed by Henry Clutton for William Stratford Dugdale, who had inherited in 1836.[9] Set high above its surrounding landscape, with far-reaching views out to the west, north and east, the mansion was built with family wealth from the coalfields on the estate between 1838 and 1844. The formal terraced gardens (*colour plate 40*), which were designed by William Andrews Nesfield after 1842, are to the rear of the Hall.[10] They begin with a top terrace of stone-edged geometrical beds forming a parterre, flanked by grass panels with yew topiary. The urns on the east terrace wall were brought to Merevale in 1926 from Drayton Manor in Staffordshire. A centrally-placed flight of stone steps with Jacobean-style balustrades leads down via a second terrace, punctuated with hornbeam arches, to a more informal area of trees and shrubs, centred by a circular pool set in a gravel sweep with more urns. To the east of this sunken enclosure, on higher ground, there is an ornamental shrubbery of deciduous trees and conifers known as The Wilderness. It is laid out with a cruciform of gravel paths, running north-south and terminated by a charming timber Arbour. To the west of the house, on a narrow terrace overlooking the view towards Rugeley power station and the coalfields at Baddesley, is a triple-arched Loggia with Jacobean-style strapwork; this contains a modern bronze bust of Sir William Dugdale, who owned Merevale for eighty-three years. Much of the planting was renewed in the 1990s by the firm of Paige & Matthew, but Nesfield's original intentions can still be discerned.

Nesfield worked at several sites in Warwickshire, most notably at Welcombe House and **Stoneleigh Abbey**. He was designing at Stoneleigh in the late 1840s, though his contribution to the area below the south front of the house was not formally acknowledged until an 1858 article in the *Midland Florist*.[11] This concerned the Conservatory (*67*), which had just been stocked with plants. Nesfield's stock-in-trade was the seventeenth-century French-style scroll-work parterres of box and coloured gravels, sometimes enlivened with flowers, their enclosures punctuated by shallow tazzas.[12] He also laid out the Italian Garden on the west front in time for a visit by Queen Victoria and Prince Albert in June 1858. She had

67 William Andrews Nesfield's Conservatory was once the centrepiece of an elaborate
series of flowerbeds and parterres at Stoneleigh Abbey

come to the county to open the People's Park at Aston Hall, which still
retains some vestiges of mid-Victorian planting, though much decayed.
For the Stoneleigh reception the royal couple were given a suite of rooms
on the south front overlooking the gardens, whose flowerbeds and
borders were illuminated at night. During the visit the 'Queen and Prince
Albert walked through the Italian Garden in front of the house where
arrangements had been made that they should plant a tree, the Queen
planted an oak and the Prince a Wellingtonia gigantia'.[13] All the formal
gardens surrounding the house survived at least until 1899, when they
were photographed for an article in *Country Life*.[14] That to the south had
stone-edged grass panels, gravel and box-edged embroidery filled with
flowers, while yews lined the perimeter. The West Garden, scene of the
royal planting, was treated in similar fashion, while on the south-west
corner was a 'Grecian Garden', whatever that means, of more open,
circular beds. A later *Country Life* article illustrates the semicircular
timber Summerhouse, which survives today by the Kitchen Garden wall,
but does not give a precise date for it.[15] Close by was the Rose Garden,
now gone, but its centrepiece fountain survives in a sad isolation of lawn.
It was originally sited at the crossing of four gravel paths surrounded by

flowerbeds.[16] By 1901 it was surrounded by an arched trellis of climbing roses, devised by Head Gardener Mr H T Martin.[17]

Nesfield's formal gardens at **Welcombe House**, just outside Stratford-upon-Avon, were, if anything, even more elaborate than the enclosures around Stoneleigh. The house is now a hotel and the gardens have been beautifully restored. Here again, as at Merevale, he designed continental-style parterres for a historicist house, this time a rather gaunt Jacobean pile by Henry Clutton and Thomas Newby. The house was built for Mark Phillips, a Manchester cotton magnate, between 1866 and 1868. Nesfield is thought to have surveyed the estate in 1862 and laid out the gardens thereafter. They combined his usual penchant for stone-edged geometric parterres on the top terrace behind the house with more labyrinthine areas of close-cut greenery below (*colour plate 41*). At the centre is a beautiful Italian fountain with cherubic mermen, which may be a later addition, and the whole is enlivened with urns and statuary. On a hill above the house an Obelisk, raised by Phillips' brother Robert Needham, who succeeded him in 1874, marks the horizon. When Welcombe was sold in 1929 sale particulars were drawn up. These give a detailed account of the gardens at that time, including a twin-towered Winter Garden, which has been demolished: 'Beautiful gardens and grounds extend from a main terrace and include an Italian Garden, Rose Garden, Lawns and Shrubberies. Sunk Rock Garden with cloistered approach. Exceptionally fine Winter Garden partly stone built with glazed walls and domed glazed roof, approached by a flight of stone steps and having a Lily Pool and Fountain'.[18]

Nesfield is also connected to **Hampton Manor** at Hampton-in-Arden, though the link is a little tenuous as the plans that survive for the house are by his son, William Eden Nesfield.[19] William Eden had recently completed the new wing at Combe Abbey, on the strength of which he was engaged in 1868 by Sir Frederick Peel to build a lodge, a row of estate cottages and an octagonal clock tower for the Manor. Today the terraced gardens are all laid to lawn, but sale particulars of 1919 describe the original gardens: 'A wide flight of stone steps with stone wing wall gives access to gardens on Lower terrace comprising Lawns, Box-bordered Beds; Rose Beds; stone carved sun dial and large stone seat with carved Coat of

Arms'.[20] While the Seat survives, most of the other furnishings have disappeared, including a 'Valuable pair of 22in Italian marble garden vases' and a similar pair of 24-inch vases 'on high marble pedestals'.[21] At Hampton there is a terraced Italian theme to the grounds, which are commanded incongruously by a dull Tudor-Gothic house.

There is a similar, somewhat desultory parterre garden at **Wroxall Abbey**, more important for its association with Sir Christopher Wren than for any designed landscape, though the fragmentary ruins of the Benedictine priory, which have been planted with yews, make a numinous approach to the gaunt barracks of a house.[22] Similarly, **Studley Castle**, on the border with Worcestershire, a brash mixture of neo-Norman and Tudor Gothic built in 1834-37 for Francis Lyttleton Holyoake, is remembered more for being an agricultural college taken over in 1903 by the Countess of Warwick than for its early Victorian gardens. The place is now a somewhat down-at-heel hotel, where fragments of a formal terraced garden – stone retaining walls and one embattled archway – laid out by William Sawrey Gilpin lie strewn about the undergrowth. It is approached via an impressive Wellingtonia avenue, which was planted after 1863.[23]

A more dramatic formal garden of topiary survives at **New Hall** in Sutton Coldfield, now a suave hotel and spa catering for Birmingham executives and their spouses. This is a romantic moated site with ranges dating from the fourteenth through to the nineteenth century. John Chadwick remodelled the grounds after he had inherited in 1854. A formal garden was laid out between the house and the moat, while further out across the water there are the remains of terraced gardens, now laid to lawn, and an umbrageous Yew Walk. Even though the Hall is of several dates, its stylistic character is generally Tudor Gothic, so the ornamental topiary accords well with the building.

Mention earlier of **Combe Abbey** and the Nesfield connection introduces one of the Victorian horticultural heavyweights, certainly the most satisfying, of all the formal parterres in the county. Furthermore, the design is entirely in keeping with the late seventeenth-century wing that faces the gardens. This is best observed in an aerial view (*68*), taken before the house was radically extended and altered when it was being converted into a hotel with the most crepuscular reception area in the country. The

68 This view of Combe Abbey from the air shows the tulip-shaped parterres devised by
the Head Gardener, William Miller, in the 1890s, rather than a plan by W A Nesfield of
the 1860s. *Cambridge University Collection of Aerial Photography; ES15*

gardens are bordered by the moat that extends out into a canal and
thence to Brown's lake beyond. Clipped hedges define the boundaries and
the central path, while the lawns either side are decorated with box-edged
parterres in the form of stylised tulips, that to the north compromised by
a single unclipped yew, now removed in a sensitive restoration (*colour plate
42*). At the centre of each parterre a stone eagle rises from a circular
enclosure. It is a perfect symmetrical compliment to the angularity of Sir

William Craven's classical west wing, both garden and house working in harmony for once.

It is thought that William Andrews Nesfield designed these formal gardens in the early 1860s, when his son William Eden was remodelling the house, and that they were laid out by the Head Gardener, William Miller, whose first plans are dated 1864.[24] However, there is confusion here. The *Journal of Horticulture and Cottage Gardener* for November 1873 includes an engraving of the west front showing steps descending from the house to the moat with nothing in between 'save the two quadrants of close-shaven velvety turf sloping down to the water'.[25] Indeed, the correspondent continues to describe Miller's laying out of the pleasure grounds – the specimen tree plantations, a flower garden to the north of the mansion by the Kitchen Garden containing a ribbon border of roses 233 yards long, a croquet lawn and a 'rosary' – but confirms that there was 'no flower garden in immediate connection with the house'.[26] It would seem that the present layout was actually designed by Miller, and that it broadly reflects a Miller plan of 1897; much later, therefore, than the 1860s and not by Nesfield.[27] The gardens are shown in a *Country Life* article of 1909, ten years after Miller's retirement, and the design corresponds closely with what is on site today, though the box enclosures are kept much lower than the flowers they embrace, while in place of the eagles there are two-tiered fountains.[28] What is most strikingly different is that the 1909 photograph presents a completely open view from the garden, along the canal and out to the lake, one that is lost today with the encroachment of trees on the north side of the canal.

Before we leave the contribution of the Nesfields to the garden history of Warwickshire, mention must be made of William Andrews' other son, Arthur Markham Nesfield, who is credited with having designed the layout at **Ardencote Manor**, Claverdon. As with so many Victorian houses in the county, Ardencote is now a hotel and country club with attendant golf course, so the grounds have been radically altered. In 1876 there was a kitchen garden, an orchard, a Conservatory, which has since been restored, a lily pond, an artificial lake with an island and bridge, and a box maze. This last is called a 'box edged Knot Garden' in sale particulars of 1937 and survives miraculously on the hotel lawns.[29]

Perhaps the greatest Warwickshire loss of the Victorian period is the landscaped grounds and gardens that Edward Milner laid out in 1879 around Joseph Chamberlain's new **Highbury Hall** at Moor Green, Moseley. The formal lawn behind the house is still edged with jelly-mould yews, but the former shrubberies beyond, interspersed with specimen conifers, are now wildly overgrown. In its heyday Highbury had a conservatory, a plant corridor, a rock fernery and several plant houses; Chamberlain and his wife were enthusiastic cultivators of orchids.[30] Later in the century Chamberlain added an 'Elizabethan Garden', a 'Dutch Garden' and a rock garden approached via a pergola. Contemporary photographs of all these features appeared in the horticultural periodicals of the time, especially *The Gardeners' Chronicle* for 26 November 1904 and *The Gardener's Magazine* for 18 April 1903. The brick pergola at Highbury, illustrated in the *Gardener's Magazine*, is reminiscent of one that survives, though ruinous, in the grounds of **Wootton Court**, Leek Wootton. The Pergola at Wootton was featured in a 1902 issue of *The Garden*, which praised the taste and horticultural knowledge of the owner, Francis Beresford Wright. Like Chamberlain, he was an informed gardener and was attempting at Wootton to produce grounds characterised by the 'entire absence of the formal style of gardening'.[31] Vestiges of his extensive planting survive on the site today, which is now partly given over to the Warwickshire Golf and Country Club. Originally there were brooms, azaleas, kalmias and rhododendrons in the pinetum or wilderness garden, while closer to the house there was a rock garden, linked to the Court by the covered Rose Walk, whose slender metal arches are currently bowing under the weight of overgrowth. Despite the correspondent's assertion that there was an avoidance of formality in the grounds, the presence of the Pergola, which would become a staple of the next generation of Edwardian gardens, suggests that owners were at last tiring of flowers and plants arranged purely for their own sake, and were looking to architectural features to give their grounds a stronger sense of design.

endnotes on pages 278-279

Old gardens and patriotic nostalgia – the Edwardians

Compton Wynyates, Ashorne Hill House, The Cottage, Brooke End
Little Compton Manor, Greys Mallory, Mallory Court, Billesley Manor
Winterbourne Botanic Garden, Moreton Hall, Moreton Paddox
Dunchurch Lodge, Skilts, Bourton Hall
Wootton Hall, Clifford Chambers Manor

THE LAST CHAPTER ENDED WITH A FAINT GLIMMER OF HOPE AT WOOTTON
Court that the Victorians had begun to see the need for a distinct connection, through hard landscaping, between the environs of a house and its
wider landscape, especially where parks were essentially tree museums. In
the early part of the century Repton and Loudon had brought back
formality to the immediate surroundings of the house through the use of
terraces, steps and balustrades, but had generally left the lawns separate,
enlivened only by isolated island beds of shrubs. After the stylistic chaos
of the high Victorian period and the subsequent dislocation between
pleasure grounds and arboreta, a new aesthetic was required to bring
coherence, where a house would become part of the gardens and landscape it commanded. Such a holistic approach could only be achieved if
the gardens merged almost imperceptibly into the park. William Andrews
Nesfield had attempted this, but his busy box and flower embroideries
had always struck a note of highly ornate formality and, as such, never
provided that easy transition between gardens and naturalised landscape.
As the century came to its close, and the Arts & Crafts movement developed, writers such as John Dando Sedding and Reginald Blomfield
reassessed the last four hundred years in garden design, advocating an
approach where architectural forms might work in conjunction with horticulture to produce a satisfying whole, one in which gardens became

extensions of the parent house and its rooms. Sedding neatly summed up this synergy in his seminal *Garden-Craft Old and New*, first published in 1890:

> It is of the utmost importance that Art and Nature should be linked together, alike in the near neighbourhood of the house, and in its far prospect, so that the scene as it meets the eye, whether at a distance or near, should present a picture of a simple whole, in which each item should take its part without disturbing the individual expression of the ground. To attain this result, it is essential that the ground immediately about the house should be devoted to symmetrical planning, and to distinctly ornamental treatment; and the symmetry should break away by easy stages from the dressed to the undressed parts, and so on to the open country, beginning with wilder effects upon the country-boundaries of the place, and more careful and intricate effects as the house is approached.[1]

Although Sedding did not specify a particular style, either of architecture or planting, it is clear from his preface that, having 'studied old gardens and the point of view of their makers', he was confident of 'the general rightness of the old ways of applying Art, and of interpreting Nature'. As a result, he was now an 'advocate of old types of design, which, I am persuaded, are more consonant to an English homestead than some now in vogue'.[2]

This desire to recreate the 'old-fashioned garden', as Sedding called it, represents a yearning in the late Victorian and Edwardian period for 'the pleasures of England, one of the charms of that quiet beautiful life of bygone times'.[3] A typical 'old-fashioned garden' was planted around that most evocative of all English country houses, **Compton Wynyates**, when the 5th Marquess of Northampton and his wife came to live in the house after their marriage in 1884. Unfortunately, access was not allowed for this study, but a postcard view (69) of about 1918 shows an excess of topiary strewn across the lawns like some giant horticultural chessboard, the yew shapes interspersed with flowering shrubs. The garden was illustrated in a *Country Life* article of 3 August 1901, where the plants overwhelm the topiary, which suggests that it must have been laid out just prior to publication.

It is not surprising, therefore, given Warwickshire's obsession with the past, that most of the landscape gardeners of the Edwardian period worked in the county, producing gardens that satisfied this patriotic, nostalgic aesthetic. They had all trained as architects, and all their designs utilise architectural forms in combination with flowers, trees and shrubs. No distinct style connects them, merely this mood of quiet reverie for an age gone by. Charles Annesley Voysey's earliest house is at Bishop's Itchington, while at Brooke End in Henley-in-Arden both house and a garden

69   An early-twentieth-century postcard of the topiary at Compton Wynyates – a typical example of the Old English Style current in the Edwardian period

plan survive to record his achievements there; Harold Peto worked at Spiers Lodge in the park at Warwick Castle and later at Bourton Hall, near Dunchurch; Thomas Mawson provided a complete landscape for Dunchurch Lodge, gardens for Skilts and a kitchen garden for Hampton Manor. Other architects who obtained commissions in the county include Edward Goldie, Percy Morley Horder and William Henry Romaine-Walker, the latter working alongside artists from the Bromsgrove Guild of Applied Arts, while that great Edwardian heavyweight, Edwin Lutyens, may well have designed the garden at Clifford Chambers Manor, working in concert with Gertrude Jekyll, when he rebuilt the house just after the end of the First World War.

Chronologically, if we accept that the Edwardian period stretches from the last decade of the nineteenth century until the outbreak of the Great War, the first significant Warwickshire house and garden of the later 1890s is **Ashorne Hill House** at Newbold Pacey, designed in a staid Elizabethan style by Edward Goldie for the American couple, Arthur and Ethel Tree. Their ownership is celebrated in a carved oak tree above the central bay window, while their joint interest in Nature and the Universe is signalled on the lintel of a door leading out into the formal gardens, with the inscription: 'Flores × Terre × Stelle'. Furthermore, a vast stone chimneypiece in the Great Hall, though originally intended to be riotously Jacobean in decoration,[4] was eventually carved with figures of Adam and Eve – presumably Arthur and Ethel – sitting beside the Tree of Life, which is topped by a peacock. Inexplicably, all the figure carving has been removed, but the bressumer frieze still has sea creatures swimming amongst the waves, while celestial bodies float below the cornice.[5] It was an extremely accomplished carving, with natural symbolism worthy of William Lethaby. This was the clearest link, in a consciously Arts & Crafts idiom, between house and garden but, sadly, the Trees' gardens have not survived to confirm their passion about the natural world. Most of the yew hedges and topiary has gone, while the vacant lawns of a sunken garden crossed by gravel paths are now given a much-needed vertical accent by David Backhouse's 1973 bronze of the Three Graces (*colour plate 43*). Further out amongst the later buildings, dating from British Steel's occupation of the Manor, there is a small Pool Garden overshadowed by conifers.

In the absence of further visual documentation it seems likely that the Trees' gardens were predictably formal, cut off from the parkland by the simple balustrade that survives along the garden front of the house. There were the stirrings of that unity and harmony proposed by Sedding at Ashorne, but these aspirations appear to have been confined to the intellectual. At C A Voysey's **The Cottage**, however, there is a clear demonstration of that Arts & Crafts symbiosis of architecture and horticulture. Here a simple walled enclosure leads down to a former dell garden, its paths edged with stones.

On our visit in August 2009 there was a pleasant, ramshackle feel to the site (70), which was under restoration, but the bones of Voysey's rustic layout were still discernible. The diminutive 1888 house, designed for Michael Lakin who owned cement works at Harbury, has his signature roughcast walls, draped in lush wisteria, while the paved garden terrace was cut with angular beds for shrubs and circular box bushes, its architectural feature a stone table constructed from a millstone supported by staddle stones.[6] It could easily have been a scene from one of Helen Allingham's cottage garden paintings, but it was, perhaps, a little too unkempt for her.

Some elements of Voysey's grounds survive at **Brooke End**, Henley-in-Arden, but fortunately the owners still possess Voysey's plan for the garden layout, so it is possible to reconstruct his original intentions.[7] Brooke End (*colour plate 44*) is a far more substantial house than The Cottage, designed for a Miss Knight in 1909 with Voysey's familiar white-washed walls, stone mullioned windows and sweeping roofs; Miss Knight's initials are carved over the projecting mini *porte cochère*. The plan (*colour plate 45*) is drafted in a light colourwash of blues, greens and pinks, with each of the features marked in italic script. The house connects with the orchard to the front via a path lined on axis with the entrance porch, and to the garden at the side via a hexagonal conservatory, which juts out from the wall plane and leads to a central 'Pergular' and then on to a 'Green House'. The Conservatory survives, though remodelled, as does the Greenhouse (71), but the pergola has disappeared. This garden enclosure originally had perimeter flower borders and four large rectangular flowerbeds, in contemporary terms described as a 'panel garden', while the entrance façade is fronted by a terrace with more borders and steps down to the orchard, where some fruit trees still blossom. To the front and the rear of the house are two arched openings, which allow views across the house and on to the garden; that to the main front terrace is marked on the plan as an 'Inspection Eye'. This is the clearest indication that Voysey was anxious to make physical and visual connections between each component of his design, at the same time bringing the house into contact with its surroundings.

Voysey is remembered more for his houses than his gardens, whereas

70 Charles Annesley Voysey's The Cottage at Bishop's Itchington is an early work of 1884, with a small enclosed garden by the house and a miniature dell garden below

71 Voysey's Greenhouse at Brooke End, Henley-in-Arden has his typical sweeping roofline

Harry Inigo Triggs practised primarily as a landscape architect, working with the architects Frederick and Gerald Unsworth.[8] Triggs specialised in sunken gardens enclosed in dry-stone walls, where rills and pools enlivened his formal parterres. These elements are all evident in the illustration of **Little Compton**, which was published in his 1902 *Formal Gardens in England and Scotland*.[9] His drawing suggests how the gardens looked in the seventeenth century and how they might, therefore, be recreated in the same spirit of formality. However, there is a confusion here, because the present house is a gabled vernacular building in Cotswold limestone, altered and extended by Archbishop William Juxon, who lived there in retirement during the Commonwealth, whereas Triggs' plate shows a classical house of about 1680. This is surrounded, appropriately, by formal gardens, which include a raised bowling green, a panel garden of grass plats terminating in a circular pool, and several parterre gardens, all enclosed in walls and separated from the house by a canalised moat. None of this is apparent at Little Compton today, which was taken over by the Reed Business School in 1971, but there are walled and yew-hedged gardens around the house that look Edwardian in character, particularly the Foliage Garden (*colour plate 46*), which has a central pool and a semicircular Summerhouse. Christopher Hussey wrote two informed *Country Life* articles on the house and its grounds in 1939 and, while he congratulated the current owner – the late Mrs Leverton Harris – on her upkeep of the gardens, he made no mention of their original designer.[10] She bought the house in 1927, but the central section and the west wing were gutted by fire the following year, so she may have had to restore both house and gardens.

The conundrum is solved by Triggs' text, which places Little Compton, a lost house, near Compton Abdale on the high Gloucestershire Cotswolds rather than near Moreton-in-Marsh. Although Triggs was not responsible for the layout of the gardens at the Warwickshire house, formerly in Gloucestershire, then they at least follow quite closely his general design principles. It is just conceivable that they were created in the 1920s, when Lady Alexandra Metcalfe, daughter of Lord Curzon, Viceroy of India, hosted her famous house parties at the Manor. The Foliage Garden is sunk below the house, accessed from the original

72 A crouching Venus fronts the Summerhouse in the swimming pool enclosure at Little
Compton Manor

entrance forecourt via steps flanked by tall piers with pineapples, its
stone-flagged paths dramatised by topiary shapes. This appears fairly
subdued in its planting in one of the 1939 articles, whereas today it is a
riot of hot colour with plants spilling all over the hard surfaces. The
Summerhouse is almost unrecognisable, as its entire roof has been
subsumed in wisteria (*colour plate 47*). After this world of enclosed heat,
there is the relief of the Rose Garden and the grassed Long West Walk,
flanked by more exuberant borders, which leads to the swimming pool, a
typical interwar feature of such gardens. This is illustrated in *Country Life*,
edged with thyme and overlooked by a little Summerhouse, now
commandeered as a changing room, and a crouching marble Venus (*72*).
As a modern sculptural counterpoint to this classical beauty there is a
gardener close by, modelled on Brian Underhill, caught in the act of clip-
ping the yew hedge.

Greys Mallory at Bishop's Tachbrook is another limestone vernacular house, but designed in a revived Jacobean style by Percy Morley
Horder between 1903 and 1904 for Alan Batchelor, a retired barrister.
Here the house and gardens work perfectly together in true Arts & Crafts
tradition, with an inviting entrance forecourt comprising house and

service range, which is walled and punctuated with gate piers. This leads down through an arched opening like Voysey's inspection eyes at Brooke End, via steps to a formal garden, now laid mostly to lawn, but separated into sectors by battlemented yews. House and gardens are connected on this side by a columned loggia overlooking the flowerbeds, which had been cleared on our visit. This physical link between house and grounds was further emphasised on the garden front, where a timber-framed open loggia gives onto a paved terrace which runs the length of the façade; this recalls several similar features by Edwin Lutyens in his Surrey houses. The entrance lodges to the house also have a sub-Lutyens feel in the sweeping-roofed vernacular of the twin cottages, which is combined with an arched Italianate classicism in the gateway.

Morley Horder's other Warwickshire commission is **Mallory Court**, now a hotel, at Tachbrook Mallory, which he designed in 1914 for James Thomas Holt, another retiree, who had made his fortune in the cotton industry. While Greys Mallory was designed in a tranquil Jacobean with Dutch-style gables, Mallory Court is more emphatically Elizabethan vernacular, with acutely angled gables and clusters of tall brick chimneystacks. The gardens are to the rear and on a higher level to the west above the forecourt.[11] A series of plans and perspective drawings by Morley Horder show his original intentions,[12] which were modified in execution, particularly the panel garden to the west (*colour plate 48*). It is now a Rose Garden with a circular pool, and leads to a tennis lawn bounded by a yew hedge. Behind the house is a Pool Garden (*73*) laid out with cruciform flagged paths, whose retaining walls have robust stone seats set into them. This is the epitome of the architectural garden advocated so forcibly by Reginald Blomfield in his polemical battle with William Robinson. Further out in the lawns is a dramatic Rock and Water Garden, designed in November 1947 by Sidney C Lillim for Sir John Black; a plan of the proposed layout with its surrounding trees – damsons, acers, plums and a magnolia – some of which survive, is preserved at the hotel.

Another Warwickshire garden in the grounds of a hotel is at **Billesley Manor**, near Alcester. It was laid out in 1905 for Charles Hanbury Tracy, possibly by the architect Detmar Blow when he altered and extended the house. The Jacobean manor was originally moated, and fragments of the watercourse exist on site, but it is the Topiary Garden that features prominently in the brochure. This wall of shaped yew hedges surrounds a rectangular area centred by a Venetian wellhead. Circular steps lead up to raised borders, while the central lawn is guarded by an odd collection of forms, some animal-like, others abstract.[13] It is a more controlled version of the overwrought chessboard of Compton Wynyates and might easily double for an illustration in Blomfield's *Formal Garden*.

73 Percy Morley Horder's 1914 Pool Garden at Mallory Court has corner bastions inset with stone seats for internal views of the garden and the house beyond

A more extensive garden of the early years of the century is now part of the University of Birmingham and has been renamed the **Winterbourne Botanic Garden**. The brick house was built by John Nettlefold, a wood-screw manufacturer, who in 1891 had married Margaret Chamberlain, daughter of Arthur Chamberlain, the younger brother of the politician, Joseph. Nettlefold bought a ten-acre parcel of meadow in 1902 and set about building a house, to designs by a local architect J L Ball, and making a garden, supervised by his wife. The University acquired it in 1943 from John MacDonald Nicolson, a Birmingham draper. Ball did all the hard landscaping, while Margaret, who was inspired by Gertrude Jeykll, carried out the planting. At the southern end of the brick-walled terrace, which separates the east front of the house from its lawns, is a small paved courtyard with a Venetian wellhead, now choked in ivy. This was originally called the Dell Garden and had a loggia, now gone; it was later renamed the Trough Garden, after the stone troughs used to grow alpines. Beyond the terrace wall, stone-walled beds punctuated by tall Irish yews have been constructed to ease the transition between house and gardens. Further out there is a Pergola with stone piers reminiscent of Lutyens' example at Hestercombe in Somerset; this is likely to have been a 1920s Nicolson addition. The surrounding grounds are more informal with a Rock Garden, a Japanese Garden and a Scree Garden planted up with alpines, the latter two introduced by Nicolson. The main interest today is in the Walled Garden, which is now laid out with flowerbeds.

These last gardens were relatively minor sorties in the battle of the styles between the formal and the informal of the first decade of the century, but with **Moreton Hall** and Moreton Paddox architecture is resolutely in control. William Henry Romaine-Walker designed both gardens in 1907-8 and 1909-15 respectively, while the layouts displayed important features by the Bromsgrove Guild. Sadly, both sites are compromised by later alterations and demolitions, but enough survives, often in atmospheric semi-dereliction, as a record of Edwardian self-confidence and swagger, and there are many photographs showing the gardens in their prime.

Moreton Hall is an extraordinary house for its time, in that it is neither Arts & Crafts in style, nor in the contemporary Beaux Arts classicism, but a revival of the Whig aristocracy's Palladian that had been current in the early eighteenth century. Indeed, it might easily be mistaken for Wilton House in Wiltshire or Sir Robert Walpole's Houghton Hall in Norfolk. It was built for a rich American, Charles Tuller Garland, who had already rented the nearby Ashorne Hill House from his fellow American, Arthur Tree. Romaine-Walker laid out a vast stepped terrace and parterre garden to the rear of the house (74), whose central feature is a circular pool. This produced on the perimeter an exedral balustrade into which he inserted stone benches. This vast garden was once criss-crossed by gravel paths, but now the entire area is laid to grass. The pool has a beautiful Fountain

74

The vast formal garden laid out in 1907-08 by W H Romaine-Walker at Moreton Hall is now laid to grass, but the central pool survives. *Warwickshire County Record Office, PH96/9*

of Diana and her Nymphs (75), designed by the Bromsgrove Guild, founded in 1898.[14] The lead is in fairly good repair, though one of the cherubs has split at the waist. Below the balustraded wall there were further formal gardens, features of which survive in deep undergrowth and require assiduous detective work. Early photographs show an Italian Garden with Lily Pond and a Tea House, Rock Garden and Pool in The Pleasance. The arcaded Tea House is now bricked up and ruinous, like a fragment from the Baths of Caracala in Rome's Forum; below it are the rock-edged steps of the Rock Garden, leading down to a silted pool in which there is an outcrop of rock that was once the base of a fountain. Finally, somewhere in the grounds, was a Rose Garden surrounded by ornamental trelliswork.

Not to be outdone by his rich relative, Major Robert Emmett, who was married to Garland's sister, also commissioned Romaine-Walker in 1909 to build him a house – **Moreton Paddox** – but this time in a neo-Jacobean style. Again, the style of the garden layout was consciously classical and formal with a vast canal centred on the garden front flanked by four parterre gardens (76). Below these was an open lawn on a lower level, terminating in exedral yew hedges, while another open glade strode off at a 45-degree angle. At the heart of this Long Terrace was another majestic fountain supplied by the Guild. Writhing on the plinth were several scantily clad nymphs attended by nude cherubs, while rising up amongst them, on a decidedly phallic term, was Bacchus, the God of wine, looking down in a most predatory manner (77). Access to the Long

75 A cast lead fountain of Diana and her Nymphs at Moreton Hall by the Bromsgrove Guild – a rare and valuable survivor of the formal parterre

76 Romaine-Walker also designed the house and gardens at Moreton Paddox. This aerial view shows the central canal flanked by parterres and the oblique-angled Long Terrace. *Cambridge University Collection of Aerial Photography*

77 Bacchus looks down upon half-naked nymphs and cherubs in one of the pools of the
Long Terrace at Moreton Paddox – another minor masterpiece by the Bromsgrove Guild

Terrace and the Bacchus Fountain was via a double-flight imperial staircase that, bizarrely, survives today in the garden of a contemporary house
(*colour plate 49*), while the Rock Garden forms the centrepiece of another
modern house on the site. Moreton Paddox was demolished in 1959 and
its grounds sold off for housing development. The sale catalogue
mentions a Sundial Garden, a Topiary Garden, a Sunken Garden and, in
the 'West Garden', in addition to the Bacchus Fountain, a 'powerfully
modelled 4ft. 8in. lead group figure of "Boy and Boar", on 27in. square
base, by the Bromsgrove Guild'.[15] This appears in an early postcard at the
centre of a flower garden.

A garden with a similar treatment of parterres close to the house, long
axes and informality in the wider pleasure grounds was achieved by
Thomas Mawson at **Dunchurch Lodge**, near Rugby. Even though the
house currently functions as a conference centre and golf club, enough
survives on site to form an impression of Mawson's original intentions.
The house was built in Queen Anne revival style by the Liverpool architect Gilbert Fraser for John Lancaster of Bilton, a self-made iron and coal
magnate.[16] It was complete by 1907 and illustrated in the November 1908
issue of *Building News*. Soon after its completion, Mawson was called in to

landscape the site and, as usual, used his family firm to implement the scheme. Although he was the most successful and prolific landscape architect of his generation, he had done little more in the county than provide a kitchen garden for Hampton Manor. His design for Dunchurch (78) reflected his interest, derived from town planning, of parallel axial lines extending from the house and further sight lines, framed by planting, fanning out into the wider grounds.

The approach is along an obliquely-sited avenue that passes the stables and then curves alongside a plantation to the entrance forecourt at the east elevation of the house. Here an open glade marches off to the east with its counterpoint – a Rose Garden laid out in lozenge-shaped beds – on the west of the house. In this western area there were also a bowling green and a Pool, the latter of which survives, enclosed now on the east by a linking corridor. As at Brooke End, the transitions between each garden space are achieved by formal archways, one of which has a beautifully detailed openwork gate.

The house itself is set high up, with a broad balustraded terrace on the garden front, where steps lead down to what was once the Tennis Lawn. Further parallel arms of lawns edged by herbaceous borders extended on both sides; these grass vistas are still in place, with yew hedges defining the boundaries. Mawson varies the profile of the stone steps to the pleasure grounds, leading the eye on down across the Tennis Lawn to the open lawns and beyond to the oval lake (79), which has an exedral-shaped promontory enlivened with balustrades and obelisks. It is a most subtle and satisfying visual connection between the separate elements of the scheme, the trees and shrubs aligned, almost subliminally, in radiating lines out from the Tennis Lawn steps to give further coherence to the layout. Early photographs show the garden soon after it was finished, with low box hedges to the beds on the top terrace, and each architectural feature, such as the Sundial enclosure, precisely defined. Now that the planting has taken over, this circular paved area is surrounded by tall trees and shrubs, so its original purpose of providing a geometrical shift between the angular terrace and the serpentine gravel walk to the lake has been lost. This is, however, a minor criticism of the sensitive care with which the grounds are currently maintained.

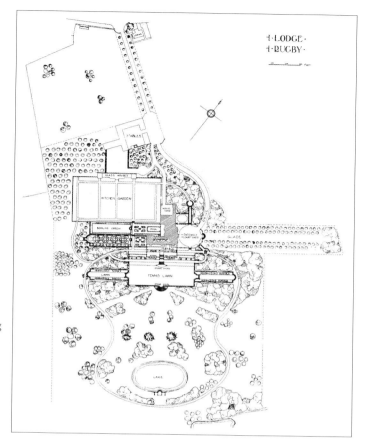

78

Thomas Mawson's
plan for the garden
and pleasure grounds
at Dunchurch Lodge
reveals his obsession
with axial vistas by
the house, which are
repeated in a subtle
patte d'oie of planting
towards the lake.
*University of Bristol,
Special Collections*

Mawson's next commission in the county was for William Jaffray, son
of the newspaper magnate Sir John Jaffray, who owned the *Birmingham
Post*. In 1908 William Jaffray extended the family house at **Skilts**, near
Studley, and brought Mawson in to design the gardens and grounds.
Fortunately, plans survive in Kendal Record Office and show two distinct
phases of the garden.[17] He designed a garden with typically strong structural lines comprising a rose garden centred by a pool edged by a pergola
near the terrace in front of the house, while an axial path ran from a
pavilion at the end of the house via a summerhouse to gates north of the
kitchen garden. This paved axis met a serpentine path, perhaps part of
the previous garden, and then continued as a lawned walkway between
trellised flower borders. Areas labelled 'this portion to remain as present',
suggest plans for later developments. A foreman's plan also survives for
new tennis courts in 1914 and shows how the garden might have evolved

79 The hard landscaping of the garden terraces at Dunchurch Lodge is continued in the steps of the Tennis Lawn and reflected in the exedral-shaped viewing platform at the other side of the lake

by that date. A round seat near the house is backed by trellis and the rose garden has a fountain surrounded by trees in tubs, but there is no sign of the pool. Semicircular steps lead out of the garden from a terraced area near the house, and the serpentine path has been changed in the centre to more angular lines. A pergola with rose arches strides down to the new sunken clock golf and tennis courts, but the western axial garden has lost some of its strength of design, now becoming a paved or gravel path with rose borders. A herbaceous border lies further to the west, while on the pathway there are two square areas containing trees. Whether this work was carried out is not known, as Jaffray died less than a month after the date of the plan for the new tennis courts. The family sold the house at some time after the Second World War. It is now owned by Birmingham City Council and used as a school for special needs children. The site of the garden is now a playing field and there is very little of the structure left to suggest that a garden ever existed. A few mature trees and an ornamental doorway with semi-circular steps are all that remain of Mawson's layout (*colour plate 50*).

Harold Peto would have approved of Mawson's deft handling of architectural spaces around the houses at Dunchurch and Skilts, particularly the
connection between the terraces and the outer lawns. Peto appears to have
worked only twice in Warwickshire, at Spiers Lodge in the park at
Warwick Castle, and when he was commissioned by J F Shaw in 1906 to
design an extension and a new Catholic chapel at **Bourton Hall**,
Bourton-on-Dunsmore. The Chapel, sited in the entrance forecourt of the
eighteenth-century house, is a small Italianate jewel with Romanesque-
style windows and Florentine Renaissance decoration to the pilasters and
doorframe; Peto's name and the date – 1908 – are inscribed on the base of
one of the pilasters. The extension is also Italian in style, with an Ionic
loggia reminiscent of the one at his own house, Iford Manor in Wiltshire,
and tripartite Venetian windows above to match the Palladian character
of the main house. This loggia and its first-floor balcony provide the
visual link between house and grounds, though the latter are now laid
mainly to lawns, the house being in corporate ownership. However, there
is a curious sunken garden on axis with the house, rising up via steps to a
rectangular pool whose walls are lined with plinths (*colour plate 51*). Photographs in the house prove that this was originally connected to the house
by an axial gravel path flanked by grass parterres, the whole enclosure
being hedged with yew.[18] Moreover, the rectangular feature was once a
gravel garden, decorated with large pots and surrounded on three sides by
a Doric pergola, a feature much favoured by Peto. The whole effect must
have been perfectly in keeping with the Italianate nature of his additions
to the house.

Peto's Mediterranean treatment was favoured by the Edwardian
owners of **Wootton Hall** at Wootton Wawen when they laid out the
'Italian Garden' to the rear of the stately 1680s house, which can be seen
from the A3400.[19] Now, only a vestige of this stony layout is evident, in
front of the reception shop for the mobile home park on the site. This is
a small rill garden with two circular pools that was once part of a vast
formal complex of sunken enclosures and a long pergola. These are illustrated in Charles Holme's 1908 study of gardens in the Midlands, and
there are also photographs preserved at the house.[20] Stony pebble and
gravel paths, stepping stones and crazy paving threaded a mini Acropolis,

where Corinthian capitals rose up from rectangular cisterns. Venetian wellheads centred courtyards, while classical busts supported on carved stone brackets looked down from the enclosing walls (*80*). Somewhat incongruously, the earlier Dovecote with its timber-framed roofline was retained and formed the backdrop to all this theatrical show. The brick- and stone-columned pergola extended from the house to an octagonal arbour enlivened by urns, with views through to the rear wall of the gardens, where a robust bench gave views back down its length (*81*). Most authorities that have written about the Hall concentrate on the building of the house by the Carringtons, and the eighteenth-century parkland surrounding it, which features the impressive weir on the river Alne. As a result, the Italian Garden has been missed, yet it must have been one of the most impressive of its date in the county. It is likely that the garden was commissioned by George Hughes of Birmingham, who bought the estate in 1904 and redecorated the interior of the Hall in a variety of styles fashionable in the Edwardian period.[21] It is just possible that Hughes is the man sitting pensively under the pergola (*82*).

Peto designed another garden at Spiers Lodge, the eighteenth-century Gothick keeper's lodge in the park at Warwick Castle, but access was not allowed for this study, so his work there must go unrecorded. Fortunately, the owners of **Clifford Chambers Manor**, just south of Stratford, were more than welcoming, so Edwin Lutyens' single commission in the county could be appraised.[22] There is, however, uncertainty surrounding the garden layout for, while Lutyens is recorded as having extended the house between 1918 and 1919, it is by no means certain that he designed the formal gardens there, either on his own, or with help and advice from Gertrude Jekyll. In addition, there was an earlier campaign of remodelling at the house, by Tudor Owen for John Gatrix in 1903-09, and both house and gardens were reconstructed by Kathleen Wills and her husband Dr Edward Douty between 1909 and 1911. Douty died in 1911, whereupon Kathleen married Lt Colonel G B Rees-Mogg. They were in occupation when the house was seriously damaged by fire in 1918, and Lutyens was commissioned to reinstate it. There are at least three separate periods, therefore, when the gardens might have been reshaped. *Country Life* published two articles on the house and gardens in 1928, when Mrs Rees-

80 The Italian Garden at Wootton Hall, Wootton Wawen in an early photograph – one of the most grievous losses in the county. *By kind permission of Ashton Hall*

81 The site of this pergola at Wootton Hall, worthy of Harold Peto or Edwin Lutyens, has now been subsumed by static homes. *By kind permission of Ashton Hall*

82 Could this pensive man be George Hughes, who bought the Wootton Hall estate in
1904? *By kind permission of Ashton Hall*

Mogg was still alive, but they offer no clue as to who designed the
layout.[23] What photographs in the articles do prove is that the gardens
have been subsequently altered and bear little relation to what must have
been laid out in the early years of the century. Added to this, a vast
timber-framed grange, south of the garden courtyard, which Lutyens
rebuilt, has been demolished, thereby opening up the courtyard to the
surviving arm of the medieval moat.

Today the main garden is on the west side of the house and features a
walled enclosure laid out as a rose garden, with clipped box shapes on the
lawns between the stone-flagged paths, which are edged with lavender
(*colour plate 52*). Beyond this is a pedimented brick Summerhouse (*colour
plate 53*), which looks seventeenth-century in date, fronted by stone gate
piers with pineapple finials. The *Country Life* caption for this reads: 'A
modern garden house and old gate piers', while in another photograph the
lawns of the walled enclosure are cut with triangular and trapezoid beds
planted with tulips; there are further ranks of tulips outside the walls.

Christopher Hussey, who is always a reliable source of information, reports that the 'garden house' was 'designed by the late Mr Edward Douty'.[24] It is likely that the brick Pergola that extends south from the Summerhouse was also built during Douty's ownership, between 1909 and 1911. Further out to the south there is a sunken area crossed by flagged paths, which leads to a wooden balustraded Bridge that looks decidedly Lutyensesque and must, therefore, be post-1918 in date. In 1928 the south courtyard was bare except for a Venetian wellhead. Now, in summer, it is beautifully unkempt, with flowers thrusting through the flagstones, shrubs cascading over walls and in the borders, and a loggia cloaked in wisteria.

It is hard to disentangle the layers at Clifford Chambers. On the furthest southern corner of the gardens, as a distant twin to the Summerhouse, there is another garden building of brick and stone dressings. Might this also be by Edward Douty, or could it date from Tudor Owen's reconstruction of 1903-09 for John Gatrix? Certainly Tudor Owen built a tree house in the grounds, supported on tree trunks and with a thatched roof, which has disappeared.[25] All that can be safely recorded is that the Garden House looks 'Edwardian'. This then is the difficulty when analysing early twentieth-century gardens, especially when they have been subsequently altered, as is often the case. However, Jane Brown, writing about Lutyens and Jekyll's collaboration, was in no doubt when she wrote about the gardens at Clifford Chambers in 1982: 'No plans have been found, but this is an interesting garden with many partnership features'.[26] Quite what those features were is not stated, but the series of garden rooms surrounding the Manor would have delighted both Lutyens and Jekyll, who did much to popularise the idea long before Lawrence Johnston perfected it at Hidcote.

endnotes on pages 279-280

The country house style and figures in the grass

Upton House, Ilmington Manor, Armscote Manor, Sherbourne Park
Barton House, Maxstoke Castle, Warmington Manor, Coughton Court
New Place, Hall's Croft, Shakespeare's Birthplace
Anne Hathaway's Cottage, Ragley Hall
Lord Leycester Hospital, Ryton Organic
Garden of International Friendship, Lady Herbert's Garden
Baginton Quarry Garden, Mill Garden, Highfield
Dorsington Manor, Dorsington House

THE EDWARDIAN CHAPTER ENDED AT CLIFFORD CHAMBERS WITH THE establishment of that ubiquitous design motif of all twentieth-century layouts: the garden room. As the century progressed this practical expedient, where separate, sheltered enclosures could be themed either by specific plants or historic iconography, inevitably led to the development of the 'country house style'. The essential elements of this are the box-edged parterre or knot; the linking pergola; the random scattering of statuary and urns on close-clipped lawns; and the symmetrical planting of fruit trees. Whenever inspiration fails, this familiar style can be re-processed again and again, just as it has in many of Warwickshire's twentieth-century gardens, particularly those associated with Shakespeare in Stratford. But its saving grace is often the modern sculpture associated with it; hence the figures in the grass of the title of this last chapter. However, it was not always thus, as the first significant garden laid out in the county after the Great War is one of the most inspired. This was due to the sophistication of the owners – Lord and Lady Bearsted – their architect, Percy Morley Horder, and the garden designer

Kathleen Lloyd Jones. Admittedly, they had an existing terrain with which to work: the spectacular viewing platform which commanded the valley at **Upton House**, but, with the help of their architect's hard landscaping, the hilltop was latticed in 1927-8 with a network of steps and dry-stone walls (*83*) to create a terraced garden worthy of the Villa d'Este, but with the fountains replaced by herbaceous borders.

Horder was aided by Lady Bearsted's garden designer, Kitty Lloyd

83   The early-twentieth-century terraced gardens at Upton House were achieved by the combined talents of the owners, Lord and Lady Bearsted, their architect, Percy Morley Horder, and the garden designer, Kitty Lloyd Jones

Jones, and a local mason who constructed the flights of steps and walls that link the several sectors of the gardens as they cascade down the hill-side.[1] These contain garden areas, but they are never as prosaic as garden rooms, for they merge one into another in a profusion of flowering shrubs and herbaceous borders linked by green axial paths. The main lawn by the house is the perfect introduction, with its calm greenery, to the busy floral displays below. It is bordered by a simple Rock Garden, designed by Lloyd Jones and dramatised by five eighteenth-century cedars of Lebanon; wisteria, clematis and climbing roses drape the rich orange walls of the house. Below the escarpment are three terraces running east-west – Top, Middle and Lower – all with elaborate borders, Lloyd Jones' speciality, which are meticulously maintained by the National Trust. The Top Terrace is for spring colour, with ceanothus, agapanthus, salvias and lavenders; the Middle is planted up with Mediterranean-type plants for summer heat, and the Lower Terrace verges on the autumnal with berberis, olearia, phlomis, genista and cistus. Lloyd Jones originally planted irises in clumps throughout the west border. That facing north is called the Aster Border, planted in the 1920s with Michaelmas daisies and yellow flag irises. Finally, there are the Scented Garden, the Wild Garden and the Mirror Lake, which last has further herbaceous borders. Even if the plants vary from those specified by Lloyd Jones, the National Trust has aimed to produce the same effects in a brilliant display throughout the three flowering seasons.

The importance of hard landscaping, such an important structural feature of the Edwardian garden, was still in evidence at **Ilmington Manor**, near Shipston-on-Stour, when Major Spenser Flower and his wife Ella Lowndes Flower of the brewery family laid out the garden around the gabled Elizabethan house in the 1920s. Prominent yew hedges provided enclosure; there were a Rock Garden, a Dutch Garden and a Rose Garden commanded by a hexagonal Summerhouse of 1924. Photographs taken for a 1983 *Country Life* article show the grounds to have been sharply manicured in the manner of Hidcote, which is just over the county border and must have inspired the Flowers.[2] Today the grounds are allowed to grow more naturally and have been enriched by several pieces of modern sculpture, including a unicorn of 1995 by Felicia Fletcher.[3] The Pond Garden has an extraordinary water tank faced with decorative carving, which may be Jacobean in date. It is now surrounded by mature shrubs rather than flanked by open lawns, as it was in 1983, but the Pond Garden still retains its twenties' character.

A similar house and semi-formal garden altered in the 1920s, this time by the architect E Guy Dawber, is **Armscote Manor**, near Stratford, but Deborah Williams, in association with Dan Pearson, has radically reshaped the garden out of all recognition. Fortunately, Armscote also featured in *Country Life,* where the correspondent delighted in the 'order and charming formality without austerity; the borders being planted with rare skill, and the house itself just sufficiently foiled with greensward to soften the architectural lines. For this the wife of the owner must receive the entire credit'.[4] Armscote is no longer a historic garden but, with its distinctly separate garden rooms, it may well be seen in future as one of the most significant contemporary designs in the country house style in Warwickshire.[5]

Somewhat better preserved, though without the panache of new land-scaping, is the 1950s garden at **Sherbourne Park**, just south of Warwick, where the Smith-Rylands had a blank canvas. They created an axial line from the house to Sir George Gilbert Scott's spired parish church, and enlivened the grounds with hedged and walled enclosures dramatised by stone sculptures, while silver willow-leaved pears *Pyrus salicifolia* Pendula were set to march across open lawns.[6] The White Garden is a shadow of its former self and the diamond-shaped parterre by the churchyard wall, photographed in 1983, survives, but in a dishevelled state.

Barton House, the most southerly property in Warwickshire, is another Elizabethan house with 1898 alterations and additions by Dawber. However, while the grounds at Armscote have undergone a complete transformation, those at Barton still retain elements of the Victorian period, principally the lawned areas around the house, though with imaginative new areas of planting set with intriguing sculpture. Most significantly, Barton has a national collection of arbutus and the catalpas are also strong elements in the gardens. This interest in rare plants is signalled by the Secret Garden alongside the Victorian entrance drive, which was created by Hamish Cathie's mother, Marian Josephine, between 1949 and her death in 1982. This is a small but profusely planted area containing, amongst others, *drimys lanceolata*, *rhododendron mucronu-latum*, *embothrium*, the Chilean fireplant, *crinodendron hookerianium* and *arbutus menziesii*, the Pacific Madrone. Further round the house the shrub-beries are threaded with paths where classical touches – a column (*84*) and a Caesar bust – lead the visitor to a tennis court guarded by a 1990 Temple with vine-encrusted terracotta columns, past a stone statue of the Hindu elephant deity, Ganesh, carved locally in Blockley, and on to a Japanese Garden of 1992. This is planted with a pagoda tree, cherries, bamboos

84

A fine garden will
always reflect the taste
and interests of its
owners – Hamish
Cathie in the grounds
of Barton House,
which contains a
national collection of
sorbus

and pines. The eclecticism of this ingenious series of enclosures climaxes
in a pair of Nepalese Pokhara bulls, carved by Alan Wright, and a curiously sedate bust of Byron. The grounds at Barton encapsulate perfectly
the taste and travels of its owner.

Another modern garden set within a historic site is at **Maxstoke
Castle** in the north of the county where Rosemary Fetherston-Dilke has
created a new Sunken Garden on top of a 1930s swimming pool. This has a
raised walk on the Castle side lined by limes, while the centre is laid out as
a box-edged parterre filled with lavenders, geraniums and penstemons with
a colour palette of pink and white which changes to blue and white. It is a
pleasant space from which to view the romantically moated quadrangular
Castle that seems never to have had a significant garden, though the

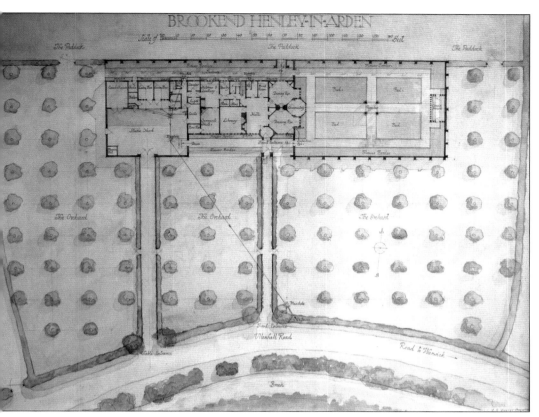

45 Voysey's 1909 plan for Brooke End proposed a simple panel garden and greenhouse aligned on the conservatory by a 'Pergular' to the east, while the grounds to the south were to be planted as orchards. *By kind permission of Marion and Tony Dowding*

46 The Foliage Garden at Little Compton Manor, essentially of the 1920s, is now meticulously gardened by the Reed Business School, which took over the house in 1971

47 The 1920s Summerhouse at Little Compton is now completely subsumed in wisteria and fronted by beds of hot colour

48 Percy Morley Horder's 1914 watercolour design for the gardens around Mallory Court – a perfect demonstration of how to connect the house with its grounds through appropriate hard landscaping. *Warwickshire County Record Office, CR1886/M47*

49 Bacchus no longer looks down lovingly on his nymphs at Moreton Paddox, nor does the
staircase give access to the top terrace of the Jacobean Revival mansion. Instead, a striking
modern house commands what is left of the features of the original Long Terrace

50 This lone archway and moon steps are all that is left of extensive formal
gardens at Skilts, which Thomas Mawson laid out in 1914; the site is now a
playing field

51 This forlorn pool at Bourton House was originally encircled by a pergola designed by Harold Peto, who was also responsible for the 1908 Chapel. The Loggia giving onto the grounds may be another Peto feature, or possibly the work of Charles Armstrong, who remodelled the house

52 An early-twentieth-century garden at Clifford Chambers, which might have been designed by Edwin Lutyens when he was extending the house between 1918 and 1919, or might possibly be earlier, by Kathleen Wills; the enclosure has since been extensively replanted

53

This remarkably accurate
seventeenth-century-style
Summerhouse at Clifford
Chambers was built
before 1911

4 Municipal planting within a scholarly recreation – the sunken Knot Garden at Shakespeare's
   New Place

55

Brutus caught in thoughtful
contemplation in the
Shakespeare Tree and
Sculpture Garden at Anne
Hathaway's Cottage – a
bronze by Isaac Graham

56

A modern urban garden with a frankly
modern civic backdrop – the Garden of
International Friendship in Coventry

7 The Quarry Garden at Baginton has hosted the annual Outside Art Garden Sculpture Exhibition, where both abstract and figurative forms blend strikingly with the plants and rockwork

8 Man on a wire – Beverly Ranger's *Swing* in the Baginton Quarry Garden

59

The Mill Garden has the best view of Warwick Castle in the town

60 Angular lines are reflected in architectural planting, while precisely laid stone courses are draped in rich foliage at Dorsington House – the county's most impressive modern house and garden

remains of a Regency Grotto can be seen in the shrubbery across the moat.

Geraint Lewis took the same approach, though on a smaller scale, when he began to redesign the gardens at **Warmington Manor** in the mid-1990s. He dressed the skirts of the Hornton stone vernacular house with geometric, box-edged parterres decorated with grey chippings. These give structure to the terrace and lawns and extend the house out into the garden. This attention to geometry is apparent in the wider grounds where there is a close-cut turf maze, while the Potager, though irregular with productive and ornamental plants, is firmly punctuated at the borders with box cubes.

A similar treatment was given to the interior courtyard at **Coughton Court**, with four box-edged beds whose linearity is extended into the grounds by two double avenues of red-twigged limes planted by students from nearby Pershore College.[7] But it is the Walled Garden, a 2-acre plot that wraps around the parish church, which is the most significant of Clare McLaren-Throckmorton's recent contributions to Coughton's garden history. She began its restoration and development in the 1990s with her daughter, the garden designer Christina Williams. Together they have created a series of asymmetrical spaces overflowing with flowers and shrubs, all linked by paths and set with specially designed seats or bowers in Gothick style to accord with the house. The centrepiece of the enclosure is the Rose Labyrinth, designed by Christina as a private gift for her mother, which includes 200 varieties of climbing and rambling roses. In 2006 the World Federation of Rose Societies gave it the 'Award of Garden Excellence'. As with other sectors of the Walled Garden, where design and sculpture has been carefully thought through, at the heart of the Labyrinth there is a statue of Rosamond Clifford, mistress of Henry II, surrounded appropriately by several bushes of *Rosa mundi*.

This sophisticated attention to detail is sadly lacking in almost all of the gardens related to Shakespeare in the county. **New Place** in Stratford has an Elizabethan-style 'Knot Garden' with balustrade and trelliswork, but is awash in summer with a garish display of flowers that are more municipal 1950s than sixteenth-century in impact (*colour plate 54*). Indeed, the show is so overwhelming that the patterns of the knot are almost impossible to read. There are similar attempts at recreating some kind of historicism at **Hall's Croft**, where John Hall has been the catalyst for a formal herb bed with plants mentioned by him in a notebook. **The Birthplace** is also uncoordinated in its garden design, with lawned areas, island rose beds and shrub borders. Finally, **Anne Hathaway's Cottage** is more successful in that its cottage garden has been allowed to grow almost unrestrained to produce the wild, unkempt effects so desired by William Robinson and beautifully evoked by the watercolours of Helen Allingham. What saves all these garden homages to the great playwright are the sculptures and artworks. These are liberally scattered around the vapid sectors of the first three, and in a separate field at the last.

At New Place there is a series of scabrous, leprosy-encrusted bronzes derived from Shakespeare's plays, often emanating chunks of his verse, by Greg Wyatt. They are undoubtedly dramatic in impact, but are almost all consciously ugly except an arching woman from *The Winter's Tale*, which must represent an awakening Perdita (*85*). They make a bizarre modern counterpoint to the bas relief sculpture of Shakespeare, moved here in 1871 from the Shakespeare Gallery in Pall Mall, London. There is another Greg Wyatt piece at Hall's Croft, the head of an ass, presumably meant to be Bottom in *A Midsummer Night's Dream*, while at the Birthplace the eye is taken, not by the suburban planting, but by the angular 1971 Sundial in front of the Shakespeare Centre: a perfect complement to the building.

There is more variety in the Shakespeare Tree and Sculpture Garden at Anne Hathaway's Cottage, which was opened in 1988 and features forty trees mentioned by the poet. The sculptures resulted from an initiative between the Birthplace Trust and the Newington-Cropley Foundation; the first pieces were added from 2001. As with the Greg Wyatt sculptures, all were inspired by Shakespeare's writings and include an oddly-titled *History Play* by Jane Lawrence, a rusted sheet of metal with an image of the British Isles cut out of it, and a brooding Brutus by Isaac Graham (*colour plate 55*). These modern sculptures are a perfect preparation for the Jerwood Sculpture Park at **Ragley Hall**, where major pieces by internationally renowned sculptors are sited enticingly around the grassy area below Robert Marnock's great Rose Garden. Indeed some are so well placed that they produce a frisson of excitement when encountered (*86*), especially Harry Everington's 1992 *Crusader* and Lynn

85

Greg Wyatt's 2008 sculpture *The Winter's Tale* – one of a series of bronzes inspired by Shakespeare's plays in the grounds of New Place, where the playwright died in 1616

86 Sculptures are carefully sited to achieve maximum visual impact in the Jerwood Sculpture Park at Ragley Hall. This is Harry Everington's 1992 *Crusader*

Chadwick's numinous 1978 *Cloaked Figure IX* with a triangular head, looking like an escapee from the annual Venice carnival. Further out in the Woodland Walk there are carved benches and more sculptures, which culminate in Elisabeth Frink's *Walking Man* of 1986.

A more significant and scholarly recreation of one of Warwickshire's important historic garden sites is the present Master's Garden at the **Lord Leycester Hospital** in Warwick, to which is appended the Millennium Knot Garden featured in the Introduction. It is roughly similar in size and prospect to the original sixteenth-century enclosure and divided into two halves, the southern section left as an orchard and lawn, while the northern area is used for fruit and vegetables. The old town wall formed the western boundary of the Garden and a terrace or promenade was built giving views across the countryside. It is known that a central walk was constructed in 1796 across the southern section of the garden;[8] this was later changed in 1852 and a lawn created, surrounded by a more fashionable serpentine walk.[9] Archive material reveals that in 1819 repairs or alterations were made to a brick stove on the ground floor of a gazebo. Repairs were also made at this time to a heated pineapple pit; the pineapples were commonly nurtured in pots immersed in a bed of tan bark. Small plants were possibly obtained from Warwick Castle pinery and grown on to become mature fruit.[10] In 1838 a Nilometer was installed, which had been donated by the Earl of Warwick: 'In the centre of the garden, on a square pedestal, stands a vase, [which] formerly crowned a Nilometer, or one of the pillars which marked the rise and fall of the Nile: This curious and beautiful relic of Egyptian art formerly stood in the centre of the grand conservatory of Warwick Castle.'[11] The form of the Garden is shown on the local 1851 Board of Health plan, and this has inspired the present reconstruction.[12] Further information came from the American writer Nathaniel Hawthorne, who described this sector of the garden in November 1857: 'Each brother has a little garden of his own, and the master has, also, a nice garden. There is a beautiful little thatched summer-house where they can go and sit in warm weather, and play at chess or checkers. Cards are prohibited entirely.'[13]

In 1993 an extensive programme of renovation and replanting began under the supervision of the garden historian Susan Rhodes and the land-

87

The Gazebo in the restored Master's Garden at the Lord Leycester Hospital, Warwick

scape architect Geoffrey Smith. The garden remains today divided into its two historic sections by a hornbeam hedge, which crosses the site from south-west to north-east. From the entrance to the Master's Garden, the square Gazebo (87) is viewed down a tunnel-like Pergola constructed of iron hoops, which is similar to one previously in the garden.[14] The Gazebo is in the same position as that in the eighteenth century, and has a practical room for tools and pots on the ground floor, with an upper room with views over the town wall and east garden. The north-east area of the garden is laid to lawn with mixed borders of flowers, and has a specimen tree planted in each corner. The south-west sector has cruciform, box-edged brick paths which join at a central *rond-point* where the sundial is sited. The four quarters are treated as a potager, with decorative plantings of seasonal fruit and vegetables.[15] Each part of the garden is cleverly masked from the next, giving elements of surprise within this beautifully maintained historic space.

One anomaly in this catalogue of twentieth-century gardens, but which has provided an important function in the development of awareness about organic gardening, is the complex of gardens at **Ryton-on-Dunsmore**, near Coventry. This is the physical home of a charity, The Henry Doubleday Research Association (HDRA), renamed Garden Organic in 2005. Founded in 1954 by the journalist and horticulturist Lawrence D Hills to promote organic gardening and research,[16] the HDRA was named after Henry Doubleday, a nineteenth-century Essex Quaker smallholder. Hills continued with Doubleday's research, setting up the charity to further investigation into organic ways of growing plants. The first headquarters were in Bocking, Essex, which was only a small site, as the HDRA was conceived as a members' club for gardeners to experiment on their own home plots. With demand increasing for practical demonstrations in organic methods, the operation was moved to a new site at Ryton.

Ryton Gardens opened on 5 July 1986 and have continued, until recently, to uphold Lawrence Hill's vision and passion for enlightening growers and the general public on the virtues of organic gardening. The site is now used to display thirty different gardens. With names such as the Herb Garden, the Bee Garden, the Paradise Garden and the Rose Garden, herbs, flowers and shrubs are plentiful, while the Vegetable Kingdom, the Mount and the Children's Garden are promoted as a magical experience for visitors. More recent plots encourage the fashion for growing vegetables in ornamental flower borders or containers, and a 'Flowers for Pleasure' garden gives tips for organic growing of flowers for display.[17] However, all is not as rosy as it seems. Webbs Garden Centre took over the retail, conference and catering facilities at Ryton in 2009. With plans for an outdoor space, a planteria selling local produce, but not all organic, launched in 2010 in association with Webbs, Lawrence Hill's purist dream appears to be unravelling.[18]

At this point it is worth a short detour into neighbouring Coventry, where an attempt to reconnect the city with its historic past through gardens animated with modern sculptures has been a mixed success. Already producing cars, bicycles and planes at the beginning of the Second World War, Coventry's war effort also included the manufacture of munitions and tanks. As a result, the city was bombed many times during the course of the war, and on the night of 14 November 1940 a mass raid by 500 German bomber planes, and the resulting fire-storm, left three-quarters of the factories destroyed, along with 4,000 homes and St Michael's Cathedral. After the destruction the Provost of the Cathedral pledged forgiveness for the city's enemies. St Michael's was left a ruin, but after the war a new Cathedral was built and developed as a World Centre for Reconciliation. The city regenerated in the 1950s and 1960s, but with the need to revitalise in the early 1990s, the Phoenix Initiative was established to create a traffic-free walkway, a 'metaphorical journey',[19] along a sculptured landscape, linking spaces representing the past, present and future of the city. The route culminates at the **Garden of International Friendship** and **Lady Herbert's Garden**. Artists Christine Browne, Alexander Beleschenko, Susanna Heron, David Ward, Kate Whiteford, Françoise Schein and Jochen Gerz, together with the poet David Morley, were commissioned to develop works of art to enhance the theme of reconciliation between past and future.[20]

By 2001 the Phoenix Initiative was complete and its ideals put into practice. At the beginning of the walkway the removal of a 1950s church hall enabled archaeological excavations to uncover the remains of the Benedictine Priory and adjoining St Mary's Cathedral. A sunken Priory Garden was incorporated into the excavated nave of the church, with a raised walk giving views of the lawn, which was scattered with foundations and Christine Browne's 2001 *Cofa's Tree*: a mosaic of objects found during the excavation. Six glass cabinets, lit at night, display archival objects and artwork, giving a 'wash of light' within the sunken space.[21] Further along the walkway is the Priory Cloister Garden, where David Ward's mixed media installation *Here* plays blue light on the old walls, while pleached limes form a rectangle, recalling the contemplative space of the cloister.[22] From the Priory Cloister, steps lead to the vibrant Priory Place, which is surrounded by shops and bars. In Susanna Heron's *Water Window*, a sheet of copper provides a backdrop for a 12-foot high waterfall cascading into a triangular pool. A bridge crosses the water and the outline of streams in the pool recreates the mediaeval millrace fed by the River Sherbourne, which still lies beneath the square.[23]

This public area is exited by a narrow passage through to Millennium Place, a fan-shaped piazza dominated by the twin stainless steel Whittle Arches, commemorating Sir Frank Whittle, who designed the jet engine at Rolls Royce in the city. The whole square is lacking in soft landscaping and the space is too busy, with artworks vying for a viewer's attention. Jochen Gerz, born in Berlin on 4 April 1940, has two installations in the piazza, linking with the concepts of memory and reconciliation. His 45-metre long *Public Bench* has plaques mounted by the people of Coventry, and, by the entrance to Lady Herbert's Garden, a glass obelisk, entitled the *Future Monument,* engages with the past and the future, with former enemies becoming friends. At the back of the site a spiral structure leads to a glass bridge over Lady Herbert's Garden. Blue etched glass fins by Alexander Beleschenko enclose the bridge, which terminates at a sandstone platform that gives views over the Garden of International Friendship, designed by Robert Rummey Landscape Architects. The garden contains The Priory Maze, designed by Kate Whiteford.[24] A curved wall is inscribed with bronze text by David Morley, inspired by the Coventry Mystery Plays, which were performed in procession outside the city walls each year by Coventry's mediaeval trading and manufacturing guilds.[25]

Lady Herbert's Garden, which is sited between Millennium Place and The Garden of International Friendship, is a small garden of one and a half acres.[26] It was created in two phases: the east garden in 1930-31, and the west garden in 1935-38, with the two areas split by the city wall that runs through the site. Sir Alfred Herbert, a Coventry industrialist, laid it out as a memorial to his second wife Florence, who died in May 1930. The land chosen for the east garden site included the only complete section of the fourteenth-century city wall.[27] The restoration of the wall and two adjoining mediaeval gates − Swanswell and Cook Street − were part of Herbert's vision for the garden. He described his ideas for the garden, envisaging a 'garden of flowers', and asked the Corporation not to 'allow it to degenerate into a mere shrubbery'; it was to be a 'haven of peace and floral beauty in an industrial city', with games and meetings strictly forbidden.[28] Albert Herbert, a cousin and Leicester architect, who had designed an extension to Leicester Museum and Art Gallery, was appointed as designer.[29] The east garden was opened on 12 April 1931.

Lady Herbert's Garden is physically separated by railings from the Garden of International Friendship, but Alexander Beleschenko's finned bridge crosses overhead, from which walkers enjoy an elevated view of both gardens and the surrounding area (*colour plate 56*).

To return to the theme of the figures in the grass or, more appropriately, the figures in the quarry, Warwickshire has a spectacular **Quarry Garden** at Russell's Garden Centre, Baginton. It is part of a 26-acre independent family nursery that has been operating for over 80 years from the same site.[30] Frederick Russell bought eight acres of land at Baginton in 1927, establishing a nursery which was further enlarged in the 1950s to 20 acres by his son, Reg.[31] David Russell and his brother Brian inherited the Centre from their father and, as a separate project, in 1984 David bought six more acres. This was a disused sandstone quarry,[32] filled with rubbish and old vehicles, at the rear of the car park.[33] The medieval quarry, which may have supplied building stone for Coventry,[34] has a spectacular 35-foot rock face of red Triassic 'Lower' Bromsgrove Sandstone, while in other areas where the rock has been exposed it has weathered to a gentle buff-green colour.[35] David Russell has painstakingly converted the quarry into a rock garden (*colour plate 57*), investing in many thousands of pounds-worth of plants, to produce what has been described a horticultural 'masterpiece',[36] with a series of ponds, streams and waterfalls, shady trees and open meadow. Designed for colour all year round, it is particularly beautiful in spring, with the flowering of magnolias and camellias followed by a spectacular display of hundreds of azaleas and rhododendrons in bloom.

For three years it has been the venue for the Outside Art Garden Sculpture Exhibition, which adds another dimension to the garden once the spring flowers are over. More than sixty sculptors, including many local artists, exhibited in 2010. The annual exhibition has quickly gained a reputation as one of the major sculpture events in the country. Commanding the whole site in 2010 was Sue Parry's *Glass Tree* and, like Amanda Noble's *Lilac Ripples*, which was set amongst the hostas, it produced an organic effect in tune with the landscape. The quarry wall and surrounding pool were reflected in the blue scimitar-shaped *Flight* by Katie Green, while nearby Susan Long's water sprite *Anya* sat with knees clasped, gazing into the still pool surrounded by gunnera and bamboo. Haunting images of Michael McEntee's giant silver wired head, *July 1st 1916*, backed by laurel bushes, and Beverly Ranger's *Swing*, a man gliding over a pool hanging from an overhead rope (*colour plate 58*), are impossible to dispel, but the recollection of Stephen Charlton's *Swinging Mouse* will raise a smile.

The Russells' other garden cowers beneath Caesar's Tower in Warwick, close to the ruined medieval bridge across the Avon and the Castle Mill. Not surprisingly, it is called the **Mill Garden** and has one of the most spectacular views of the Castle in the entire town (*colour plate 59*). Arthur Measures began it after 1938, but David and Julia Russell (née Measures) now own it and continue to garden there in the spirit of Measures' original ethos. He is recorded as having said: 'I should really like to ensure that it [the garden] remains unharmed for all time, and a peaceful place for those in need of spiritual refreshment'.[37] Despite the thunderous roar of the weir and the oppressively cliff-like walls of the Castle overhead it remains just that, a strangely tranquil spit of cottage garden fingering into the dark Avon. To walk its brick paths, almost obscured by the encroaching burst of flowers and shrubs, is to step back into the past and leave the cares of the modern world behind.

That carefree atmosphere is particularly evident in Dorsington village, south-west of Stratford-upon-Avon, at the 650-acre estate of the million-aire Felix Dennis.[38] A very successful British self-made entrepreneur, Dennis was once co-editor of *Oz*, an underground magazine, and involved in the notorious 1971 obscenity trial the Old Bailey, at which he was acquitted. These days he is more philosophical about life and writes poetry, 'a counterpoint to business' as he puts it,[39] and plants trees, setting up the Forest of Dennis charity, dedicated to planting a substantial native broadleaf forest in the Heart of England. Around twenty years ago he bought the thatched Old Manor at Dorsington, originally five cottages. Between 1995 and 1998 he also built **Highfield**, a modern 'folly' based on Robert Louis Stevenson's *Treasure Island*, to house his entertainment complex. The garden at the back of Highfield is sheltered on two sides by earth ridges that define the boundary of the garden without hiding the views across the Warwickshire countryside. On the northern ridge is a

88 An anchor, cannon and ships' figureheads enliven the front garden of Highfield in
Dorsington – Felix Dennis' homage to *Treasure Island*

living sculpture by Dave Johnson, created from the stumps of three ash
trees, entitled *Highfield's Nudes*, while to the east stands a bronze horse,
weighing nearly a ton and seven feet tall, modelled on the 'Burano', a rare
breed of war horse found near artist Brian Taylor's home in Italy. The
front gardens have ships' figureheads guarding the doorway and an anchor
and cannon on the lawn (*88*).

The Old Manor gardens at **Dorsington** have well tended lawns and
bright borders, with compartmented gardens at the front of the house,
and a smooth lawn area to the rear. In almost every direction there are
statues: a cat on a balcony railing, children reclining on seats, putti on the
door jamb to a rustic cottage, twin owls guarding steps, and in the pool a
putti and dolphin fountain. On the back gateposts two Art-Deco-style
nudes hold a garden light feature suspended on wires. A Fairy Walk
leading to a gypsy caravan runs along the side of the garden. Nearby, a
sunken garden is surrounded by a castellated hedge, with the motif on the
garden seats, gates, and bridge, echoing the reeds by the pool. Some
distance from the house is the Welshman's Barn, where Dennis now
writes his poetry. Next to it is a small arboretum, with artificially created

89 Dennis' surreal but fascinating Garden of Heroes at Dorsington finds the rock guitarist Chuck Berry strumming next to Grace Murray Hopper, the computer scientist

ponds and streams, and an extraordinary avenue of life-sized bronze figurative sculptures, which he has named The Garden of Heroes. This strangely surreal, latter-day Appian Way is a mix of significant shapers of history (*89*) that have influenced Dennis, and in many ways have defined the course of his career and his life. The heroes are too numerous to name individually, but the often jarring juxtaposition – Galileo next to Dorothy Parker – and broad cultural range of the figures is representative of Dennis' catholicity of taste and interests.

At the other end of Dorsington there is a ground-breaking, twenty-first century house and garden. As it is the most important and innovative in the county, it will provide a fitting climax to a chapter of traditional excursions into garden design. Innovative, eco-friendly and low maintenance, the house has a stark, distinctive quality (*colour plate 60*), as outlandish in the twenty-first century as Corbusier's villas proved to be in the 1920s. **Dorsington House** was conceived jointly by its owner Igor Kolodotschko, an architect and entrepreneur who worked on the Fisher Park stadium rock shows,[40] and Granville Lewis, a former City Architect

90 Dorsington House is the most significant modern house and garden in the county – the joint inspiration of its owner, Igor Kolodotschko and the architect, Granville Lewis, together with the garden firm, Reckless Orchard

of Birmingham.[41] Natural light filters into the house through large windows, and energy-saving heating and water recycling have been installed in addition to an indoor swimming pool, study with private courtyard garden, cinema and entertainment complex. The long hall has views outside to the garden and to internal spaces. To the right a lily pool and sculpted water feature are bordered by bamboo *phyllostachys fastuosa*, while to the left willows, *Salix alba* 'Birzensis', have been planted to give a multi-stemmed effect; these are underplanted with *cornus canadensis* and *vinca minor* 'Gertrude Jekyll'. The cool, cream-painted interior walls are extended outside where the firm Reckless Orchard has designed a contemporary garden with linking areas fully complementing the open plan nature of the house.

The entrance courtyard is a paved space with angular walls clad with a mixture of cream, honey and grey stone, softened by a border of alchemilla. Opposite the front door water falls from a rectangular pool into a flat area of grey cobbles, while the nearby *Liquidamber styraciflua* tree is underplanted with *Geranium macrorrhyzum* 'Album'.

Passing through a walled kitchen garden the dining terrace is reached, which is essentially an extension of the living space, hung with a sail to provide shade. Its bold water feature resembles three taps, which spout water into an oblong pool, the water cascading over the edge into the Sunken Garden below (*90*). The planting here has been planned to give fragrance throughout the year, with the grey, pink and purple flower palette designed to look its best in the last rays of the evening sun. *Geranium psilostemon, Verbena bonariensis* and *Anemone x hybrida* 'Honerine Jobert', contrast with *Allium christophii*, and *Allium schubertii*, while the seed-head birdbath and a small sculpture of a boar add structure to the space. An old, gnarled olive tree stands starkly beside the dining furniture, its base surrounded by sweet-smelling thyme.

The walled Sunken Garden has a vast raised bed planted with blue Siberian irises, *Iris sibirica* 'Ruffled Velvet', edged with golden creeping jenny, *Lysimachia nummularia* 'Aurea'. Cool cream and grey steps link the terrace to the Sunken Garden, while overhead a silver Pergola, with training wires silhouetted against the sky, echoes the metal and glass fencing surrounding the terrace. At the opposite end of this subterranean space, grey steps, bordered by creamy white walls, pass between lime trees, *Tilia europaea* 'Pallida', with box (*Buxus suffruticosa*) underplanting. The steps lead to smooth lawns which provide a visual contrast with the wild-flower meadow and the view out to the wider landscape, where natural hedges and trees have been strengthened with additional native species, including ash, field maple, hawthorn, dog rose, holly, wayfaring-tree and crab apple. A wooden summerhouse is reflected in a still pond, behind which massed herbaceous plants are interspersed with grasses, including *Miscanthus sinensis* 'Zebrinus', and *Stipa tenuissima*. The garden entrance from the back of the house is treated as an architectural space leading to a bird sculpture, while close by over 500 English lavender plants, *Lavandula angustifolia*, have been planted in five straight rows in a raised 'field'. This is stunning when seen from below, and even more so when viewed from the platform in the modern Folly, a silo with a geodesic dome where slick modern technology meets agricultural simplicity in this small rural corner of the county.

endnotes on pages 280-281

Chapter Notes Introduction

Introduction A COUNTY OF LEGENDS, HEROES AND HISTORICAL REVIVALS

1   William Dugdale, *The Antiquities of Warwickshire*, 1656, Preface, describes the river Avon as 'dividing the Wood-land ... from the Feldon'.
2   Christopher Morris (ed.), *The Illustrated Journeys of Celia Fiennes, c.1682-c.1712*, 1982, p.114.
3   Ibid., p.115.
4   Ibid.
5   The designs are in the University of Bristol, Theatre Collection. We are most grateful to Jo Elsworth for alerting us to this commission and for Sir Roy Strong's kind permission to use an image of his late wife's design for the fountain. The information is taken from JTO 47/2/2 & JTO 47/1.
6   The fish in the pool died owing to lethal amounts of dilute sulphuric acid emitted by the rock, and the weight of the fountain caused the substructure of the pool to collapse. The exhibition was dismantled in 1983; the whereabouts of the Bear is unknown.
7   Morris, *Illustrated Journeys*, p.115.
8   Ibid.
9   Ibid., p.115-16.
10 Ibid., p.116.
11 A Ewert (ed.), *Gui de Warewic: roman du XIIIe siècle* (Paris, 1932-3). For recent scholarly work on the legend see Carol E Harding, 'Dating Gui de Warewic: A Re-Evaluation', *Notes and Queries*, vol.56, no.3 (September, 2009), pp.333-5.
12 See Velma Bourgeois Richmond, *The Legend of Guy of Warwick* (New York and London, 1996).
13 James Joel Cartwright (ed.), *The Travels Through England of Dr Richard Pococke*, 2 vols (Camden Society, 1888-9), 2, p.282.
14 Ibid., p.283.
15 Ibid.
16 Ibid.
17 Ibid.
18 Ibid.
19 Ibid.
20 Ibid.
21 Ibid.
22 Morris, *Illustrated Journeys*, p.116.
23 Thomas Arnold (ed.), *Dryden: An Essay of Dramatic Poesy* (Oxford, 1918), p.67.
24 Cartwright, *Travels*, 2, p.238.
25 Levi Fox, *A Splendid Occasion: the Stratford Jubilee* (Oxford, 1973), p.8.
26 Zoffany's 1762 portrait of Garrick sitting on the chair taking tea at the Temple is illustrated in the exhibition catalogue *Every Look Speaks: Portraits of David Garrick* (Holburne Museum of Art, Bath, 16 September-17 December 2003), pp.12-13.
27 Both pictures were destroyed by fire in 1946.
28 This illustration is an engraving published much later in 1858 (University of Bristol Theatre Collection, RS/046/0075).
29 For the best account of the Jubilee see Johanne M Stochholm, *Garrick's Folly: The Shakespeare Jubilee of 1769 at Stratford and Drury Lane* (Bungay, 1964); in addition to Fox, also George Winchester Stone &

George M Kahrl, *David Garrick: A Critical Biography* (Southern Illinois University Press, 1979), pp.577-85 and Vanessa Cunningham, *Shakespeare and Garrick* (Cambridge, 2008), pp.106-12.

30   David M Little & George M Kahrl (eds.), *The Letters of David Garrick*, 3 vols (Oxford, 1963), 2, letters 553-4, pp.660-2.

31   Fox, *Splendid Occasion*, p.14.

32   Ibid., p.20.

chapter 1 MAXIMUM CONSUMPTION FOR A VISITING MONARCH – ELIZABETHAN GARDENS

1   Quoted in H M Colvin (ed.), *The History of the King's Works, Volume II: The Middle Ages*, 1963, p.685. See also John Steane, *The Archaeology of the Medieval English Monarchy*, 1993, pp.121-2.

2   See Jane Elisabeth Archer, Elizabeth Goldring & Sarah Knight (eds.), *The Progresses, Pageants, and Entertainments of Queen Elizabeth 1* (Oxford, 2007); Jean Wilson, *Entertainments for Elizabeth 1* (Woodbridge, 1980); June Osborne, *Entertaining Elizabeth I: The Progresses and Great Houses of her Time*, 1989.

3   John Nichols, *The Progresses and Public Processions of Queen Elizabeth*, 3 vols., 1788-1805, 1, p.309.

4   June Osborne, *Entertaining Elizabeth*, p.47.

5   *Oxford Dictionary of National Biography* (hereafter, *ODNB*).

6   The fields had previously belonged to the Knights Templar, hence the name.

7   Nichols, *Progresses,* 1, p.319. The phonetic spelling has been regularised for greater comprehension in this and subsequent quotations from Nichols.

8   Ibid., pp.319-20.

9   Ibid., p.320.

10   Sir Philip Sidney, *The Countess of Pembroke's Arcadia* (Clarendon Press, Oxford, 1987, edited by Victor Skretkowicz).

11   *Arcadia*, Book Three, lines 27-33.

12   Ibid, lines 8-10.

13   Ibid., lines 16-18.

14   Ibid., line 25.

15   Ibid., lines 38-40.

16   To appreciate how the landscape worked as a setting for the several events staged see Elisabeth Woodhouse, 'Kenilworth, The Earl of Leicester's Pleasure Grounds following Robert Laneham's Letter', *Garden History*, vol.27, no.1 (Summer 1999), pp.127-44.

17   Simon Adams (ed.), *Household Accounts and Disbursement Books of Robert Dudley, Earl of Leicester, 1558-1561, 1584-1586* (Cambridge University Press for the Royal Historical Society, 1995), p.94.

18   Reprinted the following year as *Turberville's Booke of Hunting*.

19   *ODNB*.

20   Nichols, *Progresses* 1, p.436.

21   Jean Wilson, *Entertainments for Elizabeth I* (Woodbridge, 1980), p.42.

22   Turberville, *Booke of Hunting*, 1576 (Oxford, 1908), p.90.

23   Ibid., p.91.

24   Ibid.

25   WL Renwick (ed.), Edmund Spenser, *The Shepherd's Calendar* (Scholartis Press, 1930), April, lines 55-63. I owe this source to Jim Bartos.

26   Turberville, *Booke of Hunting*, p.96.

27 Nichols, *Progresses*, 1, pp.473-4.

28 Ibid., p.475.

29 Ibid., p.476.

30 See Paula Henderson, *The Tudor House and Garden: Architecture and Landscape in the Sixteenth and Early Seventeenth Centuries*, 2005, pp.181-95.

31 For the Nonsuch fountain see Martin Biddle, 'The Gardens of Nonsuch: Sources and Dating', *Garden History*, vol.27, no.1 (Summer, 1999), pp.143-83; for Kelston see Timothy Mowl & Marion Mako, *Historic Gardens of Somerset* (Bristol, 2010), pp.20-2.

32 See Timothy Mowl, *Historic Gardens of Wiltshire* (Stroud, 2004), p.20.

33 Illustrated in Jacques Adrouet Du Cerceau, *Les Plus Excellents Bastiments de France* (Editions Sand/Conti, Paris, 1988), p.153.

34 I owe this suggestion to Jane Whittaker.

35 Nichols, *Progresses*, 1, p.474.

36 Ibid.

37 Ibid., pp.476-7.

38 Ibid., p.476.

39 Listed as such in a valuation of 1603-07, quoted in H Knowles, *The Castle of Kenilworth* (Warwick, 1872), cited by Mark Girouard, *Elizabethan Architecture: Its Rise and Fall, 1540-1640*, 2009, p.478, note 165.

40 Quoted by Nichols, *Progresses*, 1, pp.524-5.

41 Adams, *Household Accounts*, p.215.

42 Ibid., p.223.

43 Ibid., p.178.

44 Ibid., p.179.

45 See *Heritage Today*, May 2009, pp.14-19.

46 Ibid., p.3.

47 Adams, *Household Accounts*, p.225.

48 Frances, Lady Erskine, *Memoirs relating to the Queen of Bohemia by one of her ladies*, 1772, p.117.

49 Ibid., pp.119-20.

50 Ibid., p.120.

51 Ibid., pp.110-11.

52 Ibid., pp.111-12.

53 Ibid., pp.112-13.

54 Ibid., p.113.

55 Ibid., pp.121-2.

56 Ibid., p.122.

57 Ibid., p.121.

58 Ibid., p.123.

59 Ibid., pp.123-4.

60 Ibid., p.109.

61 Ibid., p.114.

62 Ibid., p.124.

63 Warwickshire County Record Office (hereafter WCRO), CR8/184: Survey of Combe Estate, Matthias Baker, 1778.

chapter 2 POOLS AND EARTHWORKS – LOST GARDENS OF THE EARLY SEVENTEENTH CENTURY

1   'Plan of the Manor of Wormleighton and Stoneton', from the Collection at Althorp.

2   WCRO, Z176/2/1 (U). A copy of this plan, with a delightful Chinoiserie cartouche, was made by John Corris in 1779 (WCRO, Z0176/4 (U)).

3   H Thorpe, 'The Lord and the Landscape', *Transactions of the Birmingham Archaeological Society*, vol.80 (1962), pp.51-71; plate 6.

4   Quoted in Geoffrey Tyack, *Warwickshire Country Houses* (Chichester, 1994), p.274.

5   Richard K Morriss, 'Astley Castle, Warwickshire', December, 2007.

6   Tyack, *Warwickshire Country Houses*, p.16.

7   WCRO, CR 136/M/9: 'Mapp of the Lordship of Astley by Robert Hewitt' (1696).

8   Morriss, 'Astley Castle', p.6.

9   The Landmark Trust confirms this interpretation.

10   Thomas Kemp, *A History of Warwick and its People* (Warwick, 1905), p.198.

11   Diane James, 'The Renaissance Garden of Sir Thomas and Lady Puckering, built at Warwick Priory in the year 1620', MA Garden History Dissertation, University of Bristol, 2005.

12   Shakespeare Centre Library and Archive (hereafter SCLA), DR 37/3/vol.17, 1620, Archer of Tamworth Collection, Puckering family: 'A book of accounts of my receipts and disbursements for the yere of our Lord 1620-1'.

13   Ibid., pp.42-4.

14   Ibid., p.46.

15   See Roy Strong, *The Renaissance Garden in England*, 1979, pp.34-7.

16   SCLA, DR 37/3/vol.17, p.42.

17   Strong, *Renaissance Garden*, p.83.

18   Tibbits Councillor, 'Early Twelfth-Century Pottery found in Warwick: The Story of Priory Site Excavations', *Warwick Advertiser and Leamington Gazette,* 29 January 1938.

19   British Library, Add. MSS. 29264, fol.71v: 'Thomas Ward, MS Collections for the Continuation of the Histories and Antiquities of Warwickshire by Sir William Dugdale & Dr Thomas to the present year 1830'.

20   MSS attributed to Thomas Ward in the library of W Staunton of Longbridge (now thought to have been lost in a fire) cited in Kemp, *Warwick*, p.202. Beer known as October Ales were brewed in that month and highly thought of because of their strength and extreme ageing potential.

21   SCLA, DR 37/3/vol.17, 1620, pp.42-5.

22   Ibid, pp.45-55.

23   Ibid.

24   For Campden House see Timothy Mowl, *Historic Gardens of Gloucestershire* (Stroud, 2002), pp.34-8.

25   SCLA, DR37/3/vol.17, 1620, p.28.

26   Illustrated in David Buttery, *Canaletto and Warwick Castle* (Chichester, 1992), plate 33.

27   Arthur Oswald, 'Arlescote, Warwickshire', *Country Life*, 5 September 1947; the earlier date was conveyed to us by the present owner, Ludovic de Walden.

28   See Sarah Markham, *John Loveday of Caversham 1711-1789: The Life and Tours of an Eighteenth-Century Onlooker* (Salisbury, 1984), pp.317-19.

29   For Chesterton House see Howard Colvin, *Essays in English Architectural History*, 1999, pp.179-89; also Timothy Mowl & Brian Earnshaw, *Architecture Without Kings: The rise of puritan classicism under Cromwell* (Manchester, 1995), pp.123-5.

30 Edward pulled down the old manor in about 1655 and began building the new classical house, but died in 1658 before it was completed. His wife Elizabeth supervised its completion by 1662.

31 We are indebted to Adam Mowl for the translation.

32 Colvin, *Essays*, p.187.

33 SCLA, DR 98/1823.

34 British Library, Add. MSS. 29264, f.190: Ward, MSS Collections.

35 Philip Wise, 'A Seventeenth-Century Landscape: The Chesterton Estate and the Willoughby de Broke Papers', in Robert Bearman (ed.), *Compton Verney: A History of the House and its Owners* (Shakespeare Birthplace Trust, Stratford-upon-Avon, 2000), pp.143-56; pp.153-4 speculates that the Lodge may have been built by Sir Edward's father William Peyto, who died in 1609.

36 Colvin, *Essays*, p.188; fig.164.

37 One of these is shown in an early nineteenth-century drawing of the house: Birmingham Libraries and Archives (hereafter BLA), *Country Seats & Castles*, vol.1, Aylesford Collection, f.118.

38 Warwickshire Archaeology Research Team, 'Archaeological Recordings, Church End, Chesterton, Warwickshire', Report August 2006/8, no.EFF-CE\PEYTO\2006\8\No2, fig.17.0.

39 For these and other contemporary water gardens see Paula Henderson, *The Tudor House and Garden: Architecture and Landscape in the Sixteenth and Early Seventeenth Centuries*, 2005, pp.128-41.

40 Markham's garden is illustrated in Henderson, *Tudor House and Garden*, fig.143.

41 Jeffrey Haworth, *Packwood House* (National Trust, 2000), p.4.

42 The map is hanging in the house on a first-floor landing.

43 Strong, *Renaissance Garden*, p.211.

44 Haworth, *Packwood House*, pp.24-5.

45 Ibid., p.4 and p.25 respectively. The yews are shown in an early *Country Life* article of 4 January 1902. The garden was featured again on 9 & 16 August 1924.

46 'Packwood House, Birmingham', *Country Life*, 4 January 1904.

47 Ibid., p.22.

48 Timothy Mowl, *Gentlemen & Players: Gardeners of the English Landscape* (Stroud, 2000), p.12.

49 Ralph Austen, *A Treatise of Fruit-Trees*, Dedicatory Epistle.

50 Ibid., p.36.

51 That to the west end of the Terrace Walk is probably early eighteenth-century; the north-west Gazebo has been rebuilt in the style of one shown in a 1756 drawing at Maxstoke Castle (illustrated in Haworth, *Packwood House*, p.26).

52 Ibid.

53 Timothy Raylor, 'Samuel Hartlib and the Commonwealth of Bees', in Michael Leslie & Timothy Raylor (eds.), *Culture and Cultivation in Early Modern England: Writing and the Land* (Leicester University Press, Leicester, 1992), p.92.

54 See Timothy Mowl & Dianne Barre, *The Historic Gardens of England: Staffordshire* (Bristol, 2009), pp.49-50.

55 Tyack, *Warwickshire Country Houses*, p.216.

56 Markham (ed.), *Life and Tours*, p.374.

57 Michael Warriner, *A Prospect of Weston in Warwickshire* (Kineton, 1978), p.12.

58 Ibid., p.15.

59 Ibid., p.16.

60 Ibid., p.19.

Chapter Notes chapter 3

chapter 3 CANALS, WALLED ENCLOSURES AND THE COMING OF GEOMETRY

1 Gordon Nares, 'Arbury Hall, Warwickshire-I', *Country Life*, 8 October 1953.

2 It is illustrated in Roy Strong, *The Artist and the Garden*, 2007, pp.31-2. The family spelt their name with an 'e' before the 1st Baronet altered it to an 'i' when he inherited in 1642.

3 Thomas Hill, *The Gardeners Labyrinth*, 1577, pp.22-3.

4 The account books have been used extensively to provide an overview of the garden activities by Eileen Gooder, *The Squire of Arbury: Sir Richard Newdigate, Second Baronet (1644-1710) and his Family* (Coventry branch of the Historical Association, 1990), pp.48-55. Gooder cites the following references: WCRO, CR136 V17, V23, V90, V130, pocket book: CR136 A25; Garden Labour Books: CR184 1/27, 28, 58, and Diary: CR136 B1305-B1309.

5 Ibid., p.49.

6 Ibid., p.48.

7 'Arbury Hall, Nuneaton, Warwickshire: A Brief History of the Site', Warwickshire Gardens Trust pamphlet, 1994, no pagination.

8 Gooder, *Squire of Arbury*, pp.48-9.

9 Ibid., p.50.

10 Gooder cites particularly WCRO, CR136 B1305A, 28 May 1680.

11 In his entry on Arbury in the EH Register, Jonathan Lovie gives this building to Sir Roger Newdigate.

12 Ibid., p.52.

13 Ibid., p.53, quoting WCRO, CR136 B2481A; B2480.

14 Robert Hamilton, 'Sir Roger Newdigate's Private Canals', *Canal & Riverboat*, March 1993, pp.51-3.

15 Oliver Garnett, *Charlecote Park* (National Trust, 1996), p.38.

16 Strong, *Artist and the Garden*, pp.38-9.

17 James Fish's map is in WCRO, L6/1035.

18 Garnett, *Charlecote Park*, p.31.

19 For both phases see 'Honington Hall, Warwickshire', *Country Life*, 25 June 1904 and John Cornforth, 'Honington Hall, Warwickshire-I, II & III', 21 & 28 September & 12 October 1978.

20 Jennifer Meir, 'Sanderson Miller and the Landscaping of Wroxton Abbey, Farnborough Hall and Honington Hall', *Garden History*, vol.25, no.1 (Summer, 1997), pp.81-106; p.100; see also Meir's *Sanderson Miller and his Landscapes* (Chichester, 2006), pp.105-12.

21 Tyack, *Warwickshire*, p.109.

22 We are grateful to Christopher Francis for the suggestion that this is an ecclesiastical water stoop.

23 Dianne Barre & Robin Chaplin (eds.), 'William Winde: Advice on Fashionable Interior Decoration' (pamphlet, 1983); see also Nicholas Stockton, *Castle Bromwich Hall Gardens* (Castle Bromwich Hall Gardens Trust, 1988), which includes quotes from several of the letters.

24 Barre & Chaplin, 'William Winde', p.22.

25 Illustrated in Stockton, *Castle Bromwich*, p.10.

26 Barre & Chaplin, 'William Winde', p.48.

27 Ibid., p.52.

28 Ibid., p.66.

29 Ibid., p.46.

30 Ibid., p.44.

31 'Castle Bromwich, Birmingham', *Country Life*, 4 August 1900.

32 See Joan Lane, 'Umberslade Hall, Warwickshire: A tale of architects and craftsmen', *Apollo*, July 1993, pp.37-9.

33 Bodleian Library, Gough Maps, Warwickshire, 32 ff.26-7; taken from Colen Campbell's *Vitruvius Britannicus*, vol.3 (1725).

34 Lane, 'Umberslade Hall', p.38.

35 Our thanks to John Fenwick for allowing access to the grounds.

36 Jonathan Lovie, 'Umberslade Hall, Tanworth-in-Arden' (Warwickshire Gardens Trust pamphlet, 1998), no pagination, citing the SCLA Archer Estate Papers and Accounts, states that the great western avenue existed as early as 1688.

37 Ibid.

38 WCRO, CR 299/577.

39 WCRO, EAC 27. The grounds at Malvern were subsequently landscaped when Sir John Soane was carrying out alterations to the house for Henry Greswolde Lewis. Soane's work dates from 1783-5 and included a subterranean bath in the house and a barn on the estate designed in the primitive style derived from the Greek temples at Paestum, which Lewis had visited with Soane in 1779. The original formal landscape was naturalised with a lake produced by the damming of the river Blythe; it was subsequently made more rugged by Lewis after 1811 by the addition of shrubberies and plantations.

40 Information from Bill and Jane Colman.

41 It is now held in WCRO, CR56.

42 Christopher Hussey, 'Henry Wise: Gardener to King William III and Queen Anne', *Country Life*, 9 January 1948, fig.4.

43 See Timothy Mowl, *Historic Gardens of Wiltshire* (Stroud, 2004), colour plate 7.

chapter 4 ROCOCO ECLECTICISM AND THE GREAT MASTER OF GOTHICK

1 See Meir, *Sanderson Miller*.

2 See Arthur Oswald, 'Radway Grange, Warwickshire-I & II', *Country Life*, 6 & 13 September 1943.

3 WCRO, CR125C/1; quoted in Meir, *Sanderson Miller,* p.106.

4 See Anthony Wood & William Hawkes, 'Radway: the making of a landscape', *Journal of Garden History*, vol.7, no.2 (April-June, 1987), pp.103-30. This includes a very useful map of the site drawn by Hawkes, which is based on contemporary sources.

5 Marjorie Williams (ed.), *The Letters of William Shenstone* (Oxford, 1939), 16 June 1754, p.400.

6 Wood & Hawkes, 'Radway', p.116.

7 William Hawkes, 'The Gothic Architectural Work of Sanderson Miller', in *A Gothick Symposium* (Georgian Group, Victoria & Albert Museum, 21 May 1983), no pagination.

8 Ibid.

9 William Hawkes (ed.), *The Diaries of Sanderson Miller of Radway* (Dugdale Society, Stratford-upon-Avon, 2005) vol.41, pp.135-6.

10 James Joel Cartwright (ed.), *The Travels through England of Dr Richard Pococke 1750-57*, 2 vols (Camden Society, 1888-9), 2, p.239.

11 Illustrated in Terence Davis, *The Gothick Taste* (Newton Abbot, 1974), p.52.

12 John Hodgetts (ed.), *Letters written by the Late Right Honourable Lady Luxborough to William Shenstone Esq*, 1775, Letter 55, pp.227-8.

13 Richard Jago, *Edge-Hill; or, The Rural Prospect Delineated and Moralised*, 4 vols., 1767, 1, p.3.

14 Hodgetts, *Letters*, Letter 44, 14 February 1750, p.189.

15 Meir, *Sanderson Miller*, p.101.

16 Michael Hall, 'Invisible Nymphs', *Country Life*, 26 December 1991.

17 Hawkes, *Diaries*, p.62 and 63 note.

18 Elizabeth Hamilton, *The Old House at Walton: More about the Mordaunts* (Salisbury, 1988), p.16. For Delany see Mark Laird & Alicia Weisberg-Roberts, *Mrs Delany & Her Circle*, 2009.

19 Quoted in *Country Life*, 26 December 1991.

20 Hawkes, *Diaries*, p.251.

21 Ibid., p.279.

22 The Bath House has been sensitively restored by William Hawkes and is now owned by the Landmark Trust.

23 Hawkes, *Diaries*, p.111.

24 Meir, *Sanderson Miller*, pp.159-64.

25 J Bloom, *A History of Preston-upon-Stour in the County of Gloucester*, 1896, pp.12-13; quoted in Meir, *Sanderson Miller*, p.162.

26 See John Cornforth's three *Country Life* articles: 21 & 12 September and 12 October 1978.

27 For Robins see John Harris & Martin Rix, *Gardens of Delight: The Rococo English Landscape of Thomas Robins the Elder*, 1978; also Cathryn Spence & Daniel Brown, *Thomas Robins the Elder (1716-1770): An Introduction to his Life and Work* (Bath, 2006).

28 Information from Christopher Francis.

29 For Wroxton see Timothy Mowl, *Historic Gardens of Oxfordshire* (Stroud, 2007), pp.78-83.

30 Quoted in Tyack, *Warwickshire Country Houses*, p.7.

31 Lady Luxborough, *Letters written by the Late Right Honourable Lady Luxborough to William Shenstone Esq*, 1775, Letter 13, no date, but likely to have been written in 1748, p.38.

32 Ibid.

33 Ibid.

34 Ibid., p.98.

35 Mark Laird, *The Flowering of the Landscape Garden: English Pleasure Grounds 1720-1800,* University of Pennsylvania Press, 1999); for Luxborough and Barrells see pp.109-13.

36 Luxborough, *Letters*, Letter 5, 11 August 1717.

37 Ibid., Letter 26, 23 March 1749, p.90.

38 Ibid., Letter 24, 4 January 1749, p.79. Later in the letter sequence Luxborough says that the plasterwork was done by Robert Moore of Warwick, who was under contract to Wright.

39 See Chapter Three of this study.

40 Luxborough, *Letters*, Letter 27, no date, p.96.

41 The best account of Barrells is in Audrey Duggan, *Chequered Chances: A Portrait of Lady Luxborough* (Brewin Books, Studley, 2008), pp.62-72; plate 19 is a map of the layout.

42 Cartwright, *Pococke*, 2, p.239.

43 For the house see John Cornforth, 'Farnborough Hall, Warwickshire-I & II', *Country Life*, 11 & 18 July 1996. For the threat to the landscape by the proposed M40 motorway see Clive Aslet, 'Why Farnborough's views must be saved', *Country Life*, 22 December 1983.

44 Quoted in Jeffrey Haworth, *Farnborough Hall* (National Trust, 1999), p.20.

45 George Miller, *Rambles round the Edge Hills*, 1900, p.61; quoted in Meir, *Sanderson Miller*, p.82.

46 Haworth, *Farnborough Hall*, p.25.

47 WCRO, Z403 (u).

48 Oxfordshire History Centre, JIV-5 (B20, D3).

49 Hawkes, *Diaries*, p.150.

50 Illustrated in *Upton House and Gardens* (National Trust, 2009), p.46; the date given here is 1803.

51 Hawkes, *Diaries*, p.278.

52 Of a series of articles on the house, the most definitive concerning Sir Roger's transformation is
    Michael Hall, 'Arbury Hall, Warwickshire-I & II', 7 & 14 January 1999.

53 Tyack, *Warwickshire Country Houses*, p.11.

54 For Newdigate's architectural sketches see Michael McCarthy, *The Origins of the Gothic Revival*, 1987, pp.128-39.

55 Lilian Dickins & Mary Stanton, *An Eighteenth-Century Correspondence*, 1910, pp.177-8.

56 Phillada Ballard, 'The Garden of Soho House', pamphlet available at Soho House. For more information
    on Boulton see HW Dickinson, *Matthew Boulton* (Cambridge, 1936).

57 This is illustrated in Phillada Ballard, Val Loggie & Shena Mason, *A Lost Landscape: Matthew Boulton's
    Gardens at Soho* (Chichester, 2009), p.53.

58 Ibid., frontispiece.

chapter 5 THE QUESTIONABLE CAPABILITIES OF LANCELOT BROWN

1 Uvedale Price, *Essays on the Picturesque, as compared with the Sublime and the Beautiful*, 2 vols., 1810, 2,
   Preface, p.19.

2 Thomas Page, *The Art of Shooting Flying*, 1766.

3 Particularly in his 1772 *Dissertation on Oriental Gardening*; see John Harris, *Sir William Chambers: Knight of
   the Polar Star*, 1970, pp.153-62.

4 This was a description coined by Pococke on his many travels. It was one of three distinct types of
   landscape treatment identified by him; the others being the 'farm way' and the 'wilderness way'.

5 Denbigh Papers, Newnham Paddox Building Book, 1743-1830 (now lost); quoted in Dorothy Stroud,
   Capability Brown, 1975, p.54.

6 Ibid.

7 Stroud, *Capability Brown*, p.54.

8 Ibid.

9 Ibid., pp.71-2.

10 Bodleian Library, Oxford, Gough Maps 32, f.28v.

11 Stroud, *Capability Brown*, pp.71-2.

12 WCRO, CR1707/125: Bertie Greatheed's Journal, 27 May 1825.

13 Giovanni Antonio Canal (Canaletto), *Warwick Castle: South Front*, 1748, private collection, New York;
   Giovanni Antonio Canal (Canaletto), *Warwick Castle: South Front*, 1748, Thyssen-Bornemisza Collection,
   Lugano; Giovanni Antonio Canal (Canaletto), *Warwick Castle: South Front*, 1748 (9), Paul Mellon
   Collection, Virginia; Giovanni Antonio Canal (Canaletto), *Warwick Castle: East Front*, 1752, Birmingham
   Museum and Art Gallery; Giovanni Antonio Canal (Canaletto), *Warwick Castle: East Front from the Outer
   Court*, 1752, Birmingham Museum and Art Gallery; Mary Delany, *Part of Warwick Castle and Church*, 29
   August 1753, National Gallery of Ireland, Inv. No. NGI.2722.61; Thomas Baker, *Warwick Castle from the
   River*, 1842, Herbert Art Gallery and Museum, Coventry.

14 WCRO, CR1886/M6.

15 Illustrated in David Buttery, *Canaletto and Warwick Castle* (Chichester, 1992), plate 13. It is also illustrated

in David Jacques' informative article 'Capability Brown at Warwick Castle', *Country Life*, 22 February 1979.

16   Wilmarth S Lewis (ed.), *The Yale Edition of Horace Walpole's Correspondence*, 48 vols (New Haven & London, 1937-83), 38, p.121: Walpole to George Montagu, 22 July 1751.

17   Ibid.

18   Illustrated in *Country Life*, 22 February 1979, fig.1. The original is in the Herbert Art Gallery and Museum, Coventry.

19   WCRO, CR1886/M22.

20   *Country Life*, 22 February 1979.

21   Meir, *Sanderson Miller*, pp.127-9.

22   It is illustrated in full by Marcus Binney, 'Packington Hall, Warwickshire-I', *Country Life*, 9 July 1970.

23   WCRO, L6/1460: George Lucy letter, 1 March 1761.

24   Oliver Garnett, *Charlecote Park* (National Trust, 1996), p.32.

25   Ibid.

26   WCRO, L6/1461: George Lucy letter, 29 March 1761.

27   WCRO, L6/1463: George Lucy letter, 12 April 1761.

28   WCRO, L6/1326: Brown to George Lucy, 17 April 1762.

29   Lewis, *Correspondence*, 38, p.223.

30   Ibid.

31   Cartwright, *Travels*, 2, p.237.

32   The Johnson watercolours are in the Herbert Art Gallery and Museum, Coventry.

33   British Library, Add. MS. 69795 f. 22: Letter from Lord Craven to Brown, August 1770; cited in Stroud, *Capability Brown*, p.54.

34   Samuel Ireland, *Picturesque Views on the Upper, or Warwickshire Avon*, 1795, p.88.

35   Johnson's watercolour of the East Lodge is on the back cover of this book.

36   Markham, *The Life and Tours*, p.190.

37   Stroud, *Capability Brown*, pp.141-2.

38   Ibid., p.142.

39   This has since been demolished, but it was illustrated in *Country Life*, 18 October 1913. An undated, unexecuted greenhouse design by Brown for Ashburnham Place, Sussex (East Sussex Record Office, ASH 4358) was probably re-used for Compton Verney. See Elizabeth Hingston, 'Ashburnham Place, East Sussex', *Garden History*, vol. 29, no.1 (Summer, 2001), pp.97-8.

40   SCLA, DR98/1801.

41   Ibid.

42   Leslie Harris, *Robert Adam and Kedleston* (National Trust, 1987), p.79, drawing no.66: 'Design for the Bridge and Cascade,' 1759.

43   SCLA, DR98/1741/1 & 2.

44   SCLA, DR98/1801.

45   Ibid.

46   SCLA, DR98/1802.

47   WCRO, CR1998/M21.

1   The Red Book is in the Frances Loeb Library, Harvard University, Cambridge, MA.

2   André Rogger, *Landscapes of Taste: The Art of Humphry Repton's Red Books* (Abingdon, 2007), p.147. Taylor's support for the ancient privileges of the Church of England had provoked the 'Priestley Riots'.

3   Quoted in Rogger, *Landscapes of Taste*, p.147.

4   Ibid.

5   The Red Book is held by Sandwell Community History and Archives, Smethwick Library, FP1/1.

6   BLA, 'Plan of the Estate called Warley Hall situate in the Parish of Hales-owen', by T Pinnel, 1790, Edwards Son Bigwood & Matthews Map 51.

7   This, and subsequent quotations, are taken from the Red Book.

8   WCRO, Z0141/4 (u): 'Plan of the demesne lands and park of the Rt Hon Lord Leigh at Stoneleigh Abbey, with S W prospect of Stoneleigh Abbey drawn by J Clark, made by Thomas Wilks', April 1749.

9   Jane Austen, *Mansfield Park*, vol.1, chapters 6, 9 & 10.

10   Johnson's watercolours are in the Herbert Art Gallery & Museum, Coventry.

11   Both Repton's Red Book and the 1811 letter are preserved at the house. We are grateful to Paula Cornwell and Cynthia Woodward for allowing us access to the archives.

12   This, and subsequent quotations, are taken from chapter 6.

13   See Timothy Mowl, *Historic Gardens of Gloucestershire* (Stroud, 2002), pp.113-14.

14   This, and subsequent quotations, are taken from chapter 9.

15   Ireland, *Picturesque Views*, pp.98-9.

16   Lady Theresa Lewis (ed.), *Extracts from the journals and correspondence of Miss Berry from the year 1783 to 1852*, 3 vols., 1866, 2, pp.433.

17   Ibid., p.434.

18   WCRO, CR1707/119.

19   Lewis, *Extracts*, pp.434-4.

20   Quoted in Mavis Batey & David Lambert, *The English Garden Tour: A View into the Past*, 1990, p.248.

21   This, and subsequent quotations, are taken from the Red Book.

22   The best account is that by Hazel Fryer, 'The Park and Gardens at Stoneleigh Abbey', in Robert Bearman, *Stoneleigh Abbey, The House, its Owners, its Lands* (Stoneleigh Abbey Ltd, 2004), pp.243-61; see also Clive Aslet, 'Stoneleigh Abbey, Warwickshire-II', *Country Life*, 20 December 1984.

23   Fryer, 'Park and Gardens', p.255.

24   Ibid., pp.259-260. The Italian Garden features in a later chapter on Victorian gardens.

25   The English Heritage Register (hereafter EHR) entry, compiled by Jonathan Lovie, describes it accurately as 'early C19'.

26   *Mansfield Park*, chapter 6.

chapter 7 IN THE SHADOW OF GUY OF WARWICK – HISTORY RECREATED AT GUY'S CLIFFE

1   AF Porter, *A Short History of St Mary Magdalen Chapel, Guy's Cliffe, Warwick*, 2005, pp.5-7 suggests that Dubritious was either Anglo-Saxon or Celtic, a Christian monk from the South West, who later moved to Moccas in Herefordshire, founding a monastery on an island in the River Wye.

2   Sir William Dugdale, *The Antiquities of Warwickshire*, 2 vols., 1730, 1, p.273.

3   Porter, *A Short History*, pp. 16-19.

4   Possibly by a canon of Osney for Thomas de Beaumont, Earl of Warwick (d.1242). 'Guy of Warwick', *ODNB*.

5   Julius Zupita, 'The Romance of Guy of Warwick', edited from the *Auchinleck MS* in the Advocates Library, Edinburgh and from MA 107 in Caius College, Cambridge, Part I, 1883, (Oxford, 1966), p.11.

6   Zupita, 'The Romance of Guy of Warwick', p.9.

7   Rous cited in Porter, *A Short History*, p.10.

8   Lucy Toulmin Smith (ed), *The Itinerary of John Leland: In or about the Years 1535-1543*, 4 vols., 1908, 2, p.45.

9   Ibid.

10 Ibid.

11 Porter, *A Short History*, pp.11-12; Dugdale, *Warwickshire*, 1730, p.273.

12 Smith, *Itinerary,* p.46.

13 Thelma Bourgeois Richmond, *The Legend of Guy of Warwick* (New York & London, 1996), p.134.

14 Dugdale, *Warwickshire*, p.275.

15 Sir Andrew Flammock is said to have indecently farted in front of King Henry VIII; see George Puttenham, *The Arte of English Poesie*, 1589 (Fairford, 2007), p.196.

16 AL Malkiewicz, 'An Eye-Witness's Account of the Coup d'État of October 1549 (in Notes and Documents)', *The English Historical Review*, vol. 70, no. 277 (October, 1955), p.603, fn.1.

17 WCRO, 1707/CR124: Journal of Bertie Greatheed, hereafter JBG, 23 November 1821; WCRO, CR1707/125 JBG, 29 May 1825.

18 Thomas Fuller, *History of the Worthies of England*, 3 vols., c1662 (republished 1840), 3, p.283.

19 Dugdale, *Warwickshire*,1765, p.193.

20 Jonathan Lovie, 'Bertie Greatheed and the Development of Guy's Cliffe, Warwick as a Picturesque Landscape', *Warwickshire Gardens Trust Journal* (autumn, 2002), p.4.

21 Guy De la Bédoyère (ed.), *The Diary of John Evelyn* (Woodbridge, 2004), p.92.

22 Dugdale, *Warwickshire*, 1730, p.275.

23 *The Georgian Group Annual Report and Summarised Accounts*, 2004, p.5.

24 British Library, Add. MSS. 29264 f.149: Thomas Ward, *MS Collections for the Continuation of the Histories and Antiquities of Warwickshire by Sir William Dugdale & Dr. Thomas to the present year 1830.*

25 Paget Toynbee, and Leonard Whibley (eds.), *The Correspondence of Thomas Gray*, 3 vols (Oxford, 1971), 1, pp. 409-10: Letter 192, Gray to Wharton, 18 September 1754.

26 Warwickshire County Council, *Black People in Warwickshire's Past: Part One 1600-1914* (Leamington Spa, 1994), p.3.

27 British Library, Add. MSS. 29264 f.149: Ward, *MS Collections.*

28 WCRO, CR1707/100: *Report of Master Eld*, 12 May 1758, p.9.

29 *Georgian Group Annual Report,* 2004, p.5.

30 Bob Dixon, *Guys Cliffe: Back to its roots* (2002), pp.16-17.

31 WRCO, CR1707/121 JBG, 11 October 1815.

32 Hodgetts, *Letters*, 1775, p.411.

33 British Library, Add. MSS. 29264 f.149: Ward, *MS Collections.*

34 C Bruyn Andrews (ed.), *The Torrington Diaries: containing the tours through England and Wales of the Hon. John Byng, (later fifth Viscount Torrington) between the years 1781 and 1794*, 2 vols, 1934, 1, p.228: 8 July 1785.

35 Arthur L Humphreys, *Letters to the Countess of Ossory*, 3 vols, 1903, 1, p.253.

36 Paget Toynbee & Leonard Whibley (eds.), *The Correspondence of Thomas Gray*, 3 vols (Oxford, 1971), 1, Letter 192: Gray to Wharton, 18 September 1754, pp. 409-10.

37 In 1766, while at Eton. Dixon, *Guys Cliffe*, p.20.

38 Ibid, p.23.

39 JPT Bury and J C Barry, *An Englishman in Paris: 1803. The Journal of Bertie Greatheed*, 1953, pp. xi-xii.

40 WCRO, CR1707/ 110 JBG, 11 April 1799.

41 See TWN Hargreaves-Mawdsley, *The English Della Cruscans and Their Time, 1783-1828* (The Hague, 1967).

42 The play starred the actress Sarah Siddons, who had once been a companion to Lady Mary Bertie, and became a life-long friend to her son Bertie Greatheed. Bury, *An Englishman in Paris*, p.xii.

43 *The Castle of Otranto* was first printed in 1765; Bertie Greatheed the Younger illustrated the sixth edition, 1791. Paget Toynbee (ed), *The Letters of Horace Walpole*, vol. 15, pp.394-5, cited in Bury, *An Englishman in Paris*, p.xiv.

44 Jane Austen, *Northanger Abbey* (first published 1817, reprinted Ware, 1993), p.147.

45 Bury, *An Englishman in Paris*, p.ix.

46 Dixon, *Guys Cliffe*, p.24.

47 Rev. William Field, *Memoirs of The Life, Writings, & Opinions of the Rev. Samuel Parr, L.L.D.*, 2 vols., 1828, 1, p.210.

48 WCRO, CR1707/35. *Denization of Ann Caroline Greatheed* 26 November 1805.

49 WCRO, CR1707/125 JBG, 18 March 1824. In 1824 Greatheed wrote: 'The papers full of the important debate on the Negroe emancipation. Government is acting with much prudence. I wish the improvement of that unhappy race could proceed faster, but the evil is deep rooted and must have time to be eradicated'.

50 TB Dudley, *From Chaos to Charter: The Complete History of Leamington Spa*, 1896, p.172.

51 HG Clarke, *Royal Leamington Spa, A Century's Growth and Development*, 1947, frontispiece.

52 Lady Teresa Lewis (ed.), *Extracts from the Journals & Correspondence of Miss Berry. From the year 1783 to 1852*, 1866, p.432: Wednesday 26 September 1810.

53 The inheritance was dependant upon the death of Hon. Colyear Esq., later Viscount Milsington, before he reached the age of 25. This was thought to be most unlikely, but Colyear was attacked in Italy by bandits, wounded in the struggle, dying of 'Lockd Jaw' (tetanus) in Rome in 1819 aged 23. Greatheed was awarded £7,000 a year in the will plus property in Lincolnshire and paintings from the Ancaster estate.

54 Lovie, 'Picturesque Landscape of Guy's Cliffe', p.6.

55 The idea for the Elizabethan windows came from visits to Warwick Priory in February 1821. Greatheed scrutinised the design and took a pattern for use at Guy's Cliffe.

56 William Field, *An Historical and Descriptive Account of the Town & Castle of Warwick & of the Neighbouring Spa of Leamington* (Warwick, 1815; reprinted 1969), p.260.

57 Dixon, *Guys Cliffe*, p.25.

58 Field, *An Historical Account*, p.268.

59 WCRO, CR1707/119 JBG, 30 June 1810.

60 *The Gardener's Magazine*, August 1831, Part 1, p.398.

61 EM Butler (ed), *A Regency Visitor: The Letters of Prince Pückler-Muskau*, 1957, Letter: 29 December 1826, pp.129-30.

62 Austen, *Northanger Abbey*, p.190.

63 WCRO, CR1707/125 JBG, 27 April 1824; WCRO, CR1707/125 JBG, 13 May 1824; WCRO, CR1707/125 JBG, 24 June 1824.

64 WCRO CR1707/125 December 1823-January 1824.

65 Laura Valentine, *Picturesque England: Its Landmarks and Historic Haunts as Described in Lay and Legend, Song and Story*, 1894, p.235.

66   Porter, *A Short History*, p.20.

67   NMR Number 30053, 6 December 1999. SMR Number 2233 suggests there is now doubt regarding the transcription and interpretation of the inscription and County Archivist M Farr, who visited the site, was unable to recognise more than one or two letters.

68   Field, *An Historical Account*, p.273.

69   WCRO, CR1707/124 JBG, 14 May 1822.

70   'Country Homes & Gardens Old & New', *Country Life*, 10 February 1900.

71   Field, *An Historical Account*, pp.273-74.

72   Ibid., p.274.

73   WCRO, CR1707/124 JBG, 3, 15, 16 & 20 April 1822.

74   WCRO, CR1707/123 JBG, 5 & 6 February 1821.

75   Ibid.

76   WCRO, CR1707/124 JBG, 14 May 1822; CR1707/125 JBG, 1 & 6 November 1823.

77   WCRO, CR1707/125 JBG, 22 February & 23 April 1825. This was a favourite walk of Greatheed with his family or visitors.

78   WCRO, CR1707/125 JBG. Constructed from November 1824-November 1825.

79   WCRO, CR1707117 JBG, 15 December 1806; CR1707/119 JBG, 21 December 1811.

80   WCRO, CR1707/125 JBG, 13 July 1824.

81   WCRO, CR1707/125 JBG, 8 & 13 July 1824; 12 August 1824; 21 September 1824; 20 December 1824; 19 January 1825; 15 October 1825.

82   WCRO, CR1707/125 JBG, 2 & 15 February 1825; 1 March 1825.

83   EHR.

84   WCRO, CR1707/119 JBG, 2 October 1810.

85   WCRO, CR1707/120 JBG, 29 March 1813 – 21 April 1813.

86   Mavis Batey, 'The Swiss Garden, Old Warden, Bedfordshire', *Garden History*, vol.3, no.4 (Autumn, 1975), p.40.

87   'Country Houses: Guy's Cliff', *Country Life*, 13 February 1897.

88   WCRO, CR1707/119 JBG, 11 & 14 June 1810.

89   Samuel Ireland, 'Guy's Cliff, Warwickshire', *Picturesque Views on the Upper, or Warwickshire Avon*, 1795, pp.118-19.

90   WCRO, CR1707/119 JBG, 6 March 1810. Bertie Greatheed noted replacements in his journal in 1810: 'I went with Clemens to examine my mill bridge which must be repaired, and will cost near Twenty pounds'.

91   WCRO, CR1707/120 JBG, 9 March 1813; CR1707/124 JBG, 29 April 1823.

92   Dugdale, *Warwickshire*, p.273.

93   Ibid.

94   WCRO, CR1707/124 JBG, 14 May 1822.

95   WCRO, 1707/125 JBG, 26 March 825.

96   WCRO, CR1707/124 JBG, 17 August & 1 September 1821.

97   WCRO, CR1707/125 JBG, 12 August 1824.

98   WCRO, CR1707/125 JBG, 10 June 1825.

99   Jeff Watkin, *Seeing 'Shakespeare Country': Tourists in south Warwickshire 1800-1939 ... and visiting today* (Warwick District Council Exhibition Catalogue, Leamington Spa, 2005), p.32.

100   Watkin, *Shakespeare Country*, p.31.

101   WCRO, CR1707/125 JBG, 18 March 1824.

102   WCRO, 1707/125 JBG, 21 October 1823: 'Cook received for showing the house during our 5 week absence £35. Strong the gardiner £20'.

103 WCRO, CR1707/125 JBG, 30 July 1824.

104 WCRO, CR1707125 JBG, 27 & 28 August 1824.

105 Richmond, *The Legend of Guy of Warwick*, p.388.

106 John Ashton, *Chap-Books of the Eighteenth Century*, 1882, p.139.

107 Tyack, *Warwickshire Country Houses*, p.104.

108 *Country Life*, 13 February 1897 & 10 February 1900.

chapter 8 GUINEA GARDENS, ALLOTMENTS AND A PUBLIC PARK

1 Timothy Mowl & Marion Mako, *Historic Gardens of England: Cheshire* (Bristol, 2009).

2 John Claudius Loudon, *The Gardener's Magazine*, vol. VII, 1831, p.409.

3 Twigs Way, *Allotments* (Oxford, 2008), p.15.

4 Monica Foot, *A Potted History of the Edgbaston Guinea Gardens*, 2005, no pagination.

5 Ibid, p.13.

6 Loudon, p. 409.

7 William Howitt, *Rural Life in England* (1844) describing Nottingham, quoted in David Lambert's study, *Detached Town Gardens* (English Heritage, 1994), p. 16.

8 *Supplementary Gleanings* (Birmingham 1803), p.311; quoted in Lambert, *Detached Town Gardens*, p.9.

9 See Way, *Allotments*, p.11.

10 EHR.

11 Ibid.

12 Christine Hodgetts, *Hill Close Gardens Guide Book*, p.4 (Warwick, no date).

13 Ibid, p.8.

14 Lambert, *Detached Town Gardens,* p.27.

15 EHR, May 2000.

16 Ibid.

17 Foot.

18 Sheila Hughes, 'Guinea Gardens, with Particular Reference to the Only Remaining Site', in *Rewriting the History of Birmingham* (University of Birmingham, School of Continuing Studies, 1992), p.5.

19 EHR.

20 Ibid.

21 Lambert, *Detached Town Gardens*, p.36.

22 Ibid.

23 Ibid.

24 Minutes of the General Committee of the Birmingham Botanical and Horticultural Society, 24 September 1829, quoted in Phillada Ballard, 'John Claudius Loudon and the Birmingham Botanical and Horticultural Society's Gardens and Edgbaston: 1831-1845', *Garden History*, vol. 8, no. 2 (summer, 1980), pp.66-74; p.66. Ballard has also written in great detail about the history of the Botanical Gardens in *An Oasis of Delight: The History of the Birmingham Botanical Gardens* (Studley, 2003).

25 John Claudius Loudon, 'Description of a Design made for the Birmingham Horticultural Society' *The Gardener's Magazine*, 1832, p.408.

26 Ibid., p.409.

27 Ibid., pp.408-9.

28   Ballard, *An Oasis of Delight*, p.35.

29   Ibid., p.25.

30   Loudon, 'Description of a Design', p.407.

31   Ballard, 'John Claudius Loudon', p.68.

32   Loudon, *The Gardener's Magazine*, 1832, p.428.

33   Loudon, *The Gardener's Magazine*, August 1839, p. 456.

34   Ibid.

35   Miles Hadfield, 'Garden Design Ahead of its Time', *Country Life*, 7 May 1970.

36   Ballard, *An Oasis of Delight*, p.42.

37   Birmingham Record Office, MS 1520/25/2.

38   Wilfred G Gibbons, *The Royal Baths and Pump Rooms at Royal Leamington Spa* (Bedworth: Jones-Sand Publishing, 1999), p.1.

39   Quoted in Gibbons, *Royal Baths*, p.9.

40   A detailed history of these gardens is outlined in Diane James, 'A Brief Flowering: Ranelagh Pleasure Gardens, Leamington Spa 1811-1849' (MA Garden History Essay, University of Bristol).

41   EG Baxter, *Warwickshire History*, vol. II, no 2, p.50; cited in James, 'A Brief Flowering', p.6.

42   C Hodgetts, 'Jephson Gardens, Royal Leamington Spa: Historical Report' (Warwick District Council, 1997), p.9.

43   Jeff Watkin (ed.), *The Royal Pump Rooms and the growth of Leamington Spa* (Leamington Spa, 2002), p.16.

44   Loudon, *The Gardener's Magazine*, 1840, p.585.

45   Ibid.

46   Loudon, *The Gardener's Magazine*, 1840, p.585.

47   Hodgetts, 'Jephson Gardens', p.19.

48   Wilfred G Gibbons, *The Story of Jephson Gardens* (Warwick District Council, 1996).

49   Nathaniel Hawthorne, *Our Old Home* (Boston, 1884), pp.61-2.

chapter 9 VICTORIAN REVIVALS – AN UNEASY JUXTAPOSITION BENEATH THE HOUSE

1   Shown in a JP Neale engraving of about 1821; see Tyack, *Warwickshire Country Houses*, plate 59.

2   All these early nineteenth-century features are shown on a map of about 1842: Jonathan Lovie, Warwickshire Gardens Trust pamphlet, 1997.

3   Shown in a 1930s photograph in Tyack, *Warwickshire Country Houses*, plate 62.

4   The arrangement in this area of the grounds appears to have been inspired by JC Loudon's Derby Arboretum: Jonathan Lovie, Warwickshire Gardens Trust pamphlet, 1997.

5   Quoted in EHR.

6   Lovie, Warwickshire Gardens Trust pamphlet, 1997.

7   EHR, citing documentation in WCRO.

8   Jonathan Lovie, Warwickshire Gardens Trust pamphlet, 2002.

9   See Mark Girouard, 'Merevale Hall, Warwickshire-I & II', *Country Life*, 13 & 20 March 1969.

10 We are grateful to Head Gardener David Kirkland for guiding us expertly around the grounds.

11 Fryer, 'The Park and Gardens at Stoneleigh', in Bearman, *Stoneleigh Abbey*, p.258.

12 Shirley Evans, 'Genius of the Pattern', *Country Life*, 12 May 1994.

13 Fryer, 'The Park and Gardens at Stoneleigh', p.260.

14 *Country Life*, 28 October 1899.

15 *Country Life*, 5 May 1906. The E H Register entry dates it 'early C19'.

16 See *The Gardeners' Chronicle*, 29 October 1898.

17 See *The Gardener's Magazine*, 23 February 1901.

18 National Monuments Record, Swindon, B/60622-11-12.

19 BLA, XMS 891/78.

20 WCRO, CR 3030/3; 5 June 1919.

21 Ibid.

22 The Flower Garden was laid out before 1861 by Chandos Wren Hoskyns and his wife Theodosia; it has deep, stone-edged beds. Nearby is a gabled garden Seat constructed of found timbers including some Elizabethan panelling. The Abbey is now Wroxall Mansion hotel.

23 Post-1863 Thomas Eades Walker spent £80,000 beautifying the grounds with separate areas given over to different types of plant; the beautifications included a pinetum, a lake and a suspension bridge (Tyack, *Warwickshire Country Houses*, p.188).

24 Tyack, *Warwickshire Country Houses*, p.63.

25 *Journal of Horticulture and Cottage Gardener*, 27 November 1873, p.421.

26 Ibid.

27 EHR.

28 *Country Life*, 4 December 1909.

29 WCRO, EAC 5: 11 March 1937.

30 *Journal of Horticulture and Cottage Gardener*, 12 March 1896; see also Phillada Ballard, '"Rus in Urbe": Joseph Chamberlain's Gardens at Highbury, Moor Green, Birmingham, 1879-1914', *Garden History*, vol.14, no.1 (spring, 1986), pp.61-76.

31 *The Garden*, 1 February 1902.

chapter 10 Old gardens and patriotic nostalgia – the Edwardians

1 John Dando Sedding, *Garden-Craft Old and New* (2nd ed., 1892), p.135.

2 Ibid., Preface, p.vi.

3 Ibid.

4 *The Builder*, 14 December 1895.

5 *The Builder*, 20 August 1898.

6 Voysey's design was published in *Country Life*, 19 February 1898. It was based on an unexecuted design for a cottage Lakin had seen and liked in *The British Architect* for 7 December 1888.

7 We are most grateful to Marion and Tony Dowding for allowing us access to the plan and for permission to photograph it for this study.

8 Diana Baskervyle-Clegg, 'Designs for a Garden: Formal Informality', *Country Life*, 26 October 1995.

9 H Inigo Triggs, *Formal Gardens in England and Scotland*, 1902, plate 63.

10 Christopher Hussey, 'Little Compton Manor, Warwickshire-I & II', *Country Life*, 22 & 29 July 1939.

11 We are grateful to Chris Holdsworth for an informed tour of the grounds.

12 WCRO, CR1886/M47.

13 The gardens are shown in *Country Life*, 9 July 1927. The topiary shapes are fully formed, while the lawns are cut with beds for standard roses.

14 See Quintin Watt (ed.), *The Bromsgrove Guild: An Illustrated History* (The Bromsgrove Society, 1999), pp.127-9.

15 *Gardener's Chronicle*, 1916, pp.132-3; p.137.

16 EHR.

17 Kendal Record Office, WDB 86/1/65.

18 Illustrated in W G Edwards, 'Bourton Hall: A Brief History' (pamphlet, no date).

19 Described as such in Charles Holme, *The Gardens of England in the Midland & Eastern Counties*, 1908, plate 130.

20 We are grateful to Ashton Hall for showing us these archival photographs and granting permission for their reproduction here.

21 Tyack, *Warwickshire Country Houses*, p.272.

22 We are grateful to Sir Peter Rigby and Marian Carter for allowing us access to the gardens.

23 Christopher Hussey, 'Clifford Manor, Gloucestershire-I & II', *Country Life*, 4 & 11 August 1928.

24 *Country Life*, 4 August 1928.

25 See Holme, *Gardens of England*, plate 37.

26 Jane Brown, *Gardens of a Golden Afternoon*, 1982, p.173.

chapter 11 THE COUNTRY HOUSE STYLE AND FIGURES IN THE GRASS

1 *Upton House and Gardens*, p.34.

2 Arthur Hellyer, 'Gardens that fit snugly: Ilmington Manor, Shipston-on-Stour, Warwickshire', *Country Life*, 19 May 1983. The house was also featured in an earlier *Country Life* article of 15 March 1930, which shows the gardens in their completed state.

3 Information from Martin Taylor, who gave us a spirited and informed tour of the grounds.

4 *Country Life*, 13 January 1923.

5 Another important garden, still in embryo, is at Priors Marston Manor. This has a sunken terrace parterre centred by a water feature by William Pye.

6 See Arthur Hellyer, 'Traditional styles in a new garden: Sherbourne Park, Warwickshire', *Country Life*, 1 December 1983.

7 David Wheeler, 'Spring Fanfare', *Country Life*, 7 March 1996.

8 WCRO, CR1600/29: 'Old Book' containing minutes and corporate meetings of the Master and Brethren of Lord Leycester Hospital, 1660-1921.

9 Ibid.

10 Warwickshire Gardens Trust Newsletter, Summer 1995, p.12.

11 *Cookes Guide to Warwick and Kenilworth Castles* 1847, from information given in the gazebo in the garden.

12 WCRO, CR1618/W33/158 & Z733 (u).

13 Bryan Homer, *An American Liaison: Leamington Spa and the Hawthornes 1855-1864*, Madison & Teaneck, 1998 p.220.

14 Warwickshire Gardens Trust Newsletter, Summer 1995, p.13.

15 Ibid.

16 Garden Organic website, accessed 2011.

17 Ibid.

18 *Horticulture Week*, 5 March 2010.

19 Joanna Morland, 'Coventry Phoenix Initiative', *Public Art Online Regeneration Case Studies*, 2002.

20 Ibid.

21   *Phoenix Initiative – Coventry*, case study on CABE Space website, which was archived by National Archives in January 2011.

22   Morland, 'Coventry Phoenix', 2002.

23   Ibid.

24   Coventry City Council, Phoenix Initiative, information plaque in the Garden of International Friendship.

25   Pamela King, 'Coventry Mystery Plays', *Coventry and County Heritage* Booklet No. 22, Coventry Branch of the Historical Association, 1997.

26   Maureen E Harris, *Lady Herbert's Garden, Coventry*, Warwickshire Gardens Trust, June 2001, p.1.

27   Ibid., p.2.

28   Letter of 23 June 1930, cited in Harris, *Lady Herbert's Garden*, p.3.

29   Ibid., p.2.

30   Russell's Patio & Garden Centre website, accessed April 2011.

31   Ibid.

32   *VCH*, 6, pp.22-26.

33   Colin Clark, 'Warming to Glorious Gardens', *Warwickshire Life* website, accessed April 2011.

34   *Warwickshire Geological Conservation Group*, October 2009: Report on Site Number 43, Baginton Garden Centre.

35   Ibid.

36   Barbara Goulden, 'Horticulturist fears for future of quarry "masterpiece"', *Coventry Evening Telegraph*, 20 November 2006.

37   Warwickshire Gardens Trust Journal, autumn 2005.

38   Penny Wark, 'The poetry of immense wealth', *Financial Times*, 9-10 October 2010.

39   Ibid.

40   'Hovercraft', *Building Design*, 1 October 2002.

41   'Modern – with moat', *Sunday Times*, 15 June 2003.

42   Kastel Building Systems website, accessed June 2010.

Gazetteer

The following is a list of the gardens of significant historic importance which are covered in this book and are open to the public.

Abbreviations

AG	Art Gallery
C	Council/Charity Owned
CC	Conference Centre
EH	English Heritage
GC	Garden Centre
H	Hotel
NGS	Privately owned but open occasionally as part of the National Gardens Scheme
NT	National Trust
P	Privately owned but open regularly
PO	Privately owned but open occasionally
PP	Public Park
U	University

Anne Hathaway's Cottage	C
Arbury Hall	PO
Ardencote Manor	H
Armscote Manor	NGS
Ashorne Hill House	CC
Aston Hall	C
Baginton Quarry Garden	P/GC
Barton House	NGS
Billesley Manor	H
Birmingham Botanical Gardens	C
Castle Bromwich Gardens	C
Charlecote Park	NT
Compton Verney	AG
Combe Abbey	H
Coughton Court	NT
Dorsington House	NGS
Dorsington Manor	NGS
Dunchurch Lodge	H
Ettington Park	H
Farnborough Hall	NT
Garden of Int. Friendship	C
Guy's Cliffe	PO

Hall's Croft	C
Hampton Manor	H
Highbury Hall	C
Highfield	NGS
Hill Close Gardens	C
Honington Hall	PO
Idlicote House	NGS
Ilmington Manor	NGS
Jephson Gardens	PP
Kenilworth Castle	EH
Lady Herbert's Garden	C
Little Compton Manor	NGS
Lord Leycester Hospital	C
Mallory Court	H
Malvern Hall	PO
Maxstoke Castle	NGS
Mill Garden	P
New Place	C
New Hall	H
Packington Hall	NG
Packwood House	NT
Ragley Hall	P
Ryton Organic	C
Shakespeare's Birthplace	C
Sherbourne Park	NG
Soho House	C
Stoneleigh Abbey	P
Studley Castle	H
Upton House	NT
Warley Hall	C
Warmington Manor	NG
Warwick Castle	P
Warwick Priory	PP
Welcombe House	H
Winterbourne Botanic Garden	U
Wroxall Abbey	H

The Gardens

Not all gardens shown are open to the public

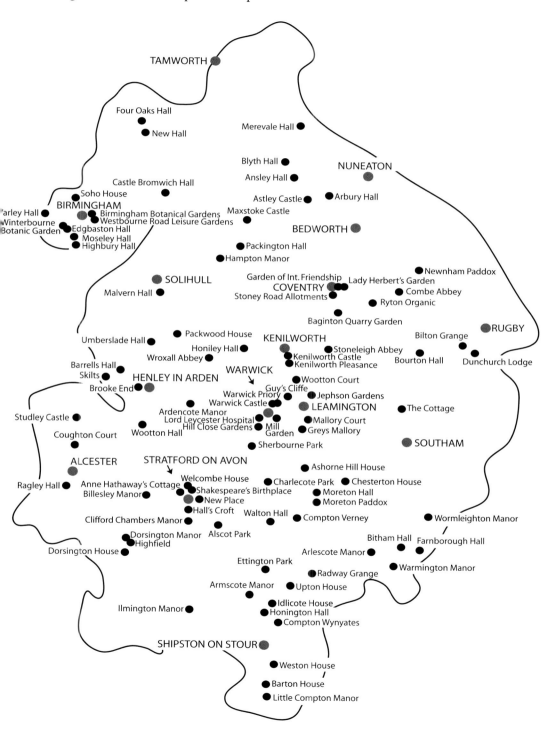

TAMWORTH

Four Oaks Hall

New Hall

Merevale Hall

Blyth Hall
Ansley Hall

NUNEATON

Castle Bromwich Hall

Soho House

BIRMINGHAM

Astley Castle
Arbury Hall

Maxstoke Castle

Parley Hall
Winterbourne
Botanic Garden

Birmingham Botanical Gardens
Westbourne Road Leisure Gardens
Edgbaston Hall
Moseley Hall
Highbury Hall

BEDWORTH

Packington Hall

Hampton Manor

SOLIHULL

Newnham Paddox

Garden of Int. Friendship
Lady Herbert's Garden

Malvern Hall

COVENTRY

Combe Abbey

Stoney Road Allotments
Ryton Organic

Baginton Quarry Garden

Umberslade Hall

Packwood House

KENILWORTH

Bilton Grange

RUGBY

Honiley Hall

Wroxall Abbey

Stoneleigh Abbey

Bourton Hall

Dunchurch Lodge

Barrells Hall
Skilts

WARWICK

Kenilworth Castle
Kenilworth Pleasance

HENLEY IN ARDEN

Wootton Court

Brooke End

Guy's Cliffe

Warwick Priory
Warwick Castle

Jephson Gardens

Ardencote Manor

LEAMINGTON

The Cottage

Studley Castle

Lord Leycester Hospital
Hill Close Gardens

Mill
Garden

Mallory Court
Greys Mallory

Coughton Court

Wootton Hall

SOUTHAM

Sherbourne Park

ALCESTER

STRATFORD ON AVON

Ashorne Hill House

Welcombe House

Charlecote Park

Chesterton House

Ragley Hall

Anne Hathaway's Cottage

Shakespeare's Birthplace

Moreton Hall
Moreton Paddox

Billesley Manor

New Place

Clifford Chambers Manor

Hall's Croft

Walton Hall

Compton Verney

Wormleighton Manor

Alscot Park

Dorsington Manor
Highfield

Bitham Hall
Farnborough Hall

Dorsington House

Arlescote Manor
Warmington Manor

Ettington Park

Radway Grange

Armscote Manor

Upton House

Ilmington Manor

Idlicote House
Honington Hall
Compton Wynyates

SHIPSTON ON STOUR

Weston House

Barton House

Little Compton Manor

283

The Historic Gardens of England

from Redcliffe Press

buy online at: www.redcliffepress.co.uk
or call 0117 973 7207

CHESHIRE

the eighth title in Tim Mowl's celebrated series

Tim Mowl and Marion Mako

'Cheshire is ducal, aristocratic, philanthropic in its Victorian entrepreneurs and richly textured in its topography and in its historic gardens.'

ISBN: 978-1-906593-14-8
288pp
60 colour and
90 black & white illustrations
Softback with flaps
£19.95

'Mowl is determined to tramp over every piece of uneven grassland and through every bramble-tangled woodland, looking for clues'

Ursula Buchan
The Spectator

From the Duke of Westminster's Eaton Hall to Lord Leverhulme's Thornton Manor and his noted garden village at Port Sunlight, there is a swagger and grandeur about the landscape and garden experiments in Cheshire. There are country-house gardens by noted designers and public parks, including Joseph Paxton's astonishing Birkenhead Park, which was the inspiration for New York's Central Park.

Other highlights include a garden laid out to symbolise John Bunyan's *Pilgrim's Progress*, a cosmic arboretum created by Sir Bernard Lovell at Jodrell Bank and England's most atmospheric rococo garden at Adlington near the border with the Peak District.

Exciting modern gardens include one based on Piet Mondrian paintings, another draws inspiration from *Alice in Wonderland* while a back garden in Sale combines brilliant planting with modern sculpture and ceramics laid out like *objets trouves* among exotic architectural planting.

STAFFORDSHIRE

the ninth title in Tim Mowl's celebrated series

Tim Mowl and Dianne Barre

Staffordshire is usually associated with the Potteries and the Black Country, the industrial heartland of the Midlands, yet it is also a county of gently rolling landscape with some of the most eccentric gardens in the country. Nothing is quite what it seems. Alton Towers, famous for its blood-curdling theme-park rides, has an historic garden with orangeries, temples and a Chinese pagoda. Trentham, best known of the county's heritage sites with a rich garden history, has a breathtaking modern garden of swaying grasses by Piet Oudolf. There are remains of Elizabethan water gardens at Gayton and Gerards Bromley and, in Izaak Walton's county, fishing pavilions in the form of a Doric temple at Calwich Abbey and a Gothic chapel at Blithbury Priory.

The county's richest period is the Georgian when Shugborough was given Chinese, Greek and Gothick garden buildings and Enville, a beautiful Gothick orangery like a Staffordshire ornament. One admiral owner at Batchacre directed mock battles on his lake with naval frigates and military forts. Most bizarrely, The Wodehouse at Wombourne had a mechanical hermit to delight visitors. The Egyptian and Chinese gardens at Biddulph Grange are the county's most important nineteenth-century designs, and even the Art Deco potter Clarice Cliff had a flower-packed garden in the suburbs of Stoke.

'an exceptional county, characterised by the whims of a succession of garden eccentrics.'

ISBN: 978-1-906593-15-5
288pp
60 colour and
100 black & white illustrations
Softback with flaps
£19.95

SOMERSET

the tenth title in Tim Mowl's celebrated series

Tim Mowl and Marion Mako

ISBN: 978-1-906593-14-8
288pp
60 colour and
90 black & white illustrations
Softback with flaps
£19.95

Somerset is still a county of deep-delved country lanes, textured manor houses and small market towns that remains agrarian and refreshingly old-fashioned. Rich in medieval deer parks, its period of greatest garden activity was the eighteenth century when a group of aesthetic rivals laid out circuits of exotic garden buildings in and around the Quantocks.

From the Italianate villa gardens of Bath to the lakeside grottoes built by Victorian industrialists at their factories around Frome, Somerset rewards exploration. In their search for lost gardens, some long forgotten, others unnoticed, Timothy Mowl and Marion Mako have visited over 100 sites.

'Artists and intellectuals of the elite group of the Souls haunted the walled enclosures at Mells Manor, where Frances Horner's friend Norah Lindsay laid out a dreamy, flower-filled garden. But the greatest expression of that pre-First World War period of weekend parties with their aesthetic longeurs is Francis Inigo Thomas' series of garden rooms at Barrow Court. Consciously planned to recapture a lost cultural heritage, they are symptomatic of the county's longing for the past. These Edwardian gardens are as characteristic of Somerset, a largely undiscovered and often passed-by county, as Arthur's vale of Avalon with its sentinel Tor, Glastonbury's own Chalice Well Garden and the 1990 stone circle in the King's Meadow at Michael Eavis' Worthy Farm. In Somerset, New Age spiritualism chimes perfectly with a reverential upper class nostalgia for an England that never was.'

HEREFORDSHIRE

the twelfth title in Tim Mowl's celebrated series

Tim Mowl and Jane Bradney

Herefordshire is a secretive county of Marcher castles, small manor houses, eighteenth-century farms, lush orchards, scattered villages and meandering rivers. It is the epitome of rural England as it was before the onset of industrialisation.

Produce from fishponds, venison from their deer parks, rabbits from the warrens and pigeon pies from their dovecotes supported the county's medieval castles.

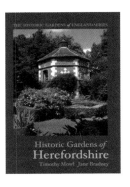

'In search of the plummy brick villages and lush valleys of Marcher Herefordshire.'

By the seventeenth century a national renaissance in cider production had brought the clergyman turned landscape fancier, John Beale, to the countryside around Backbury Hill. The view from the top inspired him to look upon Nature as a new model for garden design, a radical idea, way ahead of its time. It would take another seventy years, and the artfully informal approach of William Kent, before England achieved the Arcadian pastoral landscapes captured in Beale's time by Claude and Poussin.

In the Victorian and Edwardian periods Herefordshire was judged to be too remote for rich industrialists seeking a rural escape, consequently its Arts and Crafts legacy is small, though Charles Annesley Voysey's Perrycroft, aligned on the hill fort of the British Camp on the Malverns, and the deliciously decaying Italian Garden at How Caple Court are nationally important but like many of the county's gardens, they are virtually unknown outside Herefordshire...

ISBN: 978-1-906593-91-9
Published: Spring, 2012